# MACROECONOMIC THEORY
## A Mathematical Introduction

# MACROECONOMIC THEORY
## A Mathematical Introduction

PAUL BURROWS
and
THEODORE HITIRIS

*Economics Department*
*University of York*

JOHN WILEY & SONS
Chichester · New York · Brisbane · Toronto

Printed in Great Britain

To Barbara and Marja

Mathematics in any of its applied fields
is a wonderful servant but a very bad master.

*Kenneth Boulding*
*Economics As A Science*

# PREFACE

This text has been written with a particular objective in mind. It is to assist students at both the intermediate and advanced undergraduate levels, and also some at the first year graduate level, to bridge the widening gap between the verbal/diagrammatic exposition of macroeconomic theory in introductory and intermediate texts and the mathematical treatment commonly found in journal articles. Because we feel rather strongly that some assistance of this kind is needed we have taken the opportunity to elaborate on this theme in Chapter I and need not, therefore, pursue the matter here.

We are indebted to many of our colleagues in the Department of Economics and Institute of Social and Economic Research in the University of York for comments on parts of the book, but most of all we have benefited from the atmosphere of busy research interest in economics which has been created at York.

We must thank Professor Burley V. Bechdolt for a number of helpful comments, Peter West for working through the text in search of errors, and the secretaries in our Department and Institute for typing and retyping without complaints. Also we are grateful to Henry Pollakowski and Peter West for permission to use some unpublished work on stablization policy in section 8.3.

Finally the dedication of the book to our wives is no empty gesture: a large proportion of the credit is due to them, though they cannot share the responsibility for error which is ours and ours alone.

PAUL BURROWS
THEODORE HITIRIS

*University of York*
*July 1973*

ix

# Contents

# CHAPTER I

# Introduction

## 1.1 PURPOSE OF THE BOOK

It is fairly common practice to leave the writing of the introductory chapter of a textbook until the rest of the book has been completed. The problem with this procedure is that at the end of a long haul the author is suddenly faced with the unenviable task of trying to justify to potential readers, and to himself perhaps, the publication of yet another text. This book was started as mentioned in the Preface, because we felt that with macroeconomic theory in its present state many undergraduates, and graduate students too perhaps, are forced to tackle a major obstacle with insufficient assistance from existing textbooks. This obstacle is the transition from the verbal/diagrammatic exposition of macro-theory in the intermediate texts to the more formal, mathematical treatment of the theory in many journal articles. As far as we can see the only way this jump can be made without excessive hardship is for the student to be shown the conventional theory in a form which incorporates, *at as many points as possible*, the direct comparison of the theory in the verbal/diagrammatic form familiar to him and in the mathematical form which he wishes to understand. The juxtaposition of verbal, diagrammatic and mathematical expositions of the conventional theory is one of the main distinguishing characteristics of this book.

A second characteristic, which we think is important to the learning of macroeconomic model-building, is the presentation of the theory in a step-by-step fashion starting from simple models and gradually introducing complications until quite complex models have been developed. This is attempted by building up models sector by sector. Further we feel that macroeconomic policy is best discussed within the context of the models developed, and a determined effort has been made to avoid policy discussions which are unrelated to the theory previously presented.

1

The book is aimed mainly at economics students who have already read an intermediate macro-text† and who wish to reorientate themselves towards a more formal treatment of the theory. But there is also an increasingly large group of students of mathematics who should find the exposition suitable for the economics component of degrees which combine mathematics with economics.

It should be emphasized at the outset that this is not a book concerned with the teaching of mathematics to economists. It will be assumed that the reader has already undergone a course in calculus, and mathematical techniques will be introduced only where they are required for the formal statement of the theory. Since there is commonly a certain degree of consumer resistance to mathematics for economists, we hasten to add that the level of mathematics required for this book is no more than that taught in many mathematics-for-economists courses in universities. Section 1.4 briefly outlines the mathematics used, but any student who has worked through, say, Chiang or Allen‡ should have little difficulty. The main techniques used are total differentials and partial derivatives, together with difference equations for the dynamic models in Chapters VII and VIII. A knowledge of matrix algebra is helpful (for checking the solutions of the simultaneous models) but is not essential for an understanding of the main analysis. Students who do not know matrix algebra can easily ignore the matrices, taking the solutions as given and using them as a starting point for the formal analysis.

## 1.2   DEFINITIONS OF FREQUENTLY USED TERMS

The following is a list of the more frequently used technical terms.

### Macroeconomic model

Macroeconomic theory is the analysis of the hypothesized relationships between aggregate variables in the economy, such as national consumption, employment and exports. A macroeconomic model is an attempt to represent these relationships in an explicit and precise manner, for example in the form of mathematical equations.

### Variables, parameters and equations

Economic analysis is typically concerned with *partial* relationships, i.e. relationships between *some* variables while others are assumed or held

---

† Such as Shapiro (1970), or Lindauer (1968).
‡ Chiang (1967), Allen (1962). The text by Archibald and Lipsey (1967) is an alternative, but for our purposes is light on total differentials and difference equations and has no coverage of matrix algebra.

constant. For example, when examining the characteristics of a relationship between consumption and income we are assuming that other possible influences on consumption, such as tastes and wealth, remain unchanged. If in the analysis a particular influence is not allowed to change then it becomes a *parameter*, as distinct from those influences which are assumed to be varying which we call *variables*. Thus with the familiar functional relationship, the simple consumption function:

$$C = c_Y Y \tag{1.1}$$

income $Y$ is the only (explanatory) *variable* affecting consumption $C$, another variable. The marginal propensity to consume, $c_Y$, determines the form of the $C$–$Y$ relationship and depends on factors (e.g. tastes and wealth) not included in the relationship. These other factors are assumed constant so that $c_Y$ is a *parameter* (or structural parameter) in the analysis.

Variables can be divided into two types, *endogenous variables* and *exogenous variables*. Endogenous variables are those which are determined within the model being used, that is are explained by the model. Exogenous variables are those outside the system, ones which may affect variables *within* the model but which we make no effort to explain by the model. Clearly, which variables are endogenous and which are exogenous depends on how powerful our model is in explaining economic variables; simple models have few endogenous and many exogenous variables, whereas the complex models bring in more variables to be endogenous while leaving fewer as exogenous. In the following simple income determination model, for example, $c_0$ is an exogenous component of consumption and $\bar{G}$ (government spending) is also exogenous. The endogenous variables in the two equation model (with a linear consumption function) are income and consumption:

$$C = c_0 + c_Y Y \tag{1.2}$$

$$Y = C + \bar{G} \tag{1.3}$$

It should be noted that both the parameter, $c_Y$, and the exogenous variables, $c_0$ and $\bar{G}$, are determined *outside* the model. The difference between them is that in the analysis the parameter does not change whereas the exogenous variables may do so. In fact much analysis of economic models is concerned with deriving the implications, for the endogenous variables, of changes in exogenous variables *given* the parameters of the system.

Variables are related to one another by *equations* and in economics we distinguish between three types of equation:

(1) *Definitional equations or identities.* These are equations which define one variable in terms of other variables. For example, aggregate income is *defined* as the sum of aggregate consumption and saving:

$$Y = C + S \tag{1.4}$$

This identity should not be interpreted as a functional relationship (see (2) below); we are not saying that income is a *function* of consumption and saving, but rather that income is exactly equal to the sum of consumption and saving by definition. Equation (1.4) is not, therefore, a hypothesis; it is merely a classification of the components of $Y$ into the categories $C$ and $S$.

(2) *Behavioural equations or functional relationships.* When we hypothesize that changes in income affect people's consumption decisions we are saying that planned consumption is hypothesized to be a function of income. That is, the spending behaviour of consumers depends on their income. The consumption equation (1.2) does not say that planned consumption is *equal* to income, only that $C$ is expected to be causally related to $Y$.

(3) *Equilibrium conditions.* In addition to the behavioural equations in a model we usually wish to state the conditions under which the model will be in equilibrium (see definition below). An equation which describes the prerequisite for the attainment of equilibrium is called an equilibrium condition. An example is the condition that for the money market to be in equilibrium the demand for money must equal the supply. This can be written (see Chapter III) as:

$$L_0 + L(Y,r) = \bar{M} \tag{1.5}$$

where the left-hand side of the equation represents the demand for money (an exogenous component $L_0$ plus a component dependent on income and the rate of interest $r$) and the right-hand side the exogenous supply of money $\bar{M}$. Again in contrast to definitional equations, the demand for money *need* not be equal to the supply, though equilibrium does require it to be so.

### Equilibrium: static and dynamic analysis

In equilibrium the variables in a model have values such that there is no inherent tendency for them to change. The forces operating on the endogenous variables balance out in some sense.

Static economic analysis tells us the relationships between economic variables at a point of time, but nothing about the process by which the system adjusts before or after that time. Much of it is concerned with the conditions for equilibrium at the point of time, i.e. the conditions for *static equilibrium*. An extension of the static analysis, which will be widely used in Chapters II to VI, is the comparison of the static equilibrium resulting from one set of values of the parameters and exogenous variables and the static equilibrium resulting from another set. This is known as *comparative static analysis*. The objective will be to discover the impact on the endogenous variables, in static equilibrium, of a change in one (or more) of the exogenous variables while the parameters remain constant.

Comparative static analysis compares two equilibria but takes no account of the process by which the economic system moves from one to the other. Yet economists are interested in the characteristics of the economy through time, both in equilibrium and during a disequilibrium adjustment process. This explains the development of dynamic macro-models in which interest centres on the time paths of the values of endogenous variables and in which variables respond to one another only after some lapse of time (time lag). Since variables change through time it is necessary to specify the point of time when referring to a variable. In the simple dynamic models discussed later in this book it is assumed that variables can change *between* time periods but not within them. This leads to formulations of behavioural equations where time differences are discrete, i.e. to the use of difference equations.

One final point on statics and dynamics: it is desirable to ensure that comparative static analysis consists of a comparison of *stable* equilibria, that is equilibria which once disturbed would tend to be restored by forces operating in the system.† But in order to know whether an equilibrium is stable we require some knowledge of the dynamic characteristics of the system. For this reason we shall, on occasion, refer to the requirements of *dynamic equilibrium* even when using essentially static analysis.

## 1.3  NOTATION

Notation is a notoriously difficult problem in economics. Does one settle for a notation which is elegant and consistent but abandon the commonly used letters for variables (such as $Y$ for income, $W$ for the wage rate) or does one adhere as far as possible to the commonly used letters and adjust where necessary? We have chosen the latter course since it is difficult to 'unlearn' familiar notation (we say this with feeling having recently suffered through a seminar in which the speaker used $Q$ for price and $P$ for quantity demanded!). Where a particular letter is commonly used for two different variables (e.g. $M$ for the supply of money and for imports) we have used it for one of them and used an available letter for the other. In this way the notation has been made consistent and kept reasonably familiar.

Each of the parameters in the models has been given a subscript indicating the explanatory variable to which it relates. For example, in equation (1.2) the parameter $c_Y$, the marginal propensity to consume, concerns the relationship between $C$ and $Y$. Departing from rigorous mathematical notation the exogenous component of consumption in that equation is denoted by the same letter as the dependent variable, but with a 0 subscript. A similar form will be used in many equations. Variables which are wholly exogenous have a bar placed over the letter, such as $\bar{G}$ in equation (1.3).

In many cases it will prove possible to write our equations in a *general form*

† See Samuelson (1967), pp. 262–3.

which leaves the exact form of the relationship unspecified. For example, instead of using a linear consumption function like equation (1.2) we can write

$$C = C_0 + C(Y) \tag{1.6}$$

or perhaps

$$C = C_0 + C(Y, r) \tag{1.7}$$

where $r$ is the rate of interest and $C_0$ is an exogenous component of consumption. The relationships (1.6) and (1.7) are *general* in the sense that they may be either linear or non-linear. The exogenous component $C_0$ can be interpreted as a *shift parameter* such that a change in its value shifts the function and alters the consumption associated with a given value of the explanatory variable(s). Mathematically this is a particular form of shift parameter, one which is algebraically additive. Using this formulation of the behavioural equations is adequate for the static macroeconomic analysis to be presented. In this analysis the slope parameters, such as $dC/dY$ for equation (1.6) and $\partial C/\partial Y$ and $\partial C/\partial r$ for equation (1.7), will be assumed constant, and changes in behaviour can be represented by shifts in functions, with given slopes, such as $dC_0$ in equations (1.6) and (1.7).

On occasion it will be useful to limit our attention to the linear form of a function. In this event lower case letters will be used and the equation will be written in the form of equation (1.2) instead of (1.6).

This leads us to elaborate a little on the interpretation of an equation of the general form such as (1.7). It will be noted that in equation (1.7) we write the $C(Y, r)$ with no subscript to the $C$. The $C$ here merely indicates an undefined relationship between the dependent variable $C$ and the variables within the bracket. When we take the partial relationships between $C$ and $Y$ and between $C$ and $r$, however, we can use subscripts to specify which relationship the parameter represents. Thus, the partial relationship between $C$ and $Y$ is $\partial C/\partial Y = C_Y$, the marginal propensity to consume (when the rate of interest is held constant), and that between $C$ and $r$ is $\partial C/\partial r = C_r$, the response of consumption to a marginal change in the rate of interest (when income is held constant). For most of the functions in general form, the partial relationships will be expressed in this way. In one case a slight variation is introduced for convenience. When we write (in Chapter IV) the production function as

$$Y = Y(N) \tag{1.8}$$

where $Y$ is output (equals income) and $N$ is employment, the first derivative $dY/dN$ will be written as $Y_N'$ and the second derivative $d^2Y/dN^2$ as $Y_N''$.

### Table of symbols

To save the reader frantic searches through earlier pages to find the meaning of a particular symbol encountered, we provide a complete list of symbols, together with their definitions, at the end of the book.

## 1.4  A BRIEF SURVEY OF THE MATHEMATICS USED

As explained previously we are not attempting here to teach the mathematics required for this book. The survey which follows is intended mainly as an advance indication of the techniques used, so that students can identify any gaps in their knowledge and read the relevant parts of a book on mathematics-for-economists before proceeding.

The techniques required for a complete understanding of the mathematics used can be grouped under three headings: solving simultaneous equations, differentiation and solving difference equations. The last of these three will be omitted from this survey and be explained in Chapter VII.

### 1.4.1  Simultaneous equations

Most of the models to be considered in the theory of income determination are sets of simultaneous equations. The objective of the analysis is to solve the system for the endogenous variables and interpret the results. The first step can be achieved by either of two methods, by the elimination of variables or by using matrix algebra.

*Elimination of variables*

With a system consisting of equations (1.9) and (1.10) below, the objective is to solve for the endogenous variables $X_1$ and $X_2$:

$$a_{11} X_1 + a_{12} X_2 = b_1 \tag{1.9}$$

$$a_{21} X_1 + a_{22} X_2 = b_2 \tag{1.10}$$

First rearrange equation (1.9) to obtain the following expression for $X_1$:

$$X_1 = \frac{b_1}{a_{11}} - \frac{a_{12}}{a_{11}} X_2 \tag{1.11}$$

In order to eliminate $X_1$ from equation (1.10) we substitute for $X_1$ from (1.11) into equation (1.10):

$$a_{21} \left( \frac{b_1}{a_{11}} - \frac{a_{12}}{a_{11}} X_2 \right) + a_{22} X_2 = b_2 \tag{1.12}$$

or

$$X_2 = \frac{b_2 a_{11} - b_1 a_{21}}{a_{11} a_{22} - a_{12} a_{21}} \tag{1.13}$$

which is the *solution for* $X_2$.

Substituting the solution for $X_2$ from equation (1.13) into equation (1.11) to eliminate $X_2$ we have the *solution for* $X_1$

$$X_1 = \frac{b_1 a_{22} - b_2 a_{12}}{a_{11} a_{22} - a_{12} a_{21}} \tag{1.14}$$

This procedure may seem more familiar if we illustrate with a simple income determination model consisting of the two equations (1.2) and (1.3):

$$C = c_0 + c_Y Y$$

or
$$C - c_Y Y = c_0 \tag{1.2}$$

$$Y = C + \bar{G}$$

or
$$-C + Y = \bar{G} \tag{1.3}$$

The two unknown, endogenous variables are $C$ and $Y$, and the objective is to solve for them in terms of the knowns, i.e. the parameter $c_Y$ and the exogenous variables $c_0$ and $\bar{G}$.

In the general case initially $X_1$ was eliminated to find a solution for $X_2$; similarly $C$ is now eliminated to find a solution for $Y$. Substituting for $C$ from equation (1.2) into equation (1.3) gives:

$$-c_Y Y - c_0 + Y = \bar{G}$$

or
$$Y(1 - c_Y) = c_0 + \bar{G} \tag{1.15}$$

so that

$$Y = \left(\frac{c_0 + \bar{G}}{1 - c_Y}\right) \tag{1.16}$$

This is the equilibrium income level since it satisfies the equilibrium condition (1.3). The final step in the general case was to solve for $X_1$ by eliminating $X_2$. Similarly $Y$ is eliminated to provide the solution for $C$ by substituting the solution for $Y$, equation (1.16) into the consumption formation (1.2):

$$C = c_0 + c_Y \left(\frac{c_0 + \bar{G}}{1 - c_Y}\right) \tag{1.17}$$

This can be rearranged, by multiplying through by $(1 - c_Y)$, into the form

$$C = \frac{c_0 + c_Y \bar{G}}{1 - c_Y} \tag{1.18}$$

*Matrix algebra: Cramer's rule*

The procedure of eliminating variables becomes time-consuming when larger models are to be solved. In such cases it is an advantage to use some elementary matrix algebra to provide a short cut. Before summarizing the method of solution known as Cramer's rule, some basic terms will be defined since these will be used on occasion in the book.

Any rectangular array, **A**, of numbers (elements) $a_{ij}$ is called a *matrix*. A matrix of $m$ rows and $n$ columns is of *order $m.n$*. The matrices of order $1.n$ or $m.1$ are respectively called a row *vector* and a column *vector*. In a *square matrix* the number of columns equals the number of rows. For example, the system of two linear equations in two variables (1.9) and (1.10) can be written as:

$$\begin{bmatrix} a_{11} & a_{12} \\ a_{21} & a_{22} \end{bmatrix}\begin{bmatrix} X_1 \\ X_2 \end{bmatrix} = \begin{bmatrix} b_1 \\ b_2 \end{bmatrix} \tag{1.19}$$

or, $\mathbf{AX} = \mathbf{b}$, where the matrix of the coefficients $a_{ij}$, i.e. matrix $\mathbf{A}$, is a square matrix.

A *determinant* is a number uniquely derived from a square matrix.† More specifically, the algebraic value of a determinant consists of the sum of all possible terms, which are products of $n$ elements one from each row and one from each column, together with an appropriate sign. For example, the determinant of the square matrix of the coefficients in (1.19) can easily be evaluated by cross-diagonal multiplication; that is:

$$\begin{bmatrix} a_{11} & a_{12} \\ a_{21} & a_{22} \end{bmatrix} = a_{11}a_{22} - a_{12}a_{21}$$

However, this method of cross-diagonal multiplication is not applicable to determinants of orders higher than 3 (where the order of a determinant is defined in a way similar to that of a square matrix). For the evaluation of determinants of order higher than 3 the 'Laplace expansion' of the determinant must be applied.

The *inverse* of a matrix $\mathbf{A}$, denoted as $\mathbf{A}^{-1}$, is defined only if $\mathbf{A}$ is a square matrix and satisfies the condition $\mathbf{AA}^{-1} = \mathbf{A}^{-1}\mathbf{A} = \mathbf{I}$, where $\mathbf{I}$ is the *identity matrix*, i.e. a square matrix with 1's in its *principal* diagonal and 0's everywhere else. To find the solution of a linear-equation system $\mathbf{Ax} = \mathbf{b}$, where the co-efficient matrix $\mathbf{A}$ is *nonsingular* (i.e. $\mathbf{A} \neq 0$), first we find the inverse $\mathbf{A}^{-1}$. The product $\mathbf{A}^{-1}\mathbf{b}$ gives the solution of the system. The method of matrix inversion and the definition of the solution of a linear-equation system provide a practical way for solving such systems which is known as *Cramer's rule*. This rule states that the solution for any variable $X_j$ is found as the ratio of two determinants, the numerator being the determinant of the coefficients with the $j$th column replaced by the column of constant terms, and the denominator being the determinant of the coefficients of the system of equations.

The use of Cramer's rule can be illustrated with the two examples used previously for the elimination of variables method. For the system of equations (1.9) and (1.10), presented in matrix form in (1.19), we obtain the solution for $X_1$ as

$$X_1 = \frac{\begin{vmatrix} b_1 & a_{12} \\ b_2 & a_{22} \end{vmatrix}}{\begin{vmatrix} a_{11} & a_{12} \\ a_{21} & a_{22} \end{vmatrix}} = \frac{b_1 a_{22} - b_2 a_{12}}{a_{11}a_{22} - a_{12}a_{21}} \tag{1.20}$$

† See Chiang (1967), p. 97, and Aitken (1956).

which is the solution previously obtained, equation (1.14). For $X_2$ we have:

$$X_2 = \frac{\begin{vmatrix} a_{11} & b_1 \\ a_{21} & b_2 \end{vmatrix}}{\begin{vmatrix} a_{11} & a_{12} \\ a_{21} & a_{22} \end{vmatrix}} = \frac{b_2 a_{11} - b_1 a_{21}}{a_{11} a_{22} - a_{12} a_{21}} \tag{1.21}$$

which is the same as equation (1.13).

Turning to the income determination example, equations (1.2) and (1.3), the model in matrix notation is:

$$\begin{bmatrix} 1 & -c_Y \\ -1 & 1 \end{bmatrix} \begin{bmatrix} C \\ Y \end{bmatrix} = \begin{bmatrix} c_0 \\ \bar{G} \end{bmatrix}$$

The solution for $Y$ is:

$$Y = \frac{\begin{vmatrix} 1 & c_0 \\ -1 & \bar{G} \end{vmatrix}}{\begin{vmatrix} 1 & -c_Y \\ -1 & 1 \end{vmatrix}} = \frac{c_0 + \bar{G}}{1 - c_Y} \tag{1.22}$$

which is the same as equation (1.16), and for $C$:

$$C = \frac{\begin{vmatrix} c_0 & -c_Y \\ \bar{G} & 1 \end{vmatrix}}{\begin{vmatrix} 1 & -c_Y \\ -1 & 1 \end{vmatrix}} = \frac{c_0 + c_Y \bar{G}}{1 - c_Y} \tag{1.23}$$

the equivalent of equation (1.18).

For large equation systems this evaluation of the determinants by Cramer's rule also proves to be cumbersome. In these cases an alternative method of solution is provided by evaluating the inverse matrix and operating with it upon the vector of constants.†

### 1.4.2  Differentiation

The concepts of functions, limits and continuity are assumed to be familiar and we concentrate here on stating the elements of differentiation to be used.

To differentiate a function is to find its derivative, and the *rules of derivation* we shall need are stated in Table 1.1.

*Functions of many variables*

Partial differentiation differs from the differentiation discussed above primarily in that $(n-1)$ variables in an $n$ variable function are held constant,

† See Aitken (1956), p. 56.

TABLE 1.1

| Rule | Function | Derivative | |
|------|----------|------------|---|
| Constant function rule | $y = f(x) = \lambda,$ constant | $\dfrac{dy}{dx} = 0$ | (1.24) |
| Power function rule | $y = f(x) = x^n$ | $\dfrac{dy}{dx} = nx^{n-1}$ | (1.25) |
| Product rule | $y = g(x) \cdot h(x)$ | $\dfrac{dy}{dx} = h(x)\dfrac{d}{dx}g(x) + g(x)\dfrac{d}{dx}h(x)$ | (1.26) |
| Sum and difference rule | $y = g(x) \pm h(x)$ | $\dfrac{dy}{dx} = \dfrac{d}{dx}g(x) \pm \dfrac{d}{dx}h(x)$ | (1.27) |
| Quotient rule | $y = \dfrac{g(x)}{h(x)}$ | $\dfrac{dy}{dx} = \dfrac{h(x)\dfrac{d}{dx}g(x) - g(x)\dfrac{d}{dx}h(x)}{[h(x)]^2}$ | (1.28) |
| Chain rule | $z = f(y)$ where $y = g(x)$ | $\dfrac{dz}{dx} = \dfrac{dz}{dy} \cdot \dfrac{dy}{dx}$ | (1.29) |
| Inverse function rule | For $y = f(x)$, single valued and continuous its inverse function is written as $x = f^{-1}(y)$ | $\dfrac{dx}{dy} = \dfrac{1}{dy/dx}$ | (1.30) |

while the remaining variable is allowed to change. For example, given the function

$$y = f(x_1, x_2) \tag{1.31}$$

the partial derivatives are $\partial y/\partial x_1$ and $\partial y/\partial x_2$.

As an economic example of partial derivatives consider a model consisting of

$$C = c_0 + c_Y Y \tag{1.2}$$

$$I = i_r r \tag{1.32}$$

$$Y = C + I \tag{1.33}$$

where $i_r = \partial I/\partial r$, the interest sensitivity of investment. Substituting for $C$ and $Y$ in the equilibrium condition (1.33) we obtain

$$Y = \frac{c_0 + i_r r}{1 - c_Y} \tag{1.34}$$

To study the effect on $Y$ of a change in $c_0$, with $r$ constant, we set $dr = 0$ and obtain

$$\frac{\partial Y}{\partial c_0} = \frac{1}{1 - c_Y} \tag{1.35}$$

Similarly, setting $dc_0 = 0$ we have the partial relationship between changes in $Y$ and $r$:

$$\frac{\partial Y}{\partial r} = \frac{i_r}{1 - c_Y} \tag{1.36}$$

Numerous applications of this method will be found in subsequent chapters

## Total differentials

The total differential of a function with $n$ variables

$$y = f(x_1, x_2, \ldots, x_n) \tag{1.37}$$

is defined as

$$dy = \frac{\partial y}{\partial x_1} dx_1 + \frac{\partial y}{\partial x_2} dx_2 + \cdots + \frac{\partial y}{\partial x_n} dx_n \tag{1.38}$$

In the case of equation (1.31), for example, the total differential is

$$dy = \frac{\partial y}{\partial x_1} dx_1 + \frac{\partial y}{\partial x_2} dx_2 \tag{1.39}$$

Similarly, the total differential of the consumption function

$$C = C(Y, r) \tag{1.40}$$

is

$$dC = \frac{\partial C}{\partial Y} dY + \frac{\partial C}{\partial r} dr \tag{1.41}$$

or, in alternative notation,

$$dC = C_Y dY + C_r dr \tag{1.42}$$

The rules to be followed for finding the total differential of a function are similar to the rules of derivation previously listed. For example:

$$d(\lambda x^n) = n\lambda x^{n-1} dx \tag{1.43}$$

where $\lambda$ is a constant and

$$d(x_1 \pm x_2) = dx_1 \pm dx_2 \tag{1.44}$$

$$d(x_1 x_2) = x_1 dx_2 + x_2 dx_1 \tag{1.45}$$

$$d\left(\frac{x_1}{x_2}\right) = \frac{x_2 dx_1 - x_1 dx_2}{(x_2)^2} \tag{1.46}$$

As an illustration of the procedure consider the function

$$y = f(x_1, x_2) \tag{1.31}$$

where

$$x_2 = g(x_1) \tag{1.47}$$

and find $dy/dx_1$. From the initial function (1.31) we have the total differential:

$$dy = \frac{\partial y}{\partial x_1} dx_1 + \frac{\partial y}{\partial x_2} dx_2 \tag{1.39}$$

and dividing both sides by $dx_1$ we obtain

$$\frac{dy}{dx_1} = \frac{\partial y}{\partial x_1} + \frac{\partial y}{\partial x_2} \frac{dx_2}{dx_1} \tag{1.48}$$

which is often called the *total derivative* of the function.

As another example consider the function

$$y = f(x_1, x_2) \tag{1.31}$$

where

$$x_1 = g(t) \tag{1.49}$$

and

$$x_2 = h(t) \tag{1.50}$$

and find $dy/dt$. From the initial equation (1.31) we have the total differential equation (1.39) above and dividing this through by $dt$ we have the total derivative

$$\frac{dy}{dt} = \frac{\partial y}{\partial x_1} \frac{dx_1}{dt} + \frac{\partial y}{\partial x_2} \frac{dx_2}{dt} \tag{1.51}$$

*A note on linear homogenous functions*

The production function

$$Y = F(K^R, N) \tag{1.52}$$

is said to be linear homogenous if income, $Y$, increases or decreases *in the same proportion* as the factor inputs capital, $K^R$ and labour, $N$. Formally, function (1.52) is linear homogenous if

$$\lambda Y = F(\lambda K^R, \lambda N) \tag{1.53}$$

for any point $(K^R, N)$ and for any value of the constant $\lambda$. For a production function of the form

$$Y = (K^R)^\alpha N^\beta \tag{1.54}$$

where $\alpha > 0$, $\beta > 0$, we have

$$F(\lambda K^R, \lambda N) = \lambda^{\alpha + \beta} F(N, K^R) \tag{1.55}$$

If $(\alpha + \beta) > 1$ the production displays *increasing* returns to scale; if $(\alpha + \beta) < 1$ then *decreasing* returns to scale; and if $(\alpha + \beta) = 1$ there are constant returns to scale. [Note: the symbols $\alpha$ and $\beta$ will have different meanings in subsequent chapters.]

In much of the economic literature constant returns to scale are assumed and this assumption will be adopted at several points in later chapters.

## 1.5  PLAN OF THE BOOK

The macroeconomic theory to be presented is in two main parts: static models in Chapters II to VI plus the first two sections of Chapter VIII, and dynamic models in Chapters VII and IX and the final section of Chapter VIII.

The static theory is built up in several steps until we have a macroeconomic model of conventional form within which the effects of monetary and fiscal policy can be analysed. The first step concerns the influences which affect the decisions of households, firms and the government to make demands on available resources, that is their decisions to spend. This is the task of Chapter II. One of the influences which is mentioned in the preliminary analysis is variations in the rate of interest, but no attempt is made to explain these variations until Chapter III. In this chapter the rate of interest is viewed as the price of holding money, so that consideration is naturally given to the demand for and supply of money. By the end of Chapter III we have a macro-model consisting of an expenditure sector and a monetary sector, which can be stated in terms of the familiar *IS–LM* diagram and which essentially is a model of aggregate demand for goods and services. Despite its popularity the two-sector model suffers from the obvious weakness of ignoring supply side considerations. This deficiency is remedied in Chapter IV where, after discussion of the production-and-employment sector, this third sector is added to the two-sector model. The resulting three-sector model is used in section 4.5 to analyse the impact on aggregate income, employment, the rate of interest and the price level of changes in monetary and fiscal policy instruments. The fact that we *can* analyse the effect on *four* endogenous variables, more than one of which are policy targets (objectives), explains why a model as complicated as the three-sector model is useful. The same model is reinterpreted in Chapter V to place emphasis on the relationship between aggregate income and the price level. To this end aggregate demand and supply functions are derived and these are used, in the same chapter, to analyse the significance of the Pigou Effect and to summarize the comparative static theory of inflation. To complete the static theory, in Chapter VI, the assumption of a closed economy is dropped, and an external sector is added to the two-sector model from Chapter III to make an alternative three-sector model within which the balance of payments effects of monetary and fiscal policy can be explained. Finally in the first two sections of Chapter VIII the static theory serves to help us with an analysis of stabilization policy, including a rapid survey of the recent dogfight between 'Keynesians' and 'monetarists'.

The dynamic theory begins in Chapter VII with an income determination model which contains a dynamic consumption function, a multiplier–accelerator model of income determination, and an illustrative dynamic model of inflation. Each of these models is in difference equation form and therefore requires similar mathematical technique. The multiplier–accelerator model is later used, in the last section of Chapter VIII, to demonstrate some effects of monetary and fiscal policies which are peculiar to government decision-taking in a dynamic context. Chapter XI completes the dynamics with some simple models of growth and comments on macro-policy within such models.

### A note on the use of this textbook

It is apparent from this plan of the chapters that the book is highly integrated. Thus, Chapters II, III and IV provide the building blocks for Chapter V and section 1 of Chapter VIII, and the last section of Chapter VIII uses a model presented in Chapter VII. For this reason it is not easy, as it is with some macro-texts, to dip into this book (for example in the later stages to find the analysis of policy) since the individual chapters are not self-contained. This is one of the costs of the progressive presentation of models and of using those models for policy discussion. We would plead that there is a compensating benefit: students should not find that they complete their study of macroeconomic theory with a good picture of the various cogs of the machine but little idea of how to fit them together.

### Exercises

Exercises and essay questions are given at the end of each chapter. Where a specific algebraic or numerical answer is required the answer is given at the end of the book.

### EXERCISES

**1.1** Solve the following system for $x_1, x_2, x_3$:

$$5x_1 + 3x_2 - 2x_3 = 10$$
$$-7x_2 + 16x_3 = -6$$
$$6x_1 + x_2 + 5x_3 = 10\cdot5$$

**1.2** Given the production function $Y = Y(K^R, N)$, where both capital, $K^R$, and labour, $N$, are functions of time, that is $K^R = K^R(t)$ and $N = N(t)$, find the rate of change of output with respect to time, $dY/dt$.

**1.3**  For $y = f_1(x_1, x_2)$, where $x_1 = f_2(g, h)$ and $x_2 = f_3(g, h)$, find $\partial y / \partial g$ and $\partial y / \partial h$.

**1.4**  Assume that the following relationship exists:

$$P . X . g = M$$

where $P$ is the price level, $X$ the volume of transactions, $g$ the proportion of the money value of transactions which people plan to hold in cash and $M$ is the supply of money. Obtain the partial derivatives which show the effects on the price level of changes in the other variables.

# CHAPTER II

# The Expenditure Sector

The conventional classification of national income and expenditure distinguishes between consumption expenditure, investment expenditure, expenditure by the government and expenditure on imports. The last category will not be introduced into the analysis until Chapter VI, but the determinants of the other three types of expenditures are to be discussed in this chapter and Chapter III. We are concerned now, therefore, with the market for all goods and services in the economy, and expenditures by consumers, investors and the government constitute a demand for the real resources which are available to produce these goods and services. Subject to the limitation imposed by the maximum resource availability, output (and therefore income) is determined at the aggregate level, just as in individual markets, by the interaction of demand and supply forces. Following the discussion of aggregate demand the supply side will be introduced in Chapter IV.

In one respect the theory of expenditure to be presented is not representative of the current state of knowledge of this subject. The literature has been complicated in recent years by the analysis of many competing hypotheses about the behaviour of households, firms and governments. The exposition of the next four chapters would be extremely complex if we pursued many of these formulations of the expenditure functions. A step-by-step development of a model needs to concentrate on forward steps rather than side steps, and this will be the excuse for ignoring many of the embellishments of the theory contained in the more sophisticated literature.

## 2.1  CONSUMPTION

Decisions to consume are made by households and are subject to a wide and complex range of influences. Some of these influences are general in their effect while others represent the idiosyncracies of particular households or particular groups. To abstract from the complexities of the real world it is conventional to postulate one, or a few, major factors affecting consumers' behaviour, and to develop the theory of income (or expenditure) determination on the basis of a simplified consumption function.†

Assuming that households and firms are separate entities, and that consumption is only undertaken by households and investment only by firms, consumers can allocate their disposable income $Y$ to expenditure on goods and services $C$ or to saving $S$. Therefore

$$Y = C + S \qquad (2.1)$$

but this is merely a *definition of income*, and does not constitute a hypothesis about consumers' behaviour. What is needed is a hypothesis which attempts to explain the consumers' decisions on how $Y$ should be divided.

The simplest form of hypothesis is that the level of consumption *planned* by consumers depends on the level of their disposable income. The consumption function can then be written in a general form:

$$C = C(Y) \qquad (2.2)$$

Usually, an exogenous element $C_0$ is included in consumption expenditure subject to the restriction $C_0 \geq 0$. Planned consumption is expected to be either zero or positive at the zero income level. The function is assumed to be continuous but in this general form the parameter $C_Y$, the first derivative of $C$ with respect to $Y$ (i.e. $C_Y = dC/dY$) is subject to the limitation that, at any level of income

$$0 < C_Y < 1 \qquad (2.3)$$

However $C_Y$ is not necessarily constant at different levels of income. This derivative indicates the change in planned consumption associated with a change in income and is called the *marginal propensity to consume*. Since $C_Y$ is assumed to be positive we can recognize this assumption as the consumption function having a positive slope.

The levels of consumption and saving planned by consumers must add up to the level of income. Consequently, if consumption varies with the level of income so must saving. The savings function corresponding to (2.2) is

$$S = S(Y) \qquad (2.4)$$

If $C_0$ is included in the consumption function, $S_0$ must be included in the saving function where $S_0 = -C_0$. The *marginal propensity to save* $S_Y = dS/dY$ is subject to the restriction that

$$0 < S_Y < 1 \qquad (2.5)$$

---

† Our discussion of the variables influencing consumption decisions will be brief and assumes the student to have read the coverage of consumption functions in an intermediate text, for example Shapiro (1970), Ch. 9 and 10, or Lindauer (1968), Ch. 2.

Therefore, since income can be used *only* for consumption or for saving, we can substitute for $C$ and $S$ in the income definition. Substituting equations (2.2) and (2.4) into equation (2.1) and taking the total differential, we obtain:

$$Y = C(Y) + S(Y)$$

and

$$\frac{dC}{dY} + \frac{dS}{dY} = C_Y + S_Y = 1 \tag{2.6}$$

The division of *additional* income between planned consumption and saving is determined by the two marginal propensities which must add up to unity by definition.

The consumption function is subject to one more general restriction, that the second derivative is

$$\frac{d^2 C}{dY^2} \leqq 0 \tag{2.7}$$

which means that the marginal propensity to consume is either constant or declining as income increases. By implication $d^2 S/dY^2 \geqq 0$ which means that the marginal propensity to save is either constant or increasing as income rises.

The ratios $C/Y$ and $S/Y$ are called the average propensities to consume and save respectively. It is generally assumed that a greater proportion of total income is saved as income increases. In a formal way this can be stated as:

$$d\left(\frac{S}{Y}\right) \Big/ dY > 0$$

or

$$d\left(\frac{Y-C}{Y}\right) \Big/ dY > 0$$

Taking the derivatives and rearranging them we obtain

$$\frac{1}{Y}\left(\frac{C}{Y} - \frac{dC}{dY}\right) > 0$$

and since $1/Y > 0$, the implication is that $(C/Y) - (dC/dY) > 0$. Consequently $C/Y > dC/dY$. Therefore it is expected that as income rises, the average propensity to consume will exceed the marginal propensity to consume.

In much of this book we use the general form of the consumption function rather than limit attention to linear or non-linear forms, but we may note now some special characteristics of linear consumption functions.

Linear consumption functions, that is ones characterized by $d^2 C/dY^2 = 0$, can be divided into two types. The first is

$$C = c_Y Y \tag{2.8}$$

where $c_Y$ is the marginal propensity to consume which is constant at all income levels. Small letters will be used for the parameters and exogenous variables in linear functions. With the function of the form (2.8) planned consumption is a fixed proportion $c_Y$ of income. The proportional relationship (2.8) also has the characteristic that

$$\frac{C}{Y} = \frac{dC}{dY} = c_Y \tag{2.9}$$

Since the relationship is proportional an increase in income is divided between consumption and saving in the same ratio as total income. This means that the marginal propensity to consume equals the average propensity to consume. Figure 2.1 represents this type of function. At income level $Y_1$ the average

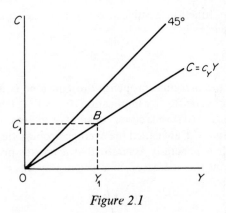

*Figure 2.1*

propensity to consume is $C_1/Y_1$ and the slope of the curve at point $B$ is the same, that is $c_Y = C_1/Y_1$.

The second type of linear function introduces an exogenous element in consumption. The planned level of consumption expenditure is now determined partly by the level of income and partly by other unspecified factors. This function is:

$$C = c_0 + c_Y Y \tag{2.10}$$

where $c_Y$ is the constant marginal propensity to consume, and $c_0$ is the exogenous element in consumption. The average propensity to consume at any income level can be found by dividing (2.10) by $Y$, which gives

$$\frac{C}{Y} = \frac{c_0}{Y} + c_Y \tag{2.11}$$

Since $c_0/Y$ is positive the average exceeds the marginal propensity to consume. Note, however, that as $Y \to \infty$, $C/Y \to c_Y$; in the limit the fixed element $c_0$ becomes an insignificant proportion of income, and the average propensity to consume approaches the marginal propensity to consume. This type of function is illustrated in Figure 2.2. At income level $Y_1$ the average propensity to consume $C_1/Y_1$ exceeds the slope of the curve at point $D$ which is

$$\frac{(C_1 - c_0)}{Y_1}$$

The savings function implied by the proportional consumption function (2.8) is

$$S = (1 - c_Y) Y$$

or

$$S = s_Y Y \tag{2.12}$$

where $s_Y = 1 - c_Y$ and $0 < s_Y < 1$. A proportional consumption function is

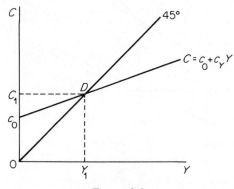

*Figure 2.2*

accompanied by a proportional savings function. With the exogenous element in consumption as in (2.10), the savings function must be:

$$S = -c_0 + (1 - c_Y) Y$$

or

$$S = s_0 + s_Y Y \tag{2.13}$$

where $s_0 = -c_0$ is the planned dis-saving (running down of assets) which is the counterpart of the positive consumption $c_0$ at zero income. Using reasoning which is analogous to the case of consumption it can be shown that with the savings function (2.13) the average propensity to save is lower than the marginal propensity to save but approaches the marginal propensity as $Y \to \infty$.

The relationship between the linear consumption and saving functions with some exogenous consumption, equations (2.10) and (2.13), is shown in Figure 2.3. The exogenous element in consumption is represented by the constant term $c_0$, which is reflected in the savings function as $s_0$.

Since $(c_0 + s_0) = 0$ and $(dC/dY) + (dS/dY) = 1$, it follows from the definition of income that the vertical summation of the two curves would produce a 45° line which has a slope of unity. By comparing the $C$ and $S$ functions in the diagram with the 45° line we see that at income levels below $Y_1$ the planned level of consumption exceeds income: the consumption function is above the 45° line and the savings function falls into the negative quadrant. At income levels above $Y_1$ planned consumption is less than income and planned saving is positive. $Y_1$ is the 'break-even' level of income at which consumers plan to spend an amount on consumption which is just equal to their total income and planned saving is zero. To avoid repetition we will subsequently refer to planned consumption (saving) as *consumption* (*saving*) unless there is a danger of confusion between planned and realized magnitudes.

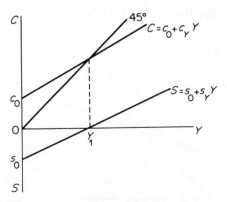

*Figure 2.3*

While restricting the analysis of the consumption function to the hypothesis that income is the main determinant, it is possible to justify on theoretical grounds the use of an income variable other than the current absolute level of income which we have used so far. The relative income hypothesis, for example, suggests that consumers adjust rapidly to a new and higher standard of living so that if income declines after a new high level has been achieved they will be resistant to downward adjustments in consumption expenditure. This attitude could lead the average propensity to consume $C/Y$ to remain relatively stable when income rises but to increase when income declines. Consumption is then related to previous peak income as well as to current absolute income and the function (in ratio form and linear) is written as:

$$\frac{C}{Y} = \Omega_0 + \Omega_Y \left(\frac{Y}{\hat{Y}}\right) \tag{2.14}$$

where $\Omega_Y < 0$ and $\hat{Y}$ is the previous peak level of income. The ratio $C/Y$ is therefore higher after the peak when $Y < \hat{Y}$.

While the relative income hypothesis emphasizes the resistance to cuts in consumption expenditure, the permanent income hypothesis supposes that consumers' reactions to income changes depend on whether the income changes are regarded as 'transitory' (windfall gains or losses) or 'permanent'.† Income is therefore divided into transitory and permanent components, $Y^Z$ and $Y^H$ respectively:

$$Y = Y^H + Y^Z \qquad (2.15)$$

and planned consumption is assumed to respond consistently and predictably only to the permanent component; that is

$$C_t = C_H(Y^H)_t \qquad (2.16)$$

where $C_H = dC/dY^H$ is the marginal propensity to consume permanent income. The $t$ subscripts represent the time period and the relationship is proportional, that is $C/Y^H = dC/dY^H$. It is usual to approximate the non-observable permanent income by hypothesizing that consumer's ideas of their level of permanent income are based on past and present actual income. Permanent income is taken to be a weighted average of past and present income, with the weights assumed to decline geometrically backwards in time:

$$(Y^H)_t = Y_t + \lambda Y_{t-1} + \cdots + \lambda^n Y_{t-n} \qquad (2.17)$$

for $n \to \infty$.

The relation between $C$ and $Y$ can be derived by substituting for $(Y^H)_t$ from (2.17) in equation (2.16):

$$C_t = C_H(Y_t + \lambda Y_{t-1} + \cdots + \lambda^n Y_{t-n}) \qquad (2.18)$$

where $0 < \lambda < 1$, and $C_H$ is constant. Lagging equation (2.18) by one period and multiplying through by $\lambda$ we have

$$\lambda C_{t-1} = C_H(\lambda Y_{t-1} + \lambda^2 Y_{t-2} + \cdots + \lambda^{n+1} Y_{t-(n+1)}) \qquad (2.19)$$

for $n \to \infty$.

Subtracting equation (2.19) from (2.18) we obtain:

$$C_t = C_H Y_t + \lambda C_{t-1} \qquad (2.20)$$

The permanent income hypothesis consequently leads us into the realm of dynamic expenditure functions. The lagged dependent variable $C_{t-1}$ in equation (2.20) introduces a continuity between time periods and consumption is no longer determined by current income alone.

The relative and permanent income hypotheses, and their implied consumption functions, represent the only theory which is introduced in this book without being integrated into the macroeconomic models to be developed. While the two theories have proved fruitful for the econometric testing of macroeconomic models‡ they have not yet been incorporated into the standard macro-theory, and we are concerned with a formal treatment of standard theory. The permanent income hypothesis is perhaps the more theoretically

† Friedman (1957), Ch. III.
‡ For a survey of the theory and econometric work in this area see Evans (1969).

productive of the two and provides a means of stepping from the static analysis
of income and expenditure to dynamic models.† However, as we shall see in
Chapter VII, there are other ways of introducing dynamic elements into the
theory of income determination, and the resulting simple dynamic models are
adequate for our purposes in Chapters VII and VIII.

The reason for explaining the two hypotheses here is that they emphasize
some of the limitations of the simple, static consumption function which will
be used for much of our subsequent analysis. Perhaps consumers do not
regard current actual income as an adequate basis for making consumption
decisions, but we shall build the theory on the assumption that consumers
behave as if it were, except on occasion to allow two non-income variables to
enter the consumption function.

Although income, somehow defined, is likely to be an important influence
on the consumption decisions of households, a number of additional or
alternative explanatory variables have been suggested. Capital gains, the stock
of durables held by consumers, the distribution of income and demographic
factors, have been postulated as factors influencing aggregate consumption,
but these will not be considered here. However, two additional variables will
be discussed. Later in this chapter the consequences for the theory of introducing the rate of interest as a determinant of consumption expenditure will be
explained (section 2.5), and subsequently consumption will often be assumed
to be interest-elastic. And in Chapter V the full model of income determination,
completed in Chapter IV, will be analysed utilizing the Pigovian hypothesis
that consumption is a function of the stock of wealth in the hands of consumers.


## 2.2   A SIMPLE MODEL OF INCOME DETERMINATION

The purpose of macroeconomic models is to explain the variation of certain
variables in the system. One variable which has received much attention is the
level of aggregate (national) income. While the simple models concentrate on
explaining this variable it is possible, as we shall see, to construct in relatively
easy steps models which can cope with a wider range of variables. The first
step will be taken by presenting a simple static model of income determination.
Since it simplifies the exposition in some respects we shall initially use a linear
model but from section 2.3.3 onwards we will build the models using the general
forms of the various functions.


### 2.2.1   Equilibrium income

To begin with the following simplifying assumptions are adopted:
(1) There are only two types of expenditure, consumption $C$ and investment $I$,

† Laidler (1968) presents a dynamic model of this kind.

of which investment is assumed to be exogenous as denoted by a bar over the symbol. The government sector is therefore eliminated, no account being taken of the government share of aggregate expenditure or of the taxation share of aggregate income. These assumptions will be dropped later in this chapter.

(2) The economy is closed, there being no external (foreign trade) sector. This assumption is dropped in Chapter VI.

(3) Saving is undertaken only by households, which implies that all earnings of firms are distributed in the form of payments to factors of production, labour, managerial skill and capital ownership. This assumption is retained throughout.

One of the main objectives of a model of income determination is to establish the conditions under which the economic system will be in (static) equilibrium. Knowledge of these conditions enables us to predict the effect on the equilibrium position of changes within the system or new (exogenous) influences from outside it. The condition for equilibrium aggregate income is equality between the aggregate demand and supply of goods and services in the economy. Aggregate demand is the sum of expenditure planned by households and firms on consumption and investment goods respectively, and aggregate supply is the equivalent of aggregate income (output) $Y$, so that the *equilibrium condition* can be stated formally as

$$Y = C + \bar{I} \tag{2.21}$$

It is worth emphasizing that $C$, $\bar{I}$ and $Y$ are *planned* magnitudes. In this sense aggregate demand and supply are not necessarily equal just as demand and supply in an individual market may not be equal. But such equality *is* required for equilibrium; without it people plan to spend more or less than is required to purchase the output planned by firms at the current price level. Equilibrium therefore requires the *compatibility of the plans* made by consumers and investors on the one hand and suppliers of goods and services on the other. If the plans are not compatible a process of adjustment (which in the static model is timeless) will eliminate the incompatibility. For example, if planned supply exceeds planned demand, firms find that their stocks of unsold goods increase and react by reducing output below the planned level. Aggregate income falls, and planned consumption also but less rapidly (since the marginal propensity to consume is less than unity), and equilibrium is at some income level below that on which the original expenditure plans had been based. Only if plans are compatible will there be no adjustment.

The equilibrium condition can be stated in another way. The level of saving planned by households is equal to the part of income which they do not plan to consume. It is apparent from equations (2.1) and (2.21) that equilibrium requires that

$$C + S = C + \bar{I}$$

or
$$S = \bar{I} \tag{2.22}$$

This is the source of the misleading statement that aggregate savings and investment must be equal. If the magnitudes in equation (2.22) are interpreted in the sense of actual or realized $C$, $S$ and $\bar{I}$ then indeed savings and investment *must* be equal. This equality of the realized $S$ and $I$ derives from the definition of income into two categories on the income uses side. That is, we are *defining* realized savings and investment to be equal.

On the other hand, interpreting equation (2.22) as a condition for equilibrium we must interpret the magnitudes as planned saving and investment. If aggregate demand and supply are to be equal the part of income which consumers do not plan to spend on consumption goods must equal the amount investors plan to spend on investment goods.

With a given consumption function and with investment exogenously determined there is only one level of income which satisfies the condition for equilibrium. Assuming a linear consumption function the model of income determination consists of two equations in two unknowns, $Y$ and $C$:

$$C = c_0 + c_Y Y \tag{2.10}$$

$$Y = C + \bar{I} \tag{2.21}$$

Substituting for $C$ from (2.10) in equation (2.21) and solving for $Y$, we have the equilibrium level of income:

$$Y = \frac{c_0 + \bar{I}}{1 - c_Y} \tag{2.23}$$

Equation (2.23) tells us the equilibrium income level, given the size of exogenous expenditure and the marginal propensity to consume. It says nothing, since the model is static, about the *stability* of that equilibrium. The static analysis is more instructive, however, if we adopt conditions for equilibrium which are known from dynamic analysis, to provide *stable* equilibrium.

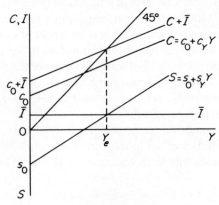

Figure 2.4

It can be shown† that stability requires $-1 < c_Y < 1$. Combined with the expectation, on economic grounds, that $c_Y$ is positive, this suggests the restriction that $0 < c_Y < 1$.

This simple model is shown in Figure 2.4. Aggregate expenditure $C + \bar{I}$ is represented by a curve parallel to the consumption function because investment, $\bar{I}$, is constant for all income levels. The 45° line conveniently locates all points at which the expenditure plans are in the aggregate equal to income. The equilibrium income level, $Y_e$, is therefore determined where the aggregate expenditure curve intersects the 45° line, where $Y = C + \bar{I}$. As we should expect from equation (2.22) at this income level the plans of savers and investors are equated, as is indicated by the intersection of the savings function and the exogenous investment line.

### 2.2.2 The multiplier

Having established the condition for equilibrium, the information can be used to analyse the effect on equilibrium income of any change in the level of exogenous expenditure $(c_0 + \bar{I})$. To this end we find the derivative of income with respect to $c_0$ and $\bar{I}$. From the equilibrium income equation (2.23):

$$\frac{\partial Y}{\partial c_0} = \frac{\partial Y}{\partial \bar{I}} = \frac{1}{1 - c_Y} \tag{2.24}$$

Since $0 < c_Y < 1$ it follows that

$$\frac{1}{1 - c_Y} > 1 \tag{2.25}$$

A unit increase in exogenous expenditure raises income by more than one unit. The derivative (2.24) is called the *income multiplier*. Mathematically it is clear that the greater is the marginal propensity to consume the greater is the multiplier $k$. The economic rationale for this characteristic of the model is that an injection of expenditure from outside the system $(d\bar{I}$ or $dc_0)$, induces an increase in income which in turn induces a rise in consumption. The induced increase in consumption creates extra income for others, who in turn spend a proportion $(c_Y)$ of this extra income. This process would continue without limit if it were not for the fact that each recipient of extra income spends only a *part* of the increase; there is a 'leakage' to saving at each stage so that the additions to consumption and income gradually diminish. This implies that as $c_Y \to 1$, $k \to \infty$. The multiplier process in this static analysis is assumed timeless, the new equilibrium level of income being established instantaneously.

The effect on equilibrium income of a change in exogenous expenditure is shown in Figure 2.5. When investment rises from $\bar{I}_1$ to $\bar{I}_2$ equilibrium income increases from $Y_1$ to $Y_2$. At income level $Y_2$ we have $C + \bar{I}_2 = Y_2$ and $\bar{I}_2 = S$.

† See Samuelson (1967), pp. 276–80, and section 7.1 below.

The increase in income is a multiple $k$ of the change in investment, and consists of the increase in investment itself, $d\bar{I}$, and the induced consumption, $dC$, in the figure.† The increase in investment plans is matched in the new equilibrium by the higher planned saving at the income $Y_2$, so that the movement from one equilibrium to another is achieved with matched changes in savings and investment plans.

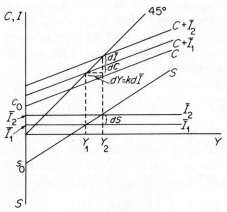

*Figure 2.5*

Finally it will be convenient for later use to restate in *general form* the equations used in linear form in this section. The model in general form consists of the equations

$$C = C_0 + C(Y) \tag{2.26}$$

$$Y = C + \bar{I} \tag{2.21}$$

Taking the differentials of equation (2.21) and rearranging terms we have:

$$dY = \frac{dC_0 + d\bar{I}}{1 - C_Y} \tag{2.27}$$

which is the general form of the differential of equation (2.23).

## 2.3  INVESTMENT

The assumption that investment is exogenously determined must now be modified. There is less general agreement on realistic formulations for investment functions than there is for consumption functions,‡ but two determinants

† Note that the figure necessarily shows discrete changes in the variables whereas the calculus is concerned with small changes.

‡ Evans (1969), Ch. 4 and 5, surveys the theory and evidence on investment functions. Shapiro (1970), Ch. 11, 12 and 13, and Lindauer (1968), Ch. 3, provide useful background for our brief coverage of the investment decision.

of investment are conventionally postulated in static income determination models. These are the level of aggregate income and the rate of interest. The discussion of the model with investment as a function of income which follows in section 2.3.1 will be extended in section 2.3.2 to cover the hypothesis that investment is affected by *changes* in aggregate income, a hypothesis which is incorporated into a dynamic model of income in Chapter VII.

### 2.3.1 Investment and income

The general form of the investment–income relationship will be

$$I = I_0 + I(Y) \tag{2.28}$$

where $I_Y = dI/dY > 0$, the marginal propensity to invest.

Assuming that planned investment consists of an exogenous component $I_0$ and an endogenous component determined by income, the *linear* form of the investment function is:

$$I = i_0 + i_Y Y \tag{2.29}$$

where $i_0 > 0$ and $i_Y > 0$ and it is assumed that $(c_Y + i_Y) < 1$, the modified condition for stability in the model to be constructed.

A number of reasons have been suggested for expecting investment decisions to be determined by the level of income. Perhaps the most generally accepted one emphasizes the influence of the availability of funds to investors. It is hypothesized that the availability of funds for investment is related to the level of profit, assuming a fixed proportion of profit to be retained by the firm, and that the level of profit is a function of the level of sales. Aggregate income can be regarded as an indicator of the quantity of sales, so that we have a predicted indirect relationship between aggregate income and the level of investment.

Incorporating the linear investment function into the model, we have three equations, the equilibrium condition (2.30) and two behavioural equations:

$$Y = C + I \tag{2.30}$$

$$C = c_0 + c_Y Y \tag{2.10}$$

$$I = i_0 + i_Y Y \tag{2.29}$$

The solution for equilibrium $Y$ is:

$$Y = \frac{c_0 + i_0}{1 - c_Y - i_Y} \tag{2.31}$$

Making investment endogenous does not alter the fundamental requirement for equilibrium that aggregate planned expenditure equals aggregate planned supply, but it does introduce an extra parameter, *the marginal propensity to invest*, into the determination of income.

The model is shown in Figure 2.6. The only difference compared with Figure 2.5 is that the investment function $I$ now has a positive slope, and the slope of the total expenditure $(C + I)$ curve is now the sum of the slopes of the $C$ and $I$ curves.

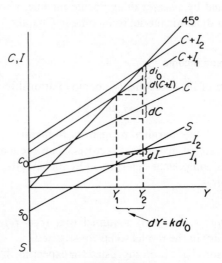

*Figure 2.6*

In the model with exogenous investment the response of expenditure within the system to a change in exogenous expenditure was confined to induced changes in consumption. With investment endogenous the responsiveness of expenditure is determined by the sum of the marginal propensities to consume and invest. The new multiplier is:

$$\frac{\partial Y}{\partial c_0} = \frac{\partial Y}{\partial i_0} = \frac{1}{1 - c_Y - i_Y} \tag{2.32}$$

which, since $i_Y > 0$, exceeds the multiplier (2.24).

The impact of an increase in exogenous expenditure can be found by manipulating the curves in Figure 2.6 in the same way as in Figure 2.5. With a given $di_0$ (or $dc_0$) the increase in income is determined by the slope of the $(C + I)$ curve and the induced increase in consumption, shown as $dC$ in Figure 2.6, is now accompanied by an induced increase in investment (shown by $dI$ in the figure and additional to $di_0$).

In general form the model, with exogenous elements in $C$ and $I$, is written as

$$C = C_0 + C(Y) \tag{2.26}$$

$$I = I_0 + I(Y) \tag{2.28}$$

$$Y = C + I \tag{2.30}$$

Differentiating equation (2.30) totally and rearranging terms we have

$$dY = \frac{dC_0 + dI_0}{1 - C_Y - I_Y} \tag{2.33}$$

where $(C_Y + I_Y) < 1$. The multiplier is now the general version of (2.32). That is

$$\frac{\partial Y}{\partial C_0} = \frac{\partial Y}{\partial I_0} = \frac{1}{1 - C_Y - I_Y} \tag{2.34}$$

### 2.3.2 The acceleration principle

A hypothesis which has been tested in many empirical studies of investment in recent years is that the level of investment planned is related to the size of the *change* in income (output) rather than to the level of output. There have been numerous versions of the hypothesis, but it is sufficient for our purposes to limit attention to the original, 'naive' form.†

Stated formally the 'accelerator hypothesis' or 'acceleration principle' is

$$I_t = a(Y_{t-1} - Y_{t-2}) \tag{2.35}$$

where the $t$ subscripts indicate time periods; $a$ is the accelerator, the ratio of investment to changes in output, which is assumed to be constant and greater than zero. The assumption that $a$ is constant implies a fixed capital/output ratio, and if $a > 1$ then fluctuations in investment, the demand for capital goods, will be greater than variations in output, as is generally the case in developed economies.

In equilibrium, where output is constant at $Y_t = Y_{t-1} = Y_{t-2}$, investment must be zero. From this it should be clear that the naive form of the accelerator hypothesis makes sense only if we interpret $I_t$ as *net* investment over and above the replacement required by depreciation. Even in equilibrium depreciation requires gross investment to be positive. This distinction between net and gross investment raises a problem for the interpretation of the hypothesis. What happens to investment when income is declining? In reality negative gross investment is limited by the rate of capital depreciation, and negative net investment at any rate greater than this requires the selling of machines for scrap. Given the costs of scrapping, the possibility that investors will not react symmetrically to increases and decreases in income is apparent. If on the other hand investment is partly determined by exogenous factors and only partly responsive to output changes then the function is

$$I_t = i_0 + a(Y_{t-1} - Y_{t-2}) \tag{2.36}$$

† Evans (1969), pp. 80–6, summarizes the developments. These have been stimulated by a number of empirical refutations of the naive accelerator hypothesis.

and if $i_0$ is sufficiently larger than zero then declines in output will result only in declines in the positive level of net investment.

The accelerator hypothesis as stated in equation (2.35) is that presented by Hicks.[†] An alternative form, and the one which will be used in Chapter VII, is due to Samuelson:[‡]

$$I_t = a(C_t - C_{t-1}) \tag{2.37}$$

Investment is expected to respond to consumption changes rather than to changes in all income (output). However, this does not alter the fundamental nature of the hypothesis, as we can see if we take the linear consumption function (2.8), and substitute for $C_t$ and $C_{t-1}$ in equation (2.37) which yields:

$$I_t = a(c_Y Y_t - c_Y Y_{t-1})$$

or
$$I_t = ac_Y(Y_t - Y_{t-1}) \tag{2.38}$$

which differs from (2.35) in terms of the lag structure and the parameters entering. The introduction of $c_Y$ into the investment equation reduces, for a given accelerator, the degree of response of investment to a change in income.

To conclude this brief explanation of the accelerator we should note that the hypothesis relies on two rather restrictive assumptions:

(1) That firms are operating their existing capacity at an optimal (most efficient) rate. If this is so then an increase in output will provide an incentive to extend the level of capacity since to rely on the existing capacity would lead to a sub-optimal rate of utilization (over-utilization). But if capacity were already being under-utilized because firms had not (yet) reacted to a previous decline in output, an increase in output could be catered for without any new investment. Clearly much depends on whether firms react quickly to all output changes, which leads us to assumption (2).

(2) That investment responds to *all* output changes. This is unrealistic because transitory output changes could often be absorbed at a lower cost using existing capacity than by adjusting capacity. The hypothesis should therefore be stated as a relationship between investment and changes in output which are expected by investors to be permanent.

Despite its theoretical limitations the naive accelerator hypothesis proves to be a useful tool, when linked with the multiplier, for constructing a simple dynamic model of income determination, as we shall see in Chapter VII.

### 2.3.3 Investment and the rate of interest

We turn now to the rate of interest as a variable affecting the level of (planned) investment expenditure. The first task is to consider why we would expect a causal relationship between investment and the rate of interest on theoretical

[†] Hicks (1950).
[‡] Samuelson (1939).

grounds. The second will be to revamp the model of income determination with the rate of interest entering the investment function.

The fundamental premise on which the argument will be based is that investments are undertaken up to the point at which the marginal investment is expected, over the lifetime of the asset, to yield returns which just cover the cost of the investment. This 'break-even' investment is the cut-off point for the investor. If investment projects are ranked according to the net (over cost) returns which they yield, those above the break-even investment will yield net returns to the investor and those below would, if they were undertaken, yield net losses. Clearly, in order to specify the cut-off point it is necessary to identify the expected returns and costs which enter the investor's decision-making.

To begin with it should be clear that £1 received now is worth more than £1 received in a later period, since the earlier the money is received the more future interest the lending of that money can accumulate. If $V_0$ is a sum of money lent in period 0 then the capital sum in period 1 is $V_0(1 + r)$, where $r$ is the rate of interest received. Lending out again this larger capital sum and receiving interest on it for period 1 produces a capital sum in period 2 of $[V_0(1 + r)](1 + r) = V_0(1 + r)^2$, and if the same process is repeated the capital sum in period 3 is $[V_0(1 + r)^2](1 + r) = V_0(1 + r)^3$, so that the capital sum accumulates over $j$ periods according to the progression

$$V_j = V_0(1 + r)^j \qquad (2.39)$$

The conclusion is that a sum $V_0$ owned in period 0 will be worth more than $V_0$ in a future period; and it follows that a sum $V_0$ which is not owned until a future period must be worth less than $V_0$ owned in period 0. If money is received in the present we *accumulate* the interest to find the future value; but if money is received in the future we *discount* it to find the present value. From equation (2.39) it is apparent that the *present value* $V_0$ of a future value $V_j$ is

$$V_0 = \frac{V_j}{(1 + r)^j} \qquad (2.40)$$

The investor, when considering a particular investment project, will have some idea of the stream of future returns (earnings) he expects to accrue to the real asset. For the years 1, 2, ..., $n$ of the life of the asset the net returns are, in terms of their value at the time they are received (i.e. in current values):

$$R_1, R_2, \ldots R_n \qquad (2.41)$$

To find the present value of all expected returns we must apply the discounting procedure to every future return $R_j$. Consequently using equation (2.40) the stream of returns (2.41) has a present value of

$$\sum_{j=1}^{n} \frac{R_j}{(1 + r)^j} = \frac{R_1}{(1 + r)} + \frac{R_2}{(1 + r)^2} + \cdots + \frac{R_n}{(1 + r)^n} \qquad (2.42)$$

The investor compares this present value of returns with the cost of the real asset $P^c$ which is incurred in period 0. The condition for the maximization of net returns over cost is that increments of investment continue until, at the margin:

$$P^c = \sum_{j=1}^{n} \frac{R_j}{(1+r)^j} \tag{2.43}$$

that is to say until the marginal investment has a present value of expected returns which just covers the initial cost. Since investment as a whole is *assumed* to be subject to diminishing marginal returns, if (2.43) is satisfied there necessarily exist intra-marginal investments which yield net returns and which are therefore undertaken.

Consider now the effect of a change in the rate of interest. An increase in $r$ raises the return on a sum of money lent and therefore increases the rate of accumulation of the capital sum. Consequently an increase in $r$ leads to future returns being discounted more heavily than before. If $R_1, R_2, ..., R_n$ are unaltered then this heavier discounting reduces

$$\sum_{j=1}^{n} \frac{R_j}{(1+r)^j}$$

because of the increase in the size of the denominator. Since the cost of the real asset remains the same a reduction in the present value of returns in equation (2.43) means that the previously marginal investment now fails to cover its costs, i.e.

$$P^c > \sum_{j=1}^{n} \frac{R_j}{(1+r)^j} \tag{2.44}$$

The consequence is that this now extra-marginal investment is not undertaken. The level of investment planned is cut back to the point at which the returns at the margin just cover costs again: this means that a previously intra-marginal investment which yielded net returns now becomes the break-even investment, i.e. the marginal investment, and some less productive investments are abandoned.

The implication of the argument is that the level of planned investment is a negative function of the rate of interest on financial assets, $r$:

$$I = I(r) \tag{2.45}$$

where $dI/dr < 0$. This investment function is shown in Figure 2.7.

It can be argued that investment plans will be responsive to changes in the rate of interest down to a certain level of the rate of interest but will be completely interest-inelastic at lower rates of interest. The rationale for this point of view is that at low rates of interest the opportunity cost of an investment is small anyway and marginal adjustments in the rate will not alter the investment

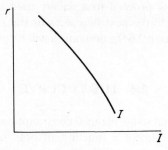

*Figure 2.7*

decision which becomes dominated by the uncertainties associated with the expectations of future earnings. If this were true then the investment function in Figure 2.7 would become vertical below a certain rate of interest since below this rate:

$$\frac{\partial I}{\partial r} = 0 \qquad (2.46)$$

Turning now to the model of income determination with the rate of interest entering the investment function, we can first modify that function to include both income and the rate of interest:

$$I = I_0 + I(Y, r) \qquad (2.47)$$

where $I_0 > 0$, $\partial I/\partial Y = I_Y > 0$ and $\partial I/\partial r = I_r < 0$.

Introducing the new investment function the model of income determination now consists of the following equations

$$C = C_0 + C(Y) \qquad (2.26)$$

$$I = I_0 + I(Y, r) \qquad (2.47)$$

$$Y = C + I \qquad (2.30)$$

As usual the equilibrium level of income is found by substituting for $C$ and $I$ in the equilibrium condition (2.30) which gives:

$$Y = C_0 + C(Y) + I_0 + I(Y, r) \qquad (2.48)$$

Taking the differential of equation (2.48) and rearranging terms we have:

$$dY = \frac{dC_0 + dI_0 + I_r dr}{1 - C_Y - I_Y} \qquad (2.49)$$

It is clear from this result that the rate of interest is another factor influencing equilibrium income. In fact the term $(I_r dr)$ enters similarly to the exogenous expenditure variables so that the interest sensitivity of investment is the critical parameter determining the impact on income of changes in the rate of interest.

The analysis can now proceed to a widely used tool of macroeconomic analysis, the *IS* curve. In the next two sections the *IS* curve will be derived algebraically and in section 2.6 the derivation will be shown diagrammatically.

## 2.4 THE *IS* CURVE

In the model developed so far planned consumption is a function of income alone and planned investment a function of both income and the rate of interest. And the condition for equilibrium is that aggregate expenditure plans equal income:

$$Y = C_0 + C(Y) + I_0 + I(Y, r) \qquad (2.48)$$

Since expenditure plans are affected by changes in income *and* the rate of interest, at any income level there will be a set of plans one for each level of the rate of interest, and similarly at any rate of interest there will be a set of plans

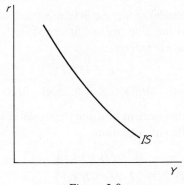

*Figure 2.8*

one for each income level. But at a given level of income only *one* rate of interest will satisfy condition (2.48), and at a given rate of interest only *one* level of income will satisfy that equation. Consequently there exists a set of combinations of *Y* and *r* which provide equilibrium. These combinations equate expenditure plans with income and, by implication, equate the planned levels of saving and investment, that is satisfy the condition

$$S_0 + S(Y) = I_0 + I(Y, r) \qquad (2.50)$$

which is the corollary of equation (2.48).

Diagrammatically, in a *Y, r* plane the locus of the combinations of these two variables which satisfy the equilibrium condition is known as the *IS curve*. Figure 2.8 shows such a curve.

Three characteristics of this equilibrium curve should be emphasized. Firstly, it must not be interpreted as a behavioural equation like the consumption function. It does not represent a direct *causal* relationship between $r$ and $Y$. Rather it represents the equilibrium condition of the model, and a change in $r$ affects the level of $Y$ (and vice versa) *only* in the sense that a change in $r$ must be compensated for by a change in $Y$ *if equilibrium is to be maintained*. Secondly, it is drawn for given values of the exogenous variables $C_0$ (or $S_0$) and $I_0$. A change in either of these will alter the position of the curve, that is alter the set of combinations of $Y$ and $r$ which yield equilibrium. Rearranging the terms of equation (2.49) we have:

$$dY = \left( \frac{dC_0 + dI_0}{1 - C_Y - I_Y} \right) + \left( \frac{I_r}{1 - C_Y - I_Y} \right) dr \qquad (2.51)$$

which is a standard function between two variables ($dY$ and $dr$) with a constant term. A change in the *position* of the *IS* curve is only possible when the constant term changes; and the constant term changes only if either $C_0$ or $I_0$ changes. From equation (2.51) we have:

$$\frac{\partial Y}{\partial C_0} = \frac{\partial Y}{\partial I_0} = \frac{1}{1 - C_Y - I_Y} > 0 \qquad (2.52)$$

and since $C_0 = -S_0$ equation (2.52) implies

$$\frac{\partial Y}{\partial S_0} = -\frac{1}{1 - C_Y - I_Y} < 0 \qquad (2.53)$$

These partial derivatives show that if there is an increase in exogenous expenditure the equilibrium level of income associated with any rate of interest is raised by an amount equal to the change in expenditure times the multiplier. In terms of Figure 2.8 the effect would be to shift the *IS* curve to the right by this amount. An increase in $S_0$, that is an upward shift in the savings function, is equivalent to a decrease in $C_0$, as a comparison of equations (2.52) and (2.53) shows. The result is a reduction in the equilibrium level of income at any rate of interest, a shift to the left of the *IS* curve. The increase in planned savings leads to a fall in the level of planned spending if investment plans remain the same. With the deficiency in planned expenditure output and income decline and (since $I_Y > 0$) planned investment falls too. Income must decline sufficiently to equate planned saving to the lower level of planned investment. The attempt by consumers to increase saving is therefore self-frustrating and depresses total income, a result often referred to as the 'paradox of thrift'.

The third characteristic of the *IS* curve is that it is drawn with a negative slope. The negative slope follows from the assumptions of the model (in particular the restrictions on the parameters $C_Y$ and $I_Y$ and $I_r$) and we can explain the result formally and then outline the reasoning behind it.

The slope of the *IS* curve indicates the change in income which must accompany a change in the rate of interest if the equilibrium condition is to be satisfied. This is given by the partial derivative $\partial r / \partial Y$ from the differential of the equilibrium condition equation (2.51):

$$\frac{\partial r}{\partial Y} = \frac{1 - C_Y - I_Y}{I_r} \qquad (2.54)$$

Given that $I_r < 0$ equation (2.54) is negative, if $(1 - C_Y - I_Y) > 0$ as is conventionally assumed.† Alternatively this condition can be written as $(S_Y - I_Y) > 0$ which implies that $S_Y > I_Y$: the marginal propensity to save must exceed the marginal propensity to invest.

An increase in the rate of interest, *ceteris paribus*, must be accompanied by a decline in income if equilibrium is to be maintained. The increase in *r* reduces the level of expenditure planned by investors. If nothing else in the system changed this would imply that expenditure plans would fall short of income; the new level of investment plans would be lower than the planned saving associated with the original equilibrium income level. Consequently there is a reduction in the level of income at which planned saving matches planned investment. The implication of the condition for equilibrium is that high (low) equilibrium income levels are associated with low (high) equilibrium rates of interest.

## 2.5 THE *IS* CURVE WITH SAVING A FUNCTION OF THE RATE OF INTEREST

No account has yet been taken of the possibility that saving and consumption decisions are sensitive to changes in the rate of interest. The rate of interest is the reward for sacrificing consumption and increases in the rate produce a substitution effect in favour of increasing the proportion of income saved.‡ The consumption function which recognizes this interest sensitivity is:

$$C = C_0 + C(Y, r) \qquad (2.55)$$

where $C_0 > 0$, $C_Y > 0$ and $C_r < 0$. The new equilibrium condition, the equation of the *IS* curve is

$$Y = C_0 + C(Y, r) + I_0 + I(Y, r) \qquad (2.56)$$

Taking differentials and rearranging terms we have

$$dY = \left( \frac{dC_0 + dI_0}{1 - C_Y - I_Y} \right) + \left( \frac{C_r + I_r}{1 - C_Y - I_Y} \right) dr \qquad (2.57)$$

---

† On the implications of dropping this assumption see Silber (1971) and Burrows (1974).

‡ We ignore the possibility that increases in the rate of interest have an income effect in favour of consumption which, if it outweighs the substitution effect against consumption, would make $C_r > 0$.

which is analogous to equation (2.51) except that now the equilibrium level of income responds to changes in the interest rate through both investment *and* consumption plans:

$$\frac{\partial r}{\partial Y} = \frac{1 - C_Y - I_Y}{C_r + I_r} \tag{2.58}$$

Equation (2.58), the slope of the *IS* curve, is again negative given that $(1 - C_Y - I_Y) > 0$, and $(C_r + I_r) < 0$.

If consumption and investment were responsive to changes in the rate of interest above a certain rate, $r_1$ in Figure 2.9, and completely insensitive below that rate, the *IS* curve would have a negative slope above $r_1$ but it would be vertical below $r_1$. Formally it is clear that as $(C_r + I_r) \to 0$ from equation (2.58) we have for the slope of the *IS* curve $\partial r/\partial Y \to -\infty$.

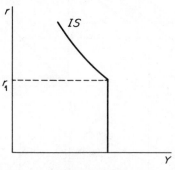

Figure 2.9

## 2.6 DERIVING THE *IS* CURVE DIAGRAMMATICALLY

An important advantage of the mathematical derivation of the *IS* curve is that it can easily be applied to models in which the expenditure sector is extended to include elements of the government budget and of the balance of payments. Diagrammatic derivation, on the other hand, is not easy even for the simple model and becomes excessively complicated when the model is developed further. However, one of the generally acknowledged dangers of the *IS–LM* framework of analysis is that it hides from view the fundamental changes (such as shifts in the consumption function reflecting changes in the behaviour of consumers) which cause variations in the equilibrium level of income. The diagrammatic derivation may help us to remember that the *IS* curve (and the *LM* curve yet to be discussed) trace out a locus of *equilibrium* points which are based upon the functions representing consumption and investment behaviour. This derivation will not, however, be repeated later for the model in its more elaborate forms.

In Figure 2.10(a) we have a family of savings functions, one for each rate of interest, $r_1 < r_2 < r_3$ etc. Linear curves are used for simplicity although this restriction is not necessary. The lower the rate of interest the lower is the level of saving planned at any level of income ($S_r > 0$). There are numerous combinations of the level of income and the rate of interest which produce any particular level of savings, say $S_4$. In Figure 2.10(a) these combinations are illustrated by

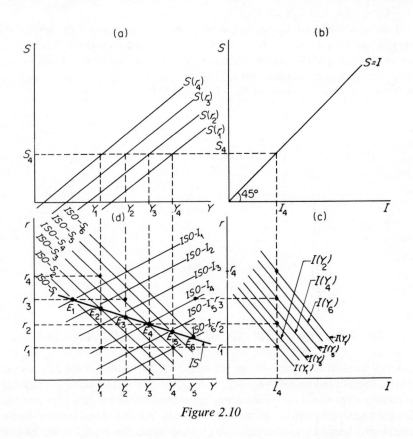

*Figure 2.10*

$Y_1$ and $r_4$, $Y_2$ and $r_3$, $Y_3$ and $r_2$, $Y_4$ and $r_1$. Since all of these combinations produce the same level of saving, $S_4$, they can be represented as an *ISO-saving* curve, *ISO-$S_4$*, shown in Figure 2.10(d). Any point on this curve shows an $r$, $Y$ combination which will result in the level of planned savings $S_4$. Different levels of saving, $S_1$, $S_2$, $S_3$, $S_5$ and $S_6$ for example can be represented by a family of *ISO-S* curves as in Figure 2.10(d). As we move from *ISO-$S_1$* to *ISO-$S_2$* and up to *ISO-$S_6$* the level of saving is increasing. Any movement in a north-easterly direction necessarily increases the level of saving because both income and the rate of interest are increasing and $S_Y > 0$ and $S_r > 0$.

Now we set the level of planned saving, say $S_4$, equal to the level of planned investment, as is required for equilibrium. The line in Figure 2.10(b) simply shows points at which $S = I$, and through it the level of planned saving $S_4$ is equated to the level of planned investment $I_4$. This particular level of investment $I_4$ can also be brought about by various combinations of income and the rate of interest. We have postulated that the higher is the level of income the higher will be the level of investment, and the lower the rate of interest the higher the level of investment. Consequently, the level of investment will only remain at $I_4$, as income increases ($Y_1 < Y_2 < Y_3$ etc.) and we move to higher investment curves, if the rate of interest also rises, for example from $r_1$ to $r_4$ as shown in Figure 2.10(c).

The combinations which produce $I_4$ are therefore $Y_1$ and $r_1$, $Y_3$ and $r_2$, $Y_5$ and $r_3$, and $Y_7$ and $r_4$, and this information can be transferred to part (d) of the figure in the form of an *ISO*-investment curve (*ISO–$I_4$*). For different levels of investment $I_1$, $I_2$, $I_3$, $I_5$ and $I_6$ we have different *ISO–I* curves, the family of such curves being shown in Figure 2.10(d), such that the level of investment increases as we move in a south-easterly direction from *ISO–$I_1$* to *ISO–$I_6$*. The level of investment planned increases as income rises *and* the rate of interest falls because $I_Y > 0$ and $I_r < 0$.

Finally, there is a point of intersection in Figure 2.10(d) between each *ISO–S* curve and the *ISO–I* curve to which it corresponds, that is the one representing the same level of investment as saving. For example we have *ISO–$S_1$* and *ISO–$I_1$* intersecting at $E_1$, *ISO–$S_2$* and *ISO–$I_2$* at $E_2$ and so on. These intersections represent the combinations of $Y$ and $r$ which equate the level of planned saving and investment. Each of them is therefore a point on the *IS* curve, and we can draw the *IS* curve through the points as shown in Figure 2.10(d).†

Each point on the *IS* curve therefore represents an intersection between an *ISO–S* curve and the corresponding *ISO–I* curve. Any shift in the family of savings functions or in the investment functions will alter the *ISO–S* and *ISO–I* curves respectively and alter the position of the *IS* curve as the intersection points shift. For example, an upward shift in the savings functions ($dC_0 < 0$) reflecting an increased desire to save at any income level, causes the following changes. The level of income which produces $S_4$ at rate of interest $r_1$ is now lower. This shifts the *ISO–$S_4$* curve to the left and the intersection between *ISO–$S_4$* and *ISO–$I_4$* moves in a south-westerly direction. Conse-

---

† We have drawn the case of the downward sloping *IS* curve. The condition for a negative slope is that (for a given level of $r$) the change in income required to move us from any *ISO–S* curve to a higher one, e.g. from *ISO–$S_4$* to *ISO–$S_5$*, is less than the change in income required for a corresponding *ISO–I* move, i.e. from *ISO–$I_4$* to *ISO–$I_5$*. Diagrammatically this means that any pair of *ISO–I* curves must be further apart (horizontally) than the corresponding pair of *ISO–S* curves. Mathematically this condition for a negative slope is stated as $S_Y > I_Y$ (as we found from equation (2.54)) which means that the response of planned saving to a change in income must exceed that of planned investment.

quently, an increase in the desire to save shifts the *IS* curve to the left. The reader can verify that a fall in the level of planned investment ($dI_0 < 0$) also shifts the *IS* curve to the left.

The derivation of the *IS* curve in Figure 2.10 can be summarized in a formal way as follows:†

*Figure 2.10(a)* It is assumed here that

$$S = f_1(Y, r) \tag{2.59}$$

Where $r$ is treated as a constant, so that with linear functions

$$S_j = (s_0 + s_r r_j) + s_Y Y \tag{2.60}$$

With $r_j$ constant we have an $S - Y$ curve for a given rate of interest. For different $r_j$'s there is a family of $S - Y$ curves, for example as for $j = 1, 2, 3, 4$ in the figure.

*Figure 2.10(b):* The equilibrium condition is stated as $S = I$ which is represented by the 45° line.

*Figure 2.10(c):* Here it is assumed that

$$I = f_2(Y, r) \tag{2.61}$$

where $Y$ is treated as a constant so that

$$I_j = (i_0 + i_Y Y_j) + i_r r \tag{2.62}$$

With $Y_j$ constant there is an $I - r$ curve for the given income level. For different $Y_j$'s there is a family of $I - r$ curves, for example as for $j = 1, 2, ..., 7$ in the figure.

*Figure 2.10(d):* In this section an equilibrium relationship is established between the variables $r$ and $Y$ which affect saving and investment plans. Treating saving as a constant $S_j$ we construct from the relationship

$$r = \left(\frac{S_j - s_0}{s_r}\right) - \left(\frac{s_Y}{s_r}\right) Y \tag{2.63}$$

for different $S_j$'s a family of curves with the characteristic that saving remains constant along each one of them. These are the *ISO–S_j* curves of the figure. Further, by treating investment as a constant $I_j$, a family of *ISO–I_j* curves is constructed from the relationship

$$r = \left(\frac{I_j - i_0}{i_r}\right) - \left(\frac{i_Y}{i_r}\right) Y \tag{2.64}$$

Along each *ISO–I* curve, investment remains constant for various combinations of $r$ and $Y$.

Any point of intersection between an *ISO–S* curve and an *ISO–I* curve,

† The remainder of section 2.6 can be skipped on a first reading with no loss of continuity.

where the level of saving and investment are the same (such as point $E_1$ where $S_1 = I_1$), satisfies the condition

$$s_0 + s_r r + s_Y Y = i_0 + i_r r + i_Y Y \qquad (2.65)$$

which can of course alternatively be rewritten as

$$Y = c_0 + c_r r + c_Y Y + i_0 + i_r r + i_Y Y \qquad (2.66)$$

The intersection points $E_1$ etc. are therefore points on the *IS* curve, in this case the linear form. Differentiating equation (2.66) and rearranging terms we have

$$\frac{\partial r}{\partial Y} = \frac{1 - c_Y - i_Y}{c_r + i_r} \qquad (2.67)$$

which is the slope of the linear *IS* curve in Figure 2.10(d).

## 2.7 GOVERNMENT TAXATION AND EXPENDITURE

The governments in many developed economies today account for approaching 30 per cent of aggregate expenditure. It is therefore incumbent upon us to modify the model of income determination to allow for the fiscal operations of the government. While these operations are in practice extremely complex, at the level of abstraction used in much standard macroeconomic theory it is not difficult to introduce the government.

It will be assumed that the government receives revenue from taxes alone and that the tax revenue is partly related to income and partly exogenously determined. Any tax with a tax base (e.g. taxable income) related to income will produce an amount of revenue which is determined within the model. For simplicity we assume an income tax with a single tax rate on all income $Y$, i.e. a proportional income tax, and the tax revenue ($T$) function is

$$T = T(Y) \qquad (2.68)$$

where $T_Y = dT/dY$. The change in tax revenue resulting from an increase in income $T_Y$ is the tax rate.† Adding to the income tax revenue an exogenous part of tax revenue $T_0$ which denotes revenue from taxes not related to the level of income, the tax revenue equation becomes

$$T = T_0 + T(Y) \qquad (2.69)$$

With the government now taking a share in total income the *definition of income* equation (2.1), must be modified to

$$Y = C + S + T \qquad (2.70)$$

† If the tax rate is different for different income brackets the tax structure is no longer proportional and the parameter of the tax function would be the average tax rate on all income which would differ from the marginal tax rate, the first derivative of the tax function. However, we will assume for simplicity that the tax rate is not different for different income brackets.

Households' income is now used for consumption, saving and the payment of taxes, and discretion is exercised by the households only over their use of income after tax, disposable income $Y^d$ which is defined as

$$Y^d = Y - T = Y - (T_0 + T(Y))$$ (2.71)

and for changes we have the differential

$$dY^d = -dT_0 + (1 - T_Y) dY$$ (2.72)

On the expenditure side we must recognize the contribution of the government to aggregate expenditure. As with the tax side government expenditure could be divided into an element which is exogenous and one related to income. However, it simplifies the analysis if we assume that only transfer payments are endogenous and include them in $T$ as negative taxes, so that $T_Y$ is interpreted as the tax rate net of transfers. Planned government expenditure on goods and services is treated as exogenous $\bar{G}$.

The condition for equilibrium remains as equality between planned expenditure and income, but planned expenditure now includes that undertaken by the government. Consequently we rewrite equation (2.30) as

$$Y = C + I + \bar{G}$$ (2.73)

Alternatively, from equations (2.70) and (2.73), this equilibrium condition can be written as

$$C + S + T = C + I + \bar{G}$$

or $$S + T = I + \bar{G}$$ (2.74)

The requirement for equilibrium is, therefore, that planned private saving plus tax revenue (i.e. income withheld from consumption) be equal to planned private investment and government expenditure on goods and services.

Before the solution for the equilibrium level of income can be found one further qualification of the model is necessary. There is some disagreement concerning the appropriate formulation of the consumption function when the government is taxing part of consumers' incomes in order to provide goods and services (some of which will be consumption goods) either free of charge to the user or at a subsidized price. Do consumers in the aggregate regard these government-provided goods as perfect substitutes for their own consumption and the tax payment as equivalent to paying the price? If they do then the government taxation and spending procedure does nothing, if the budget is balanced, to affect the consumption function: consumers would have done the same thing on their own account if the government had not intervened.

However, in practice there are many reasons for expecting consumers to make consumption decisions independently of the provision of consumption goods by the government, that is to regard private and public consumption goods as poor substitutes. Lack of information on what is provided by the government is one reason. Another is that the government may deliberately provide goods which do not enter individual consumers' preference functions. Yet another is that the private and publicly provided goods may be physically different (for example, a park may be a poor substitute for one's own garden).

We will henceforth adopt the conventional, extreme assumption that private consumption decisions are based on disposable private income and that tax payments are not regarded as equivalent to private income nor publicly provided goods as substitutes for private ones.† The new consumption function is

$$C = C_0 + C(Y^d, r) \tag{2.75}$$

which is the same as (2.55) except that *disposable* income is now the relevant income variable.

The model of income determination in general form and with a government consists of the following equations:

$$C = C_0 + C(Y^d, r) \tag{2.75}$$

$$I = I_0 + I(Y, r) \tag{2.47}$$

$$Y = C + I + \bar{G} \tag{2.73}$$

Substituting (2.75) and (2.47) into (2.73) we have

$$Y = C_0 + C(Y^d, r) + I_0 + I(Y, r) + \bar{G}$$

or $\qquad Y = C_0 + C(Y - T, r) + I_0 + I(Y, r) + \bar{G} \tag{2.76}$

Differentiating equation (2.76) totally and rearranging terms we obtain:‡

$$dY = \left( \frac{dC_0 + dI_0 - C_Y dT_0 + d\bar{G}}{1 - C_Y(1 - T_Y) - I_Y} \right) + \left( \frac{C_r + I_r}{1 - C_Y(1 - T_Y) - I_Y} \right) dr \tag{2.77}$$

Equation (2.77) is the differential of the *IS* curve when the government is included and should be compared with its predecessor in the development of this model, equation (2.57). They are different in two respects. In the first place the slope of the *IS* curve is now affected by the tax rate, $T_Y$. From equation (2.77) we have the slope of the *IS* curve

$$\frac{\partial r}{\partial Y} = \frac{1 - C_Y(1 - T_Y) - I_Y}{C_r + I_r} < 0 \tag{2.78}$$

The slope of the new *IS* curve, equation (2.78) is greater (in absolute terms) than the old slope, equation (2.58), because the numerator is increased by the tax. Since the multiplier is the reciprocal of the numerator this implies that the tax reduces the size of the multiplier.

† The implications of the alternative extreme assumption for the single sector income determination model can be found in Bailey (1971), Ch. 9.
‡ The derivative $C_Y$ is in fact $C_{Y^d}$, but for simplicity the former symbol will be retained.

The explanation of this decline in the multiplier is that, with the level of tax revenue related to the level of income, as income rises at each 'round' of the multiplier part of the induced increase in income leaves the private sector for the Exchequer. There is a continuous 'leakage' of income out of the hands of private spenders, and assuming that the government does not spend the extra revenue ($G = \bar{G}$) the effect of the induced increase in tax revenue is to dampen the response of total income to an initial change in expenditure, that is to reduce the multiplier.

The second difference with the new *IS* curve is that the curve can now be shifted by variations in exogenous expenditure resulting from changes in the government's tax and expenditure decisions. From equation (2.77) the partial derivatives with respect to the four exogenous components of expenditure are

$$\frac{\partial Y}{\partial I_0} = \frac{\partial Y}{\partial C_0} = \frac{\partial Y}{\partial \bar{G}} = \frac{1}{1 - C_Y(1 - T_Y) - I_Y} \qquad (2.79)$$

and

$$\frac{\partial Y}{\partial T_0} = -\frac{C_Y}{1 - C_Y(1 - T_Y) - I_Y} \qquad (2.80)$$

The effect on income of a change in exogenous government expenditure on goods and services is the same as the effect of a change in $C_0$ and $I_0$. But the response of income to a unit change in tax revenue is smaller than the response to a unit change in exogenous expenditure. This is because a certain proportion (equal to $1 - C_Y$) of a unit reduction in revenue is saved by the recipients of that part of income which is no longer taxed away. The initial expenditure effect is in this case $C_Y$ times the unit reduction in revenue, and the total expenditure effect is this times the multiplier as is shown by the derivative (2.80). From the point of view of efficiency in altering total income, $\bar{G}$ is preferable to $T_0$ in this model† since (ignoring signs) $\partial Y/\partial \bar{G} > \partial Y/\partial T_0$. In terms of the *IS* curve analysis, increases in $C_0$, $I_0$ and $\bar{G}$ shift the *IS* curve to the right, and a reduction in $T_0$ also shifts the curve to the right but by a smaller amount.

It is the difference between the expenditure impact of a cut in tax revenue and an expansion of government goods-and-services expenditure which suggests that increases in the size of a *balanced* government budget may not be neutral with respect to total expenditure and income. We will consider here a budget which is balanced at the outset (*ex ante*), that is $d\bar{G} = dT_0$, and will ignore the fact that as income changes endogenous tax revenue changes also, because $T_Y > 0$, and the budget will become unbalanced *ex post*.‡

---

† The same is not true of government expenditure on transfer payments. These are treated as negative taxes so that the partial derivative is the same as (2.80) but with the opposite sign. Transfer payments and exogenous taxes are equally efficient in this respect.

‡ See Chapter 8 for a discussion of fiscal policy when the government is faced with a budget constraint and must balance the revenue and expenditure *ex post*.

The effect on income of a change in the size of a balanced budget is:

$$dY = \frac{\partial Y}{\partial \bar{G}} d\bar{G} + \frac{\partial Y}{\partial T_0} dT_0 = \left(\frac{\partial Y}{\partial \bar{G}} + \frac{\partial Y}{\partial T_0}\right) d\bar{G} \tag{2.81}$$

where

$$\frac{\partial Y}{\partial \bar{G}} + \frac{\partial Y}{\partial T_0} = \frac{1 - C_Y}{1 - C_Y(1 - T_Y) - I_Y} \tag{2.82}$$

The interesting question is whether we can establish the conditions under which (2.82) is greater than zero. Assuming the conditions $0 < C_Y < 1$, $I_Y > 0$ and $T_Y > 0$, for (2.82) to be positive the denominator must be positive because the restriction on $C_Y$ guarantees a positive numerator. We therefore require

$$1 - C_Y(1 - T_Y) - I_Y > 0 \tag{2.83}$$

or

$$1 + C_Y T_Y > (C_Y + I_Y) \tag{2.84}$$

which is satisfied because $1 > (C_Y + I_Y)$ in a stable system.

The balanced budget multiplier is positive given the assumed values of the parameters $C_Y$ and $I_Y$ and a positive tax rate. The reason is that when the balanced budget is increased income is redistributed from the private sector (tax payers) to the public sector. The marginal propensity to spend this redistributed income would have been smaller than unity in the private sector but is equal to unity in the public sector ($\partial \bar{G}/\partial T_0 = 1$). The result is an initial net impact on expenditure of $(1 - C_Y)$, which multiplied by the multiplier, as in equation (2.82), gives the effect on income.

A special case which created much interest in the 1940s and 1950s was Gelting and Haavelmo's balanced budget multiplier of one.† If investment is exogenous ($I_Y = 0$) and all taxes are also exogenous ($T_Y = 0$), equation (2.82) reduces to

$$\frac{\partial Y}{\partial \bar{G}} + \frac{\partial Y}{\partial T_0} = \frac{1 - C_Y}{1 - C_Y} = 1 \tag{2.85}$$

We can check that a multiplier of one is consistent with the general condition for a multiplier greater than zero by setting $I_Y = 0$ and $C_Y T_Y = 0$ in equality (2.84). The resulting requirement that $C_Y < 1$ is of course consistent with the value we have assumed for $C_Y$.

The effect of an increase in the size of a balanced budget can be illustrated using an *IS* diagram. Starting in Figure 2.11 from point $A$ on $IS_1$ with an existing rate of interest $r_1$, the impact on $Y$ can be divided into two parts. First, the increase in $\bar{G}$ shifts the *IS* curve to $IS_2$, an increase in income at the interest rate $r_1$ of $k\,d\bar{G}$ where $k$ is the multiplier, equation (2.79). Second, the equivalent increase in tax revenue ($dT_0 = d\bar{G}$) shifts the *IS* curve from $IS_2$ to $IS_3$, the change

† The balanced budget multiplier of one was discovered by Gelting (1941). It has also been associated with Haavelmo (1945) as a result of his paper.

in income being $kC_Y d\bar{G}$. The net effect of the balanced budget change is an increase in income by the amount $(k\,d\bar{G} - kC_Y d\bar{G})$. In the Gelting–Haavelmo case, since $k = 1/(1 - C_Y)$, the expression $(k\,d\bar{G} - kC_Y d\bar{G})$ reduces to $d\bar{G}$.

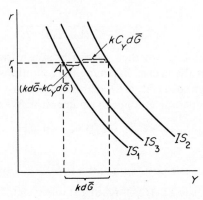

*Figure 2.11*

## EXERCISES

**2.1**  Consider the model of income determination below and answer the questions which follow:

$$Y = C + I + \bar{G}$$
$$C = 10 + 0.60\,Y$$
$$I = 20 + 0.20\,Y$$
$$\bar{G} = 10$$

(a)  Write the model in matrix form.

(b)  Solve the model to find the equilibrium values of all of the endogenous variables.

(c)  Show the solutions, obtained in question (b), diagrammatically.

**2.2**  Modify the model given in question 2.1 to include a proportional tax with a tax rate of 1/3 of income.

(a)  What is the new equilibrium income?

(b)  Does the government run a surplus or a deficit in equilibrium?

(c)  Find the balanced budget multiplier. Is the result surprising?

**2.3**  With the following model of income determination:

$$Y = C + I$$
$$C = 10 + 0.60\,Y$$
$$I = 20 + 0.1\,Y - 6.0r$$

(a) What is the equation of the *IS* curve?

(b) Obtain the new *IS* curve if exogenous consumption rises to 15.

(c) Obtain the new *IS* curve if the marginal propensity to consume rises to 0·70, with exogenous consumption equal to 15, and state the effect of the rise in the Marginal Propensity to Consume on the *IS* curve.

# CHAPTER III

# The Monetary Sector

The aim of the analysis in Chapter II was to present a conventional model of income determination containing hypothesized expenditure functions. One of the variables entering these functions is the rate of interest, but no attempt has been made to recognize that the rate of interest is determined within the economic system and may therefore in turn respond to changes in expenditure plans.

The development of the model is continued in this chapter by incorporating an explanation of the rate of interest. This entails an analysis of the demand for and supply of money because the rate of interest is the price of holding money in preference to some interest-bearing asset.

## 3.1 THE DEMAND FOR MONEY

There are several approaches to the theory of the demand for money to be found in the writings of specialists in monetary theory.† We will use the simplest theory which is compatible with the assumptions of the model as it will be developed in this chapter and in Chapter IV.‡

† These are surveyed by Laidler (1969), Ch. 3–6, Shapiro (1970), Ch. 18 and Lindauer (1968), Ch. 6.

‡ One assumption which is adopted later, in section 3.8, is that if a change in any price occurs it is not expected to be repeated. This rules out speculation and we avoid formulations of the demand for money in terms of the speculative motive since this depends on the expectation of future changes in the price of bonds. The Tobin approach, despite its theoretical appeal, is not used either because it requires the introduction of risk and of the preference patterns between risk and return of asset-holders, and because its interpretation of macro-economics terms depends on the particular form which the preference patterns take. See Tobin (1958).

A utility-maximizing asset-holder will plan to hold money to the extent that the holding offers expected net returns over cost at the margin. These money-holding plans like the ownership of any asset, are subject to the constraint imposed by the individual's titles to property, that is his wealth. The expected returns to money-holding are the convenience yielded by ready cash and the avoidance of the cost of credit incurred if the payment of bills is delayed while non-liquid assets are realized. As with other assets, however, the marginal utility of money-holding is expected to decrease as the stock of money held increases.

The expected cost of holding money is the expected return foregone on the most lucrative alternative asset plus the expected capital loss (or minus the expected gain) of value of the money held. If the price level is *expected* to remain constant then the latter component of cost is zero, because the money stock has a constant expected real value, and the expected return on assets is the rate of interest with no capital gains or losses. Taking a particular rate of interest as representative of the many rates in practice we can say that, given the expected gross returns from holding money, the expected net return after deduction of cost varies inversely with the rate of interest. Consequently, with a given budget (wealth) constraint more money and less bonds (and other interest-yielding assets) will be demanded at low rates of interest than at high rates of interest.

If the budget constraint is relaxed to some extent by an increase in income it is to be expected that the demand for money at any rate of interest will increase. This tendency will be reinforced by any increase in the returns to money-holding which results from the rise in the value of transactions undertaken with the higher income.

In the light of the above reasoning the total demand for money is expected to be a positive function of the level of aggregate income and a negative function of the rate of interest. If we introduce into the demand for money ($L$) function an exogenous element $L_0$ representing changes in liquidity preference which are independent of $Y$ and $r$ (due for example to changes in the methods of making payments for goods and services) we have

$$L = L_0 + L(Y, r) \tag{3.1}$$

where $L_0 > 0$, $\partial L / \partial Y = L_Y > 0$, and $\partial L / \partial r = L_r < 0$.

This demand function is shown in Figure 3.1 (for income levels $Y_1 < Y_2 < Y_3$) with an added restriction. This restriction is that at some low rate of interest $r_1$ the demand for money becomes infinitely sensitive to changes in the rate of interest ($L_r \to -\infty$). At this low rate of interest the rate of return on non-money assets is so low that asset-holders do not find it worthwhile to incur the costs of transferring money into other assets (and out again as the need arises). The demand for money is consequently unlimited and asset-holders will hold any amount which is put into circulation at the rate of interest $r_1$. The main reason for introducing this 'liquidity trap' situation is that it will provide a limiting case of the theory which, while it *may* not occur in practice,† will suggest the implications for the analysis of income determination of values of $L_r$ which are (negatively) large rather than small.

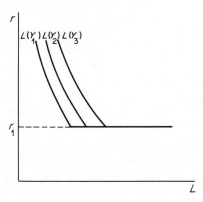

*Figure 3.1*

## 3.2  THE SUPPLY OF MONEY

The question of whether the supply of money $(M)$ is fixed exogenously by the monetary authorities, or should be regarded as endogenous to the system which determines the levels of income, rate of interest and so on, has been the subject of much recent debate (see p. 168). In macroeconomic theory $M$ has generally been assumed to be exogenous. In practice monetary authorities do to some extent adjust the money supply passively in response to changes in endogenous variables such as the rate of interest, so there is a case for explaining the money supply within our models. However, the comparative static analysis of the models to be developed is not substantially affected by the assumption that

$$M = \bar{M} \tag{3.2}$$

so we will assume for simplicity that the money supply is exogenous and constant unless the monetary authority makes a deliberate change.

## 3.3  MONETARY EQUILIBRIUM

The condition for equilibrium in the monetary sector is that the demand for money equals the supply of money. Using the demand function (3.1) and the

† There is some evidence of a minimum rate of interest of 2 per cent in the 1930s in the United States (see Evans (1969), p. 312). Studies using data for non-depression years or for the twentieth century as a whole dispute the existence of a liquidity trap in practice though of course, in the post Second World War years in particular, interest rates as low as, say, 2 per cent have not been frequently experienced so that strictly the *possibility* of a liquidity trap is not refuted by these tests. Cf. Laidler (1969), pp. 97–8.

exogenously determined supply of money (3.2) we can write the equilibrium
condition formally as

$$L_0 + L(Y,r) = \bar{M} \qquad (3.3)$$

In Figure 3.2 the vertical line $\bar{M}$ indicates the exogenous money supply, and
the family of curves $L(Y_1)$ etc. represent the demand for money at various
income levels in the absence of the liquidity trap. For a given level of income,
say $Y_1$, there is only one rate of interest $r_1$ at which the quantity of money

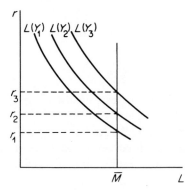

*Figure 3.2*

demanded is equal to the supply of money $\bar{M}$. Consequently the equilibrium
condition (3.3) is satisfied, if the income level is $Y_1$, only when the rate of
interest is $r_1$. At any rate above $r_1$ there is excess supply of money in circulation
which means that money-holders in the aggregate must be holding more money
than they desire at the prevailing rate of interest. The excess money balances
are used to buy bonds (or other interest-yielding assets) with the result that
bond prices are raised, and a decline in the rate of interest towards $r_1$ is initiated.
The rate of interest will decline until the desire to hold money is stimulated
sufficiently for money-holders to feel satisfied with holdings equal to $\bar{M}$.
Similarly at rates of interest below $r_1$ there is excess demand for money,
money-holders adjust their asset portfolios in favour of money and the rate of
interest rises towards $r_1$.

For any level of income there is only one equilibrium rate of interest, but at
different income levels there are different demand for money functions, each
yielding a different equilibrium rate of interest, $r_1$, $r_2$ and $r_3$ in the figure. The
higher is the level of income the greater will be the demand for money at any
rate of interest and the higher the rate of interest which provides equilibrium
in the money market with a given supply of money.

Consider now the impact on the rate of interest of changes in the exogenous component of the demand for money $L_0$ and changes in the supply of money $\bar{M}$. Differentiating (3.3) totally we have

$$dL_0 + L_Y\,dY + L_r\,dr = d\bar{M}$$

and rearranging terms

$$dr = \frac{d\bar{M} - dL_0 - L_Y\,dY}{L_r} \tag{3.4}$$

In order to find the effect of changes in $L_0$ and $\bar{M}$ on the rate of interest when the level of income is given and constant, we find from (3.4) the partial derivatives

$$\frac{\partial r}{\partial L_0} = \frac{-1}{L_r} \tag{3.5}$$

and

$$\frac{\partial r}{\partial \bar{M}} = \frac{1}{L_r} \tag{3.6}$$

Remembering that $L_r < 0$, an increase in the exogenous component of the demand for money (with the supply of money given) increases the rate of interest, as shown by relation (3.5). And an increase in the supply of money (with the demand for money function given) reduces the rate of interest, as shown by relation (3.6). These results are illustrated in Figure 3.3(a) and (b).

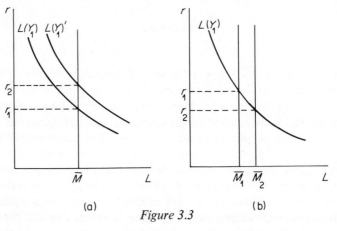

(a)                                           (b)

*Figure 3.3*

In Figure 3.3(a) an increase in $L_0$ shifts the demand for money curve, at income level $Y_1$, to the right from $L(Y_1 r)$ to $L(Y_1 r)'$. The result is an excess demand for money at $r_1$ which initiates the rise in the rate of interest towards $r_2$. The extent of the increase in the rate of interest for a unit increase in $L_0$ is determined by the slope of the $L(Y_1, r)$ curve, that is by $L_r$. This explains why the partial derivative (3.5) is determined by the size of $L_r$. In Figure 3.3(b) an increase in the supply of money from $\bar{M}_1$ to $\bar{M}_2$ reduces the rate of interest from $r_1$ to $r_2$. An initial excess supply of money at $r_1$ reduces the rate of interest towards $r_2$. Again the extent of the change in the rate of interest depends on the slope of the $L(Y_1, r)$ curve so that the partial derivative (3.6) depends on $L_r$. In the limiting case of the liquidity trap, a change in $L_0$ or $\bar{M}$ does not affect the equilibrium rate of interest. This can be seen by setting $L_r \to -\infty$ in both equation (3.5) and (3.6); the consequence is that the partial derivatives then tend to zero. The situation can be shown by redrawing both parts of Figure 3.3, as in Figure 3.4(a) and (b) where it should be self-evident that the rate of interest does not change in either case.

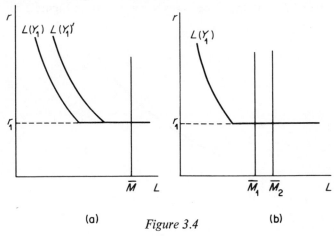

(a)    *Figure 3.4*    (b)

The liquidity trap is a situation in which people are willing to hold any amount of money made available in the money market at the prevailing rate of interest ($r_1$ in Figure 3.4). An increase in the demand for money at any interest rate above $r_1$, shown by the shift to $L(Y_1)'$ in Figure 3.4(a), does not affect the demand for money at $r_1$ since this is unlimited anyway. Similarly an increase in the supply of money, as from $\bar{M}_1$ to $\bar{M}_2$ in Figure 3.4(b), does not affect the rate of interest because, with the unlimited demand, no excess supply of money can be created which would be used to buy bonds and drive down the rate of interest.

## 3.4 THE *LM* CURVE

In Chapter II it was convenient to summarize the condition for equilibrium in the expenditure sector in terms of a curve, the *IS* curve, representing the combinations of income and the rate of interest compatible with expenditure equilibrium. We can now follow a similar procedure for the monetary sector and obtain the *LM* curve which represents the combinations of income and the rate of interest which are compatible with monetary equilibrium. Like the *IS* curve, the *LM* curve is not to be interpreted as representing a direct *causal* relationship between $r$ and $Y$. Rather it shows the $r$ which must accompany $Y$ if the demand for money is to be kept equal to the given supply of money.

The monetary equilibrium condition (3.3) is the equation of the $LM$ curve. Equation (3.4) is the differential of the $LM$ curve which implies the following partial derivative, the slope of the $LM$ curve:

$$\frac{\partial r}{\partial Y} = -\frac{L_Y}{L_r} \tag{3.7}$$

Since $L_r < 0$ and $L_Y > 0$, the slope is positive as shown in Figure 3.5.

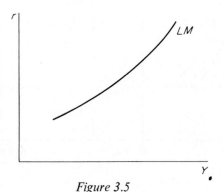

Figure 3.5

The position of the $LM$ curve is determined by the liquidity preference of money-holders and the level of the money supply. An increase in liquidity preference ($dL_0 > 0$) with the money supply constant decreases the equilibrium level of income at any given rate of interest as can be seen from the partial derivative from equation (3.4):

$$\frac{\partial Y}{\partial L_0} = -\frac{1}{L_Y} < 0 \tag{3.8}$$

The effect is to shift the $LM$ curve to the left. An increase in the money supply, on the other hand, shifts the $LM$ curve to the right because the equilibrium rate of interest associated with any level of income (and hence any demand for money) has fallen. Formally, the result from equation (3.4) is

$$\frac{\partial Y}{\partial \bar{M}} = \frac{1}{L_Y} > 0 \tag{3.9}$$

In the limiting case of the liquidity trap, setting $L_r \to -\infty$ we have from equation (3.7)

$$\frac{\partial r}{\partial Y} \to 0 \tag{3.10}$$

This means that the liquidity trap produces a horizontal section of the *LM* curve, as in Figure 3.6.

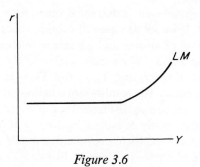

*Figure 3.6*

## 3.5 DIAGRAMMATIC DERIVATION OF THE *LM* CURVE

The derivation of the *LM* curve using diagrams is an easier task than the diagrammatic derivation of the *IS* curve. The reason is that in the monetary sector the equilibrium condition is simplified by the fact that the money supply is exogenous. In Figure 3.7(a) there is a family of demand for money curves, one for each level of income. Taking a particular level of the demand for money,

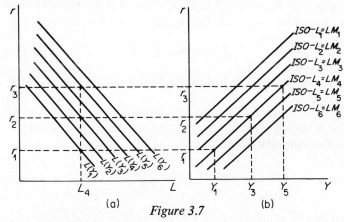

*Figure 3.7*

$L_4$, it is apparent that numerous combinations of income and the rate of interest will lead to this level of demand, $r_1$ and $Y_1$, $r_2$ and $Y_3$, $r_3$ and $Y_5$ and so on. As income rises the demand for money is stimulated and the rate of interest must increase if the level of demand is to be kept down to $L_4(L_Y > 0$ and $L_r < 0)$. In Figure 3.7(b) a line is drawn through the $r$, $Y$ combinations which yield $L_4$, and the curve is called an *ISO–L* curve, *ISO–$L_4$*. At all points on this curve the demand for money is equal to $L_4$. For different levels of the demand for money, $L_1$, $L_2$ etc. we have different *ISO–L* curves so that there is a family of such curves in Figure 3.7(b).

The condition for equilibrium is that the demand for money be equal to the supply of money, $\bar{M}$. If we set $\bar{M}$ equal to (say) $L_4$, because the level of $\bar{M}$ is independent of the level of income and the rate of interest $\bar{M}$ it will remain at $L_4$ however we change $Y$ and $r$. The condition that $\bar{M} = L_4$ is therefore satisfied at *all* the $Y$, $r$ combinations ($r_1$ and $Y_1$, $r_2$ and $Y_3$, $r_3$ and $Y_5$ etc.) which are points on the *ISO–$L_4$* curve. The equilibrium condition is satisfied at all points on *ISO–$L_4$* so that this curve must in fact *be* the *LM* curve (*$LM_4$*) which corresponds to this particular supply of money. Setting $\bar{M}$ at other levels places us on different *ISO–L* curves and therefore on different *LM* curves. The resulting family of *ISO–L*, or *LM*, curves in Figure 3.7(b) shows that an increase in the supply of money shifts the *LM* curve to the right. For example, if $\bar{M}$ rises from $\bar{M} = L_4$ to $\bar{M} = L_5$ the *LM* curve shifts from *$LM_4$* to *$LM_5$*. Equilibrium is achieved, for any level of income, at a lower rate of interest. A movement to the right in the demand for money curve ($dL_0 > 0$), on the other hand, shifts the *LM* curve to the left because the rate of interest (at any level of income) needed to keep the demand for money down to the fixed supply of money is increased.

Let us summarize formally the procedure of the construction of the *LM* curve.† It is assumed that the demand for money is a function of income $Y$, and the rate of interest, $r$; that is $L = L(Y,r)$. In Figure 3.7(a) income is treated as a constant, $Y_j$, so that the demand for money function in linear form is

$$L_j = l_0 + l_Y Y_j + l_r r \qquad (3.11)$$

For different $Y_j$'s a family of demand for money curves is drawn, as $j = 1, \ldots, 6$ in Figure 3.7(a).

In Figure 3.7(b) the equilibrium relationship between income and the rate of interest is shown. Treating the demand for money as a constant, $L_j$, we construct from the relationship

$$r = \left(\frac{L_j - l_0}{l_r}\right) - \frac{l_Y}{l_r} Y \qquad (3.12)$$

for different $L_j$'s a family of *ISO–L* curves with the characteristic that $L$ remains constant along each one of them as, for example, for $j = 1, \ldots, 6$ in the figure. A given supply of money $\bar{M}$ is equal to (say) $L_4$ at all points on the curve *ISO–$L_4$* which is therefore the *LM* curve for $\bar{M} = L_4$. For different money supplies, different *LM*'s are constructed as, for example, *$LM_1$*, ..., *$LM_6$* in the figure.

† The remainder of this section can be omitted on a first reading with no loss of continuity.

## 3.6 THE TWO-SECTOR MODEL

We have established the conditions for equilibrium in the expenditure and the monetary sectors when each sector is considered in isolation. The analysis is now extended to incorporate the interrelationships between the two sectors and to find the conditions for equilibrium in the two sectors simultaneously. The two-sector model presented in this section is a straightforward combination of the models of the expenditure and monetary sectors, and ignores output and employment considerations (introduced in Chapter IV).

The equilibrium condition for the expenditure sector is equation (2.76):

$$Y = C_0 + C(Y - T, r) + I_0 + I(Y, r) + \bar{G} \tag{2.76}$$

and that for the monetary sector is equation (3.3)

$$L_0 + L(Y, r) = \bar{M} \tag{3.3}$$

Equilibrium in the two-sector model requires equilibrium in both of the sectors simultaneously.

The analysis of this model will be presented in two steps. The first illustrates the derivation of the expressions for equilibrium income and the rate of interest using the linear form of the model. The second step investigates the impact of changes in exogenous variables on the equilibrium values of the endogenous variables in the system, i.e. undertakes a comparative static analysis. This second step reverts to the general form of the model and this form will then be retained for the remainder of the book.

The two-sector model consists of two equations in two unknowns, and the equilibrium expressions for $Y$ and $r$ can be found if the functions on which it is based (for $C$, $I$, $L$ and $T$) are explicit; i.e. if the exact form of the parameters is specified as in the case of linear relationships. To illustrate, let us derive the equilibrium $Y$ and $r$ from the linear form of the model which is:

$$Y = c_0 - c_Y t_0 + c_Y(1 - t_Y) Y + c_r r + i_0 + i_Y Y + i_r r + \bar{G} \tag{3.13}$$

$$l_0 + l_Y Y + l_r r = \bar{M} \tag{3.14}$$

where in the linear functions $l_0$, $l_r$ and $l_Y$ correspond to $L_0$, $L_r$ and $L_Y$. As explained in Chapter I, either by substitution or by solving the matrix

$$\begin{bmatrix} 1 - c_Y(1 - t_Y) - i_Y & -(c_r + i_r) \\ l_Y & l_r \end{bmatrix} \begin{bmatrix} Y \\ r \end{bmatrix} = \begin{bmatrix} c_0 + i_0 - c_Y t_0 + \bar{G} \\ \bar{M} - l_0 \end{bmatrix}$$

we obtain from the two equation system, (3.13) and (3.14), the solutions:

$$Y = \frac{(\bar{M} - l_0)(c_r + i_r) + (c_0 + i_0 - c_Y t_0 + \bar{G}) l_r}{(1 - c_Y(1 - t_Y) - i_Y) l_r + (c_r + i_r) l_Y} \tag{3.15}$$

$$r = \frac{(\bar{M} - l_0)(1 - c_Y(1 - t_Y) - i_Y) - (c_0 + i_0 - c_Y t_0 + \bar{G}) l_Y}{(1 - c_Y(1 - t_Y) - i_Y) l_r + (c_r + i_r) l_Y} \tag{3.16}$$

This solution is represented in diagrammatic terms by the intersection of the *IS* and the *LM* curve and the simultaneous determination of equilibrium income and the rate of interest, as is shown in Figure 3.8.

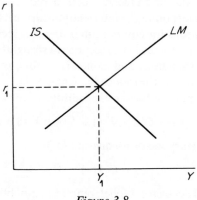

*Figure 3.8*

With the exception of the $Y_1$, $r_1$ combination all points in the $Y$–$r$ plane are characterized by disequilibrium in one or both sectors. Ignoring the $Y_1$, $r_1$ combination, points on the *IS* curve represent expenditure sector equilibrium and monetary sector disequilibrium, while points on the *LM* curve represent monetary sector equilibrium and expenditure sector disequilibrium. The points

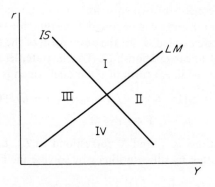

I   Deficiency of demand for goods, excess supply
    of money
II  Deficiency of demand for goods, excess demand
    for money
III Excess demand for goods, excess supply of money
IV  Excess demand for goods, excess demand for money

*Figure 3.9*

on neither curve are associated with disequilibrium in both sectors and we can divide the field of such points into four areas, as shown in Figure 3.9.

Looking first at the situation in the expenditure sector, for all $Y$, $r$ points to the right of the $IS$ curve (areas I and II) there is a deficiency of total demand for goods. At any income level the rate of interest is too high for the planned savings at that income level to be matched by planned investment. Analogously, for the points to the left of the $IS$ curve (areas III and IV) at any income level the rate of interest is so low that the planned savings at that income level are exceeded by planned investment, and there is consequently excess demand for goods.

Consider now the situation in the monetary sector at different $Y$, $r$ points. Those to the left of the $LM$ curve are associated with excess supply of money. At any income level the rate of interest is too high to induce people to hold all of the available supply of money in preference to interest-yielding assets. Conversely, to the right of the $LM$ curve at any income level the rate of interest is low enough to induce people to want to hold more money than is available.

The result of this two-way classification is the division of the disequilibrium points into the four areas in Figure 3.9. At any point there will be forces in the goods and money markets which induce changes in income and/or the rate of interest to move the system towards the two-sector equilibrium combination of income and the rate of interest.

We revert now to the general form of the model, equations (2.76) and (3.3), and investigate its comparative static qualities. Differentiating totally equations (2.76) and (3.3) and rearranging terms we have:

$$(1 - C_Y(1 - T_Y) - I_Y) \, dY - (C_r + I_r) \, dr = dC_0 + dI_0 - C_Y \, dT_0 + d\bar{G} \quad (3.17)$$

$$L_Y \, dY + L_r \, dr = d\bar{M} - dL_0 \quad (3.18)$$

or in matrix form

$$\begin{bmatrix} 1 - C_Y(1 - T_Y) - I_Y & -(C_r + I_r) \\ L_Y & L_r \end{bmatrix} \begin{bmatrix} dY \\ dr \end{bmatrix} = \begin{bmatrix} dC_0 + dI_0 - C_Y \, dT_0 + d\bar{G} \\ d\bar{M} - dL_0 \end{bmatrix}$$

Solving for $dY$ and $dr$ we obtain

$$dY = \frac{(d\bar{M} - dL_0)(C_r + I_r) + (dC_0 + dI_0 - C_Y \, dT_0 + d\bar{G}) L_r}{D} \quad (3.19)$$

$$dr = \frac{(d\bar{M} - dL_0)(1 - C_Y(1 - T_Y) - I_Y) - (dC_0 + dI_0 - C_Y \, dT_0 + d\bar{G}) L_Y}{D} \quad (3.20)$$

where

$$D = (1 - C_Y(1 - T_Y) - I_Y) L_r + (C_r + I_r) L_Y < 0 \quad (3.21)$$

because

$$(1 - C_Y(1 - T_Y) - I_Y) > 0,$$
$$(C_r + I_r) < 0,$$
$$L_r < 0 \quad \text{and} \quad L_Y > 0$$

From (3.19) and (3.20) we can find the partial derivatives of the endogenous variables $Y$ and $r$ with respect to any exogenous variable ($C_0, I_0, T_0, \bar{G}, \bar{M}$ or $L_0$). They will indicate the impact of changes in these exogenous variables on the *equilibrium* level of income and the rate of interest.

Consider first in the comparative static analysis the effect of changes in exogenous expenditure. From equation (3.19) we obtain:

$$\frac{\partial Y}{\partial C_0} = \frac{\partial Y}{\partial I_0} = \frac{\partial Y}{\partial \bar{G}} = \frac{L_r}{D} > 0 \tag{3.22}$$

$$\frac{\partial Y}{\partial T_0} = \frac{-C_Y L_r}{D} < 0 \tag{3.23}$$

and from equation (3.20)

$$\frac{\partial r}{\partial C_0} = \frac{\partial r}{\partial I_0} = \frac{\partial r}{\partial \bar{G}} = \frac{-L_Y}{D} > 0 \tag{3.24}$$

$$\frac{\partial r}{\partial T_0} = \frac{C_Y L_Y}{D} < 0 \tag{3.25}$$

We can most clearly interpret these results if they are related to the exposition of the model in terms of *IS* and *LM* curves. Equation (3.22) shows that

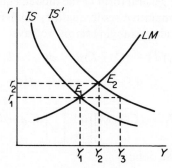

*Figure 3.10*

an increase in $C_0, I_0$ or $\bar{G}$, i.e. an upward shift in the consumption or investment function or a rise in exogenous government expenditure, has the effect of increasing the equilibrium level of income.

In Figure 3.10, where $E_1$ is the initial equilibrium position, the increase in $C_0, I_0$ or $\bar{G}$ shifts the *IS* curve to *IS'* and the equilibrium level of income rises from $Y_1$ to $Y_2$, the extent of the increase being given by the partial derivative (3.22).

But as the level of income increases the demand for money increases and, with a given supply of money, the rate of interest is pushed up, from $r_1$ to $r_2$ in the figure. As a result the partial derivatives (3.24) are positive. The fact that the demand for money is dependent on $Y$ provides a link between the expenditure and the monetary sectors. In addition, the increase in the rate of interest 'feeds back' to the expenditure sector and reduces the response of $Y$ to the exogenous expenditure increase. This can be seen by writing out the partial derivatives (3.22) in full and dividing through by $L_r$:

$$\frac{\partial Y}{\partial C_0} = \frac{\partial Y}{\partial I_0} = \frac{\partial Y}{\partial \bar{G}} = \frac{1}{(1 - C_Y(1 - T_Y) - I_Y) + (C_r + I_r)\frac{L_Y}{L_r}} > 0 \qquad (3.26)$$

The impact on income of a change in exogenous expenditure is smaller the greater is the responsiveness of the demand for money to income changes, $L_Y$, and the smaller is the response of the demand for money, $L_r$, and the greater is the response of consumption and investment $(C_r + I_r)$, to changes in the rate of interest. As income increases from $Y_1$, and equilibrium moves away from $E_1$, in Figure 3.10, if $L_Y$ is large the demand for money increases substantially. With a given supply of money the resulting shift to the right of the liquidity preference curve has a great effect on the rate of interest if the curve is steep ($L_r$ is small in absolute terms). And the more $C$ and $I$ respond to a given change in $r$ the greater is the dampening effect on expenditure. The monetary effect via the rate of interest therefore reduces the size of the multiplier, as long as the expression $(C_r + I_r)(L_Y/L_r)$ is not zero. In Figure 3.10 the increase in income is $(Y_2 - Y_1)$ which is less than the increase in income $(Y_3 - Y_1)$ that would have occurred in the absence of the dampening monetary effect. The larger increase $(Y_3 - Y_1)$ is equal to the change in exogenous expenditure times the multiplier $1/[1 - C_Y(1 - T_Y) - I_Y]$ and can occur only if either expenditure is insensitive to interest rate changes or the liquidity trap exists, that is if $(C_r + I_r) \rightarrow 0$ or $L_r \rightarrow -\infty$ in equation (3.26), assuming that $L_Y > 0$.

It is apparent from a comparison of the partial derivatives (3.22) and (3.23) and of (3.24) and (3.25), that a change in exogenous tax revenue, $T_0$, has less impact on income and the rate of interest than does an equivalent change in $C_0$, $I_0$ or $\bar{G}$. As we have seen before this is due to the fact that the change in tax payments comes partly from (or goes partly to) private saving. The initial expenditure impact which stimulates the multiplier effect is reduced by the proportion of the income change saved. Consequently equation (3.23) is (3.22) multiplied by $C_Y$, and (3.25) is (32.4) multiplied by $C_Y$, though of course with opposite signs in each case.

To complete the analysis of the exogenous expenditure changes the results for changes in $\bar{G}$ and $T_0$ can be used to find the balanced budget multiplier. From equations (3.22) and (3.23) with $d\bar{G} = dT_0$ we have:

$$dY = \left(\frac{\partial Y}{\partial \bar{G}} + \frac{\partial Y}{\partial T_0}\right) d\bar{G} \qquad (3.27)$$

where

$$\left(\frac{\partial Y}{\partial \bar{G}} + \frac{\partial Y}{\partial T_0}\right) = \frac{L_r}{D} - \frac{C_Y L_r}{D} = \frac{1 - C_Y}{(1 - C_Y(1 - T_Y) - I_Y) + (C_r + I_r)\frac{L_Y}{L_r}} \quad (3.28)$$

Even assuming the special case with investment and tax revenue exogenous (i.e. $I_Y = 0$ and $T_Y = 0$) we find that

$$dY = \left[\frac{1 - C_Y}{(1 - C_Y) + (C_r + I_r)\frac{L_Y}{L_r}}\right] d\bar{G} \quad (3.29)$$

This means that the balanced budget multiplier of unity is destroyed by the responsiveness of the rate of interest to changes in income together with the responsiveness of consumption and investment plans to changes in the rate of interest.

We turn now to the impact on the equilibrium levels of income and the rate of interest of changes in liquidity preference, $L_0$, and the supply of money, $\bar{M}$. From equation (3.19):

$$\frac{\partial Y}{\partial L_0} = \frac{-(C_r + I_r)}{D} < 0 \quad (3.30)$$

$$\frac{\partial Y}{\partial \bar{M}} = \frac{(C_r + I_r)}{D} > 0 \quad (3.31)$$

and from equation (3.20)

$$\frac{\partial r}{\partial L_0} = \frac{-(1 - C_Y(1 - T_Y) - I_Y)}{D} > 0 \quad (3.32)$$

$$\frac{\partial r}{\partial \bar{M}} = \frac{(1 - C_Y(1 - T_Y) - I_Y)}{D} < 0 \quad (3.33)$$

These four partial derivatives indicate that an increase in $L_0$, i.e. a shift in the liquidity preference curve to the right which represents an increase in the demand for money at any rate of interest, or a fall in the supply of money, raises the equilibrium rate of interest and reduces the equilibrium income level. Either of these exogenous changes shifts the *LM* curve to the left, as from *LM* to *LM'* in Figure 3.11. With the new curve *LM'*, the initial position $E_1$ would become associated with an excess demand for money at the interest rate $r_1$. The implied deficiency of demand for bonds raises the rate of interest and a movement towards $r_2$ is initiated. Planned expenditure declines as the rate of interest rises (a movement to the left on the *IS* curve) with the result that the equilibrium level of income falls to $Y_2$ at the interest rate $r_2$.

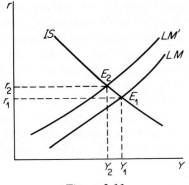

*Figure 3.11*

## 3.7 THE TWO-SECTOR MODEL IN LIMITING CASES

The comparative static analysis of the previous section assumed non-extreme values of the parameters of the various functions. The next task is to consider the implications of the limiting cases, interest-insensitive expenditure and the liquidity trap.†

Setting $(C_r + I_r) \to 0$ in equations (3.19) and (3.20) we have the partial derivatives for exogenous expenditure changes when expenditure is interest-insensitive:

$$\frac{\partial Y}{\partial C_0} = \frac{\partial Y}{\partial I_0} = \frac{\partial Y}{\partial \bar{G}} \to \frac{1}{1 - C_Y(1 - T_Y) - I_Y} > 0 \tag{3.34}$$

$$\frac{\partial Y}{\partial T_0} \to \frac{-C_Y}{1 - C_Y(1 - T_Y) - I_Y} < 0 \tag{3.35}$$

$$\frac{\partial r}{\partial C_0} = \frac{\partial r}{\partial I_0} = \frac{\partial r}{\partial \bar{G}} \to \frac{-L_Y}{(1 - C_Y(1 - T_Y) - I_Y)L_r} > 0 \tag{3.36}$$

$$\frac{\partial r}{\partial T_0} \to \frac{C_Y L_Y}{(1 - C_Y(1 - T_Y) - I_Y)L_r} < 0 \tag{3.37}$$

and also the corresponding results for exogenous changes in the monetary sector:

$$\frac{\partial Y}{\partial L_0} \to 0 \tag{3.38}$$

$$\frac{\partial Y}{\partial \bar{M}} \to 0 \tag{3.39}$$

$$\frac{\partial r}{\partial L_0} \to \frac{-1}{L_r} > 0 \tag{3.40}$$

$$\frac{\partial r}{\partial \bar{M}} \to \frac{1}{L_r} < 0 \tag{3.41}$$

† A third limiting case will be considered in section 8.2.2; this is the interest-insensitivity of the demand for money (the monetarist limiting case).

These results can be compared with those, in the absence of any limiting case, given in the previous section. We will indicate only the main points of difference.

An increase in the level of exogenous expenditure raises income by this amount times the full multiplier, that is without any dampening feedback effect through the monetary sector, as equations (3.34) and (3.35) show. The increase in income ($Y_2 - Y_1$) in Figure 3.12(a) is equal to the shift in the *IS* curve (contrast the movement from $Y_1$ to $Y_2$, rather than to $Y_3$, in Figure 3.10). The expansion of income does provoke an increase in the rate of interest but expenditure does not react to this increase. The effect on the rate of interest is shown in equations (3.36) and (3.37), and by the movement from $r_1$ to $r_2$ in the figure.

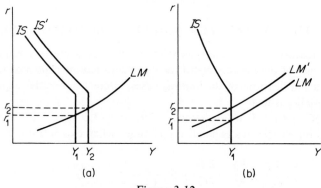

Figure 3.12

An increase in $L_0$ or a decline in $\bar{M}$, as we have seen, shifts the *LM* curve to the left, from *LM* to *LM'* in Figure 3.12(b). But in this limiting case the resulting increase in the rate of interest, given by equations (3.40) and (3.41) and the movement from $r_1$ to $r_2$ in the diagram, does not alter the equilibrium level of income, $Y_1$. The failure of these changes in the monetary sector to alter the level of income is reflected in the zero partial derivatives (3.38) and (3.39). The explanation of this failure is that, in this model, the only link between the monetary sector and expenditure decisions is the rate of interest, but in the limiting case being considered changes in the rate of interest are irrelevant to the decisions of consumers and investors.

The effects of changes in exogenous variables in the case of the liquidity trap are found by setting $L_r \to -\infty$ in equations (3.22) to (3.25). For changes in the expenditure sector we have:

$$\frac{\partial Y}{\partial C_0} = \frac{\partial Y}{\partial I_0} = \frac{\partial Y}{\partial \bar{G}} \to \frac{1}{1 - C_Y(1 - T_Y) - I_Y} > 0 \qquad (3.42)$$

$$\frac{\partial Y}{\partial T_0} \to \frac{-C_Y}{1 - C_Y(1 - T_Y) - I_Y} < 0 \qquad (3.43)$$

$$\frac{\partial r}{\partial C_0} = \frac{\partial r}{\partial I_0} = \frac{\partial r}{\partial \bar{G}} \to 0 \qquad (3.44)$$

$$\frac{\partial r}{\partial T_0} \to 0 \qquad (3.45)$$

and for changes in the monetary sector:

$$\frac{\partial Y}{\partial L_0} \to 0 \qquad (3.46)$$

$$\frac{\partial Y}{\partial \bar{M}} \to 0 \qquad (3.47)$$

$$\frac{\partial r}{\partial L_0} \to 0 \qquad (3.48)$$

$$\frac{\partial r}{\partial \bar{M}} \to 0 \qquad (3.49)$$

The effect on income of an increase in exogenous expenditure, equations (3.42) and (3.43), is similar to that in the previous limiting case (equations (3.34) and (3.35)), the expenditure increase being multiplied by the multiplier with no dampening monetary effect. The reason in the case of the liquidity trap is not

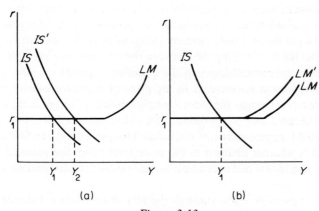

(a)                    (b)

*Figure 3.13*

that expenditure fails to react to a change in the rate of interest, but that the rate of interest itself does not increase as the rise in income stimulates the demand for money. Therefore, equations (3.44) and (3.45) tend to zero. In Figure 3.13(a) the shift in the $IS$ curve is associated with an increase in income $(Y_2 - Y_1)$ equal to the shift but the rate of interest remains at $r_1$.

It is apparent from (3.46), (3.47), (3.48) and (3.49) that in the limit a high interest-sensitivity of the demand for money neutralizes the effects of changes in $L_0$ and $\bar{M}$. As in the case of zero interest-sensitivity of expenditure, the expenditure sector is isolated from monetary variables. The significance of the liquidity trap for the control of expenditure decisions by adjustments in monetary variables becomes clear, assuming of course, as the model does, that the rate of interest is the only link between the two sectors. Figure 3.13(b) illustrates the point that shifts in the *LM* curve cannot alter the rate of interest and cannot therefore affect the equilibrium level of income either.

### 3.8   THE PRICE LEVEL AS A VARIABLE: A RE-STATEMENT OF THE TWO-SECTOR MODEL

No mention has been made up to this point of changes in the price level. Implicitly we have assumed that the price level is exogenously determined and remains constant. In this section the assumption that prices are exogenous will be retained but they will be allowed to vary so that we can trace the impact of changes in prices on other variables in the system. It will be possible to make the price level endogenous only when the supply side of the market for goods has been introduced in Chapter IV. Combined with the theory of the demand for goods, which has been presented in terms of the theory of planned expenditure, the analysis of supply provides us with a model capable of determining the price level as well as the levels of real income and the rate of interest.

For the moment, then, let us consider the effect of price changes by modifying the model contained in section 3.6. When the price level is fixed no distinction is needed between the real and monetary values of variables. But with a changeable price level we must distinguish between the increases in a variable, such as income, which represent changes in the quantity of goods it represents, and those which represent an increase in the price of a given quantity of good. The former is a real change, the latter a purely monetary change in the variable.

Defining the real value of a variable as the value measured in constant prices (that is deflated for price increases and inflated for price cuts), the first question to be settled is whether changes in the price level affect the planned level of real expenditure, that is real consumption, real investment and real government spending.

Ignoring the possible effect through the real value of cash balances, to be discussed in Chapter 5, changes in the price level will leave decisions on real expenditure unaffected if the following assumptions are adopted, as they shall be in the subsequent analysis:

(1) *A change in the general price level does not alter the relative prices of particular products.* In other words the prices of all products change by the same proportion, so that price level changes do not affect the pattern of demand for goods.

(2) *A change in the price level does not change the distribution of real income.* This will be the case if any price level change alters everyone's real income level

by the same proportion. The prices of all factors of production change by proportionately the same amount.

(3) *There is no money illusion.* This implies that those making expenditure decisions can distinguish between changes in their real income and income changes which are purely monetary; that is they do not suffer from the illusion that an increase in money income necessarily implies an increase in real income. Consequently simultaneous increases in money income and in the price level which leave the level of real income the same will not affect spending.

(4) *A price level change does not create an expectation of further such changes.* In other words all changes in the price level are expected, by those making expenditure decisions and by money-holders, to be once-and-for-all events. This rules out changes in planned expenditure arising from speculation about the future prices of goods, and also the holding of money for speculative purposes.

If people do not confuse proportionately equal increases in money income and the price level with increases in real income and if decisions to spend are based on real income, then such increases in the price level will not affect consumers' allocation of real income between consumption and saving.

The inclusion of the income variable in the investment function was based on the assumption that the availability of funds to investors is correlated with the level of income. If the real level of investment is affected by the availability of funds in real terms, which in turn depends on the real level of income, then proportionately equal money income and price changes will not change the real investment decision. Similarly, if both the return on and value of bonds rise by the same percentage as the price level, the rate of interest remains the same. With the rate of interest independent of the price level there is no need to distinguish between nominal and real rates.†

Real government expenditure plans are also not affected if the government sets its level of expenditure in real terms. Only if real taxable income increases will its real tax revenue increase and will expenditure in real terms be raised. We assume, therefore, that the government sets its *ex ante* budget surplus, deficit or perfect balance in real terms and maintains this by exactly compensating for price increases by raising proportionately the money level of expenditure. In the simple case of the proportional tax used here, the revenue from taxation in money terms increases proportionately with the price level.

Under these assumptions therefore, real expenditure is independent of the price level. The price level does not enter the equilibrium condition for the expenditure sector, and the condition remains as equation (2.76) except that *all variables are now defined in real terms* (i.e. $Y$ means $Y/P$, $T_0$ is $T_0/P$ and so on):

$$Y = C_0 + C(Y - T, r) + I_0 + I(Y, r) + \bar{G} \tag{3.50}$$

† It is possible to extend the theory to allow for differences between the nominal and real rates of interest. This will not be attempted here, but see Bailey (1971), Ch. 4, sections 2 and 3.

Differentiating and rearranging terms we have the following differential of
the *IS* curve:

$$dY = \frac{dC_0 - C_Y dT_0 + dI_0 + d\bar{G} + (C_r + I_r)\, dr}{1 - C_Y(1 - T_Y) - I_Y} \tag{3.51}$$

Since the price level does not enter (3.51), it must be the case that

$$\frac{\partial Y}{\partial P} = 0 \tag{3.52}$$

Changes in the price level do *not* alter the equilibrium level of real income, at
any rate of interest, in the expenditure sector; this means that the position of
the real *IS* curve is independent of the price level given the assumptions which
have been adopted.

The price level does, however, play a significant role in the monetary sector.
The demand for money in real terms is independent of the price level, but the
real value of the supply of money varies inversely to changes in prices. Money
is held because it offers an immediate command over goods and services. It is
assumed that the money-holder decides, at any given level of income and the
rate of interest, to have command over a certain *quantity* of goods and services.
If the value of this given quantity changes he will adjust his holdings in nominal
(or money) terms by the same percentage and thereby retain a constant holding
of money in real terms. The demand for money in real terms is then independent
of changes in the price level.

When there is an increase in prices the real value of a given supply of money
declines: less can be bought with the available supply of money. Such falls in
the real money supply can be prevented only if the government actively raises
the nominal value of the supply of money just sufficiently to compensate for
the change in prices. We will assume that the government does not vary the
nominal value of the money supply in this way, but allows the real value of a
given nominal money supply to be determined within the system.†

With the real demand for money independent of *P*, and the real supply of
money dependent on *P*, the equilibrium condition for the monetary sector,
equation (3.3), is written as

$$L_0 + L(Y, r) = \frac{\bar{M}}{P} \tag{3.53}$$

where the demand for money, *L*, and income, *Y*, are expressed in real terms.

Equation (3.3) is assumed to be linear homogeneous with respect only to *Y*
(otherwise it will not be independent of the monetary units which are used to

† There is an asymmetry between this assumption and the earlier assumption that the
government sets $\bar{G}$ at a certain level in real terms. We accept this asymmetry purely for
simplicity. It would complicate the analysis if the real value of $\bar{G}$ were determined within the
system, since the real *IS* curve would then shift with changes in prices, a possibility which is
not introduced until Chapter V.

measure $Y$ and $\bar{M}$). Therefore $\lambda \bar{M} = \lambda L_0 + L(\lambda Y, r)$ where $\lambda > 0$. If $\lambda = 1/P$, where $P$ is the price level, we have equation (3.53). In equation (3.53) $\bar{M}$ is in nominal terms, and $(\bar{M}/P)$ is the real value of the supply of money; an increase in $P$ results in a proportionate reduction in $(\bar{M}/P)$.

Consider the effect of a price change on the level of real income which provides, at a particular rate of interest, equilibrium in the monetary sector. Differentiating equation (3.53) and rearranging terms we have the new differential for the *LM* curve:

$$dY = \frac{\dfrac{d\bar{M}}{P} - \dfrac{\bar{M}\,dP}{P^2} - dL_0 - L_r\,dr}{L_Y} \qquad (3.54)$$

If the equation of the *LM* curve in the constant price model, equation (3.4), is solved for $dY$ and then compared with the real *LM* equation (3.54), it is

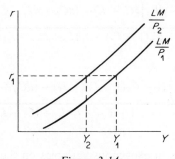

*Figure 3.14*

clear that there is now an additional factor affecting the (real) income level which, at any rate of interest, yields equilibrium in the monetary sector: this is the change in the price level, $dP$. Consequently we have from equation (3.54) the additional partial derivative:

$$\frac{\partial Y}{\partial P} = -\frac{\bar{M}}{L_Y P^2} < 0 \qquad (3.55)$$

In the model with constant prices the position of the *LM* curve was determined by the levels of $L_0$ and $\bar{M}$ but with variable prices the position is determined by $L_0$, $\bar{M}$ and $P$. The negative partial derivative (3.55) indicates that an increase in the price level, with $L_0$ and $\bar{M}$ constant, reduces the equilibrium real income level at any rate of interest, that is shifts the real *LM* curve $(LM/P)$ to the left. This is shown in Figure 3.14 where $LM/P_1$ is the real *LM* curve at price level $P_1$, and $LM/P_2$ the curve at the higher price level $P_2$. At the rate of interest $r_1$ for example, monetary equilibrium is achieved at real income $Y_1$ if the price level is $P_1$, but at $Y_2$ if the price level rises to $P_2$. The explanation for this is that, as we have seen, when the price level rises the real value of the given supply of money is cut.

The illustration in Figure 3.14 does not mean that the rate of interest *will* in fact remain constant; on the contrary when prices are allowed to rise in the two-sector model we will find that (in non-limiting cases) the rate of interest *does* increase. Rather it means that if the rate of interest were to remain constant, then equilibrium could only be restored when the level of real income has declined sufficiently (from $Y_1$ to $Y_2$) to eliminate the excess demand for money by reducing the real demand for money to equal the new lower real supply of money.

We are now in a position to restate the two-sector model to allow for variable prices. The model consists of the two equilibrium conditions (3.50) and (3.53), which in differential form are equations (3.51) and (3.54). Solving simultaneously for $dY$ and $dr$ yields:

$$dY = \frac{\left(\dfrac{d\bar{M}}{P} - \dfrac{\bar{M}\,dP}{P^2} - dL_0\right)(C_r + I_r) + (dC_0 + dI_0 - C_Y\,dT_0 + d\bar{G})L_r}{(1 - C_Y(1 - T_Y) - I_Y)L_r + (C_r + I_r)L_Y} \tag{3.56}$$

$$dr = $$

$$\frac{\left(\dfrac{d\bar{M}}{P} - \dfrac{\bar{M}\,dP}{P^2} - dL_0\right)(1 - C_Y(1 - T_Y) - I_Y) - (dC_0 + dI_0 - C_Y\,dT_0 + d\bar{G})L_Y}{(1 - C_Y(1 - T_Y) - I_Y)L_r + (C_r + I_r)L_Y}$$

$$\tag{3.57}$$

The impact of changes in exogenous variables on the equilibrium levels of income and the rate of interest are studied, as usual, by finding the partial derivatives from equations (3.56) and (3.57). However, the results for changes in $C_0$, $I_0$, $\bar{G}$, $T_0$, $L_0$ and $\bar{M}$ must be the same as before, that is the same as equations (3.22) to (3.25) and equations (3.30) to (3.33). This is because we have not introduced the price level as an endogenous variable in the system so that it does not affect the reactions within the system to exogenous changes. But with the price level variable we can add some conclusions on the impact of exogenous price changes on $Y$ and $r$:

$$\frac{\partial Y}{\partial P} = \frac{-(C_r + I_r)\dfrac{\bar{M}}{P^2}}{D} < 0 \tag{3.58}$$

$$\frac{\partial r}{\partial P} = \frac{-(1 - C_Y(1 - T_Y) - I_Y)\dfrac{\bar{M}}{P^2}}{D} > 0 \tag{3.59}$$

where

$$D = (1 - C_Y(1 - T_Y) - I_Y)L_r + (C_r + I_r)L_Y < 0.$$

An increase in the price level reduces the equilibrium level of income and raises the equilibrium rate of interest. The reason is the decline in the supply of money in real terms noted before. If $r_1$ and $Y_1$ in Figure 3.15 are the initial equilibrium rate of interest and real income, and the price level rises from $P_1$ to $P_2$, the $LM/P$ curve is shifted from $LM/P_1$ to $LM/P_2$ but the real $IS$ curve is not affected on the assumptions adopted.

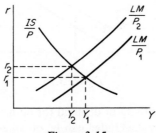

Figure 3.15

The initial effect is to create an excess demand for money (in real terms) at the rate of interest $r_1$. The selling of bonds by money-holders who are trying to maintain their real money-holdings at the level represented by $\bar{M}/P_1$ reduces the price of bonds. The consequent increase in the rate of interest reduces the level of planned expenditure (in real terms) and the equilibrium level of real income falls, from $Y_1$ to $Y_2$.

The implications of an increase in the price level in the two limiting cases can be briefly stated. With expenditure decisions unresponsive to changes in the rate of interest we have, by setting $(C_r + I_r) \to 0$ in equations (3.56) and (3.57)

$$\frac{\partial Y}{\partial P} \to 0 \qquad (3.60)$$

$$\frac{\partial r}{\partial P} \to -\frac{\bar{M}}{L_r P^2} > 0 \qquad (3.61)$$

The decline in the real supply of money raises the rate of interest but this has no impact on expenditure plans so that all the adjustment to a new equilibrium combination of $Y$ and $r$ must be through the increase in the rate of interest. This is illustrated by the move from $r_1$ to $r_2$ at the same income level $Y_1$ in Figure 3.16.

In the case of the liquidity trap, by setting $L_r \to -\infty$ in equations (3.56) and (3.57) we have

$$\frac{\partial Y}{\partial P} \to 0 \qquad (3.62)$$

$$\frac{\partial r}{\partial P} \to 0 \qquad (3.63)$$

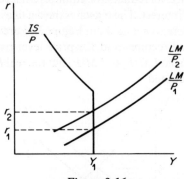

*Figure 3.16*

The high interest-sensitivity of demand for money means that adjustments
in the amount of money demanded can be obtained with small (in the limit
infinitesimal) changes in the price of holding money, that is in the rate of
interest. Consequently when an increase in the price level reduces the real
money supply, the quantity of money demanded adjusts to this lower level
with an increase in the rate of interest which tends to zero as $L_r \rightarrow -\infty$. With
no change in the rate of interest the level of real income remains the same, so
that the shift from $LM/P_1$ to $LM/P_2$ in Figure 3.17 leaves us at $r_1$ and $Y_1$.

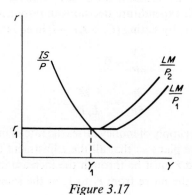

*Figure 3.17*

## EXERCISES

**3.1**   The following equations represent a monetary sector:

$$L = 50 + 0\cdot5\,Y - 5\cdot0r$$
$$\bar{M} = 200$$

(a) Find the equation of the *LM* curve.

(b) Calculate the impact on the slope of the *LM* curve of a change in the interest sensitivity of the demand for money from $-5{\cdot}0$ to $-500{\cdot}0$.

(c) Does it affect the comparative static characteristics of the model in qualitative terms if the money supply is a function of the rate of interest?

**3.2**  Solve the following two-sector model for the equilibrium values of income and the rate of interest:

$$C = 200 + 0{\cdot}6\,Y$$
$$I = 100 - 1000r$$
$$\bar{G} = 200$$
$$L = 250 + 0{\cdot}2\,Y - 500r$$
$$\bar{M} = 400$$

**3.3**  The equilibrium conditions of the two-sector model in linear form are:

$$Y = c_0 - c_Y\,t_0 + c_Y(1 - t_Y)\,Y + c_r r + i_0 + i_Y\,Y + i_r r + \bar{G}$$
$$l_0 + l_Y\,Y + l_r r = \bar{M}$$

Using this model answer the following questions for the limiting case of zero sensitivity of the demand for money to changes in the rate of interest ($l_r = 0$):

(a) Obtain the partial derivatives $\dfrac{\partial Y}{\partial \bar{G}}, \dfrac{\partial r}{\partial \bar{G}}, \dfrac{\partial Y}{\partial \bar{M}}$ and $\dfrac{\partial r}{\partial \bar{M}}$,

(b) Can you show these results using *IS* and *LM* curves?

(c) What is the significance of this limiting case for the effectiveness of monetary and fiscal policy?

# CHAPTER IV

# The Production and Employment Sector

The two-sector model of income determination in the previous chapter concentrated on factors which influence the expenditure decisions of consumers and investors. Attention was therefore limited to the demand for goods and services in the economy while nothing was said explicitly about the way in which the incomes which households spend are generated. An analysis of the generation of income must examine the production decisions of firms which determine the supply of goods and services forthcoming and the employment of factors of production. It is for this purpose that we now extend the model to include a sector which provides an explanation of the level of production.

The introduction of the third sector considerably complicates the model, so perhaps we should try to convince the reader that the imminent hardship is worthwhile by outlining the problems which the extended model will enable us to tackle.

(1) The explanation of the level of production requires the introduction of an analysis of the demand for and supply of factor inputs. In the model used in this chapter the emphasis is on the market for labour with the result that the level of employment, and by implication of unemployment, is explained within the model. This theoretical framework can then be used to study the effects of changes in variables, including instruments of policy, on the level of employment.

(2) In the three-sector model the possibility can be recognized of a discrepancy between the level of income which provides equilibrium in the expenditure and monetary sectors and that level which is associated with the full employment of labour.

(3) The introduction of the production and employment sector makes it possible to examine the effect, on any variable explained within the model, of

imperfections in the labour market such as the inflexibility of the money or the real wage rate.

The analysis of the three-sector model will be presented in *four stages*. First, a demand curve for labour will be derived from the relationship between firms' factor inputs and their output. Second, a supply of labour curve will be hypothesized. Third, the demand for and supply of labour functions will be used to state the condition for equilibrium in the production and employment sector. Fourth, the third sector will be incorporated into the model (section 4.4) and the full model will be used to analyse the implications of some imperfections in the operation of the labour market (section 4.5) and of the conventional limiting cases (section 4.6).

## 4.1 PRODUCTION AND THE DEMAND FOR LABOUR

The starting point is the relationship between output and the level of employment of labour. It will be assumed throughout that only two factors, labour and capital, are required for production and that only the labour input is variable, the stock of real capital, $K^R$, and techniques of production being fixed. The analysis is consequently applicable only to the short run. In addition both factors are taken to be homogeneous so that the labour input can be measured in terms of man-hours per time period.

In a model with labour as the only variable input and with given technical knowledge, variations in output can be achieved only by altering the level of the employment of labour. Increases in the labour input raise the level of output but, by assumption, at a diminishing rate; that is we assume diminishing returns to labour. This relationship between output (equals income, $Y$) and the level of employment of labour, $N$, can be written as

$$Y = Y(N) \tag{4.1}$$

which is called the *production function*. The assumption that labour is subject to diminishing returns can be stated formally in terms of restrictions on the first and second derivatives of the production function. These are

$$Y'_N = \frac{\partial Y}{\partial N} > 0$$

and

$$Y''_N = \frac{\partial^2 Y}{\partial N^2} < 0$$

which respectively mean that the marginal product of labour is positive and that it declines as the level of employment increases. These characteristics are represented in Figure 4.1(b), which illustrates the production function (equation (4.1)), by the positive but declining slope of the curve.

The production function for the whole economy is the aggregate of corresponding functions for individual firms. We will now digress into microeconomic
theory in order to establish the amount of labour which will be demanded by
firms and supplied by workers at different real wage rates.

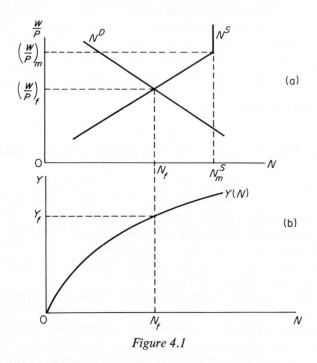

*Figure 4.1*

In the short run, the output of the $i$th firm, which we call $Q_i$, is a function of
the fixed stock of real capital with which the firm is endowed, $\bar{K}_i^R$, and the
quantity of labour which the firm chooses to employ, $N_i$. This firm's production
function can therefore be written as

$$Q_i = Q(N_i, \bar{K}_i^R) \tag{4.2}$$

the function being subject to the restrictions that the marginal product of
labour is positive, $\partial Q_i/\partial N_i > 0$, and declines as the level of employment
increases, $\partial^2 Q_i/\partial N_i^2 < 0$.

Establishing the relationship between the firm's variable input and its output
in this way does not tell us which position on its production function the firm
will choose, and therefore what quantity of labour it will employ in equilibrium.
To find this we must specify an objective pursued by the firm and derive from
this the firm's demand for labour. The analysis henceforth will assume that all
firms are *profit maximizers* in the short run, and also that product and factor
markets are perfectly competitive. The consequence of the latter assumption

is that individual industrial firms and workers are price takers since they can exert no influence over the market real wage rate, $W/P$, at which they demand or supply labour.

The marginal cost of production in this idealized economy is equal to the real wage rate because the capital stock is fixed and the cost of the unit of labour required to produce the marginal unit of output is the real wage rate paid.

The profit of the firm expressed in real terms is defined as total real revenue (i.e. total product) minus total real cost. For the individual firm total cost is the sum of total variable cost of employing labour, $(W/P)N_i$, and the fixed cost of capital, the total interest foregone on the funds tied up in the capital stock, $r\bar{K}_i^R$. We can write the expression for the total real profit of the firm ($\pi_i$) as

$$\pi_i = Q(N_i, \bar{K}_i^R) - \left(\frac{W}{P}N_i + r\bar{K}_i^R\right) \tag{4.3}$$

—i.e. total revenue minus total cost. Profits are maximized where the marginal profit is zero, i.e. (with $d\bar{K}_i^R = 0$)

$$\frac{\partial \pi}{\partial N_i} = \frac{\partial Q_i}{\partial N_i} - \frac{W}{P} = 0 \tag{4.4}$$

which simply says that the condition for profit maximization (and therefore equilibrium) is that marginal revenue (product) $\partial Q_i / \partial N_i$ minus marginal cost $W/P$ is zero.

For the aggregate of all firms this equilibrium condition (4.4) can be written as

$$\frac{\partial \pi}{\partial N} = Y_N' - \frac{W}{P} = 0 \tag{4.5}$$

Profits are maximized when individually and in the aggregate firms set marginal revenue equal to marginal cost.

If the real wage rate increases then the firm is faced with a higher real marginal cost of output so that, with the production function and consequently the real marginal revenue given, the equilibrium level of employment will be reduced until a higher marginal product is reached which is equal to the higher marginal cost. If all firms do the same, there will be a total demand for labour function $N^D$ of the general form

$$N^D = N^D\left(\frac{W}{P}\right) \tag{4.6}$$

where $\partial N^D / \partial(W/P) < 0$. The function is shown in Figure 4.1(a). It is important to note that all points on the labour demand curve represent equilibrium positions for firms since at all points the equilibrium condition (equation (4.4)), and consequently also the aggregate equilibrium condition (equation (4.5)), is satisfied. The $N^D$ curve is therefore the locus of points at which the marginal product of labour is equal to the real wage rate.

## 4.2   THE SUPPLY OF LABOUR

Remembering that we have adopted the assumption that individual workers cannot, through their decisions to offer or withdraw their labour, affect the real wage rate, each worker has the choice of using any hour of his time for leisure or for work which is remunerated at the market real wage rate. He is therefore confronted with a market determined set of alternative combinations of real income (equals the real wage rate) and leisure which form his 'budget line'. On the other hand, the worker has a preference pattern which ranks alternative combinations of income and leisure on an ordinal scale of 'more' or 'less-preferred'. The indifference curves implied by this preference pattern are assumed to be convex from below which indicates that the marginal rate of substitution of income for leisure diminishes.† The condition for the maximization of utility by the $j$th worker is that

$$\frac{\partial D_j}{\partial N_j} = \frac{W}{P} \tag{4.7}$$

where $D$ is the disutility associated with the loss of leisure and $\partial D_j/\partial N_j > 0$. Labour will be supplied up to the point at which the real wage rate just compensates the worker for his loss of leisure. In aggregate the condition for workers as a group to be in equilibrium is that

$$\frac{\partial D}{\partial N} = \frac{W}{P} \tag{4.8}$$

As the real wage rate rises the budget line pivots and another quantity of leisure, and by implication quantity of work, is chosen. We assume that at least up to a particular real wage rate $(W/P)_m$ all workers offer more labour as the real wage rate increases. In the aggregate the amount of labour supplied $N^S$ is therefore a positive function of the real wage rate:

$$N^S = N^S(W/P) \tag{4.9}$$

where $\partial N^S/\partial(W/P) > 0$. At real wage rates above $(W/P)_m$ the supply of labour is assumed to be fixed at $N_m{}^S$ and the labour supply function then takes the form shown in Figure 4.1(a).

## 4.3   THE EQUILIBRIUM LEVELS OF EMPLOYMENT AND OUTPUT

The production and employment sector consists of the production function, equation (4.1), and the demand and supply of labour functions, equations (4.6) and (4.9). The sub-sector of equations (4.6) and (4.9) represents the labour

† See Hicks (1939), Ch. 1.

market and determines the equilibrium levels of the real wage rate and employment.

The level of employment when the labour market is in equilibrium is called the *full employment level of employment* $N_f$ and is associated with the *full employment real wage rate* $(W/P)_f$. This equilibrium in the labour market is achieved when all of the labour offered by workers at the current real wage rate is taken on by employers, and all employers are able to obtain the amount of labour they prefer at that wage rate. That is, in equilibrium the demand for labour equals the supply of labour, so that the equilibrium condition can be written as

$$N^D = N^S \tag{4.10}$$

In diagrammatic terms the equilibrium level of employment $N_f$ is given by the intersection of the $N^D$ and $N^S$ curves in Figure 4.1(a), and the corresponding equilibrium real wage rate is $(W/P)_f$ in the figure. As long as the labour market is competitive and the real wage rate is perfectly flexible this equilibrium is stable, meaning that an excess demand for, or supply of, labour cannot be maintained. An excess demand for labour will bid up the real wage rate, and an excess supply will bid it down, towards $(W/P)_f$.

At all points on the $N^D$ curve firms are maximizing profits, the equilibrium condition, equation (4.5), being met, and at all points on $N^S$ workers are maximizing their utility, condition (4.8) being met. At the intersection of the two curves equilibrium conditions (4.5) and (4.8) are both met so that

$$Y'_N = \frac{\partial D}{\partial N} = \frac{W}{P} \tag{4.11}$$

The marginal product of labour, the marginal utility of leisure (sacrificed if the work is undertaken) and the real wage rate are all equal when the labour market is in equilibrium. In subsequent discussion frequent use will be made of the equilibrium condition (4.11) from the point of view of the firm, that is

$$Y'_N = \frac{W}{P} \tag{4.12}$$

The equilibrium level of employment, $N_f$, resulting from the real wage rate $(W/P)_f$, can be introduced into the production function to determine the position on the function which is chosen by the firms. The equilibrium of the third sector requires that the level of income (output) is consistent with labour market equilibrium. The equilibrium *full employment income level* is $Y_f$, in Figure 4.1(b), which is produced by the equilibrium level of employment $N_f$, and which therefore satisfies the technical equation of the production sector

$$Y = Y(N_f) \tag{4.13}$$

A characteristic of the third sector *as it has been formulated here* is that it is self-contained and completely independent of the other two sectors. No variable from the expenditure or the monetary sector enters the determination of the full employment level of real income. This characteristic will be considered further when the three sectors are brought together and solved simultaneously in the next section.

## 4.4  THE THREE-SECTOR MODEL AT FULL EMPLOYMENT EQUILIBRIUM

The third sector can now be added to the model of income determination and the qualities of the three-sector model be investigated using the familiar comparative static analysis. To begin with we will adopt the assumptions that the model is working:

(a) with perfect flexibility of all prices; that is, there are no constraints on the market determination of the prices of goods and of factors (wages and the rate of interest), and
(b) in the absence of the limiting cases.

Assumption (a) will be dropped in section 4.5 and assumption (b) in section 4.6.

Before stating the equations of the three-sector model it is necessary to emphasize one aspect of the model, already mentioned, which is central to an understanding of its operation. This is that both the expenditure and the monetary sector contain variables, $C_0$, $I_0$, $\bar{M}$ and $L_0$ for example, which are exogenous and are assumed to be changeable in the short run, whereas the production and employment sector as formulated in section 4.3, contains no *changeable* exogenous variables. In the short run model the capital stock, techniques of production and productivity of labour are fixed so that the production function, and the demand for labour function, cannot change. In addition it is assumed that the tastes of workers as regards the choice between work and leisure are fixed in the short run and that the size of the labour force can change only in the long run, with the result that the supply of labour function cannot change. In the absence of exogenous influences on the third sector we cannot undertake a comparative static analysis of the impact of changes in the production function. However, this does not prevent us investigating the effects of an exogenously determined constraint on the model, such as an exogenous money wage rate to be considered in the next section.

As formulated so far the third sector does not include any variables from other sectors, any changeable exogenous variables or any exogenous constraints. As a result the full employment equilibrium levels of employment and income, $N_f$ and $Y_f$, are constant and do not alter when changes are made in the other two sectors. The equilibrium condition of the third sector (equation (4.13)) therefore, as we shall see, has a differential of zero: no change in $Y_f$ is possible in the short run.

It is evident, from the discussion of the government's role in the two-sector model and from the statement of the third sector, that the fiscal activities of the government in the three-sector model will be limited to its taxation and expenditure. No attempt will be made to recognize the direct effect of the government's own employment of labour. The government in this model can be seen *either* as a decision-taking unit in the expenditure sector alone which spends money on goods and services produced in the private sector, *or* as a spending unit and a direct employer of labour but an employer which makes employment decisions on the same basis as private employers, i.e. using a profit maximization criterion. Whichever view is taken the presence of the government does not effect the equations of the production and employment sector.

Bringing together the equilibrium conditions for the two-sector model with variable prices, and for the third sector, we have the following model:

*The expenditure sector.*

$$Y = C_0 + C(Y - T, r) + I_0 + I(Y, r) + \bar{G} \tag{3.50}$$

*The monetary sector.*

$$L_0 + L(Y, r) = \frac{\bar{M}}{P} \tag{3.53}$$

*The production and employment sector.*

$$Y = Y(N_f) \tag{4.13}$$

Taking the differentials of the three equations and rearranging terms we have

$$[1 - C_Y(1 - T_Y) - I_Y] dY - (C_r + I_r) dr = dC_0 + dI_0 - C_Y dT_0 + d\bar{G} \tag{4.14}$$

$$L_Y dY + L_r dr + \frac{\bar{M} dP}{P^2} = \frac{d\bar{M}}{P} - dL_0 \tag{4.15}$$

$$dY = Y'_N dN_f = 0 \tag{4.16}$$

The differentials for the expenditure and monetary sectors, equations (4.14) and (4.15), are the same as in the two-sector model with variable prices. The differential of the third-sector equilibrium condition, equation (4.16), is zero for the reason already given. Since $N_f$ cannot change it cannot bring about changes in any of the endogenous variables in the system and consequently it does not enter the solutions for the endogenous variables, equations (4.17), (4.18) and (4.19) below. This is not to say that $N_f$ is unimportant in the model. In fact quite the reverse is true. Equilibrium in all three sectors simultaneously, which we shall call the *overall equilibrium* of the model, can be achieved only when the income level in the expenditure and monetary sectors is equal to the equilibrium income level in the third sector $Y_f$. And $Y_f$ is a fixed amount determined by the equilibrium level of employment in the labour market $N_f$.

The system represented by the three equilibrium conditions in differential form, equations (4.14), (4.15) and (4.16), is written in matrix form as:

$$\begin{bmatrix} [1 - C_Y(1-T_Y)-I_Y] & -(C_r+I_r) & 0 \\ L_Y & L_r & \dfrac{\bar{M}}{P^2} \\ 1 & 0 & 0 \end{bmatrix} \begin{bmatrix} dY \\ dr \\ dP \end{bmatrix}$$

$$= \begin{bmatrix} dC_0 + dI_0 - C_Y\,dT_0 + d\bar{G} \\ \dfrac{d\bar{M}}{P} - dL_0 \\ 0 \end{bmatrix}$$

And the solutions of the model for the three endogenous variables are:

$$dY = 0 \tag{4.17}$$

$$dr = \frac{(dC_0 + dI_0 - C_Y\,dT_0 + d\bar{G})\dfrac{\bar{M}}{P^2}}{\varDelta} \tag{4.18}$$

$$dP = \frac{-\left(\dfrac{d\bar{M}}{P} - dL_0\right)(C_r + I_r) - (dC_0 + dI_0 - C_Y\,dT_0 + d\bar{G})L_r}{\varDelta} \tag{4.19}$$

where

$$\varDelta = -(C_r + I_r)\frac{\bar{M}}{P^2} > 0 \tag{4.20}$$

The solution of the model for $Y$, $r$ and $P$ will not be given mathematically but is illustrated in Figure 4.2. The vertical line at $Y_f$ indicates the fixed level of income which is produced when the labour market is in equilibrium at full employment. As usual the $IS/P$ curve represents the expenditure sector equilibrium combinations of $Y$ and $r$, and the $LM/P$ curves represent the $Y$ and $r$

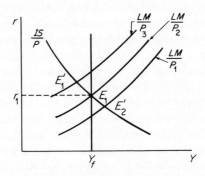

*Figure 4.2*

combinations which provide monetary equilibrium at different price levels. There is only one price level $P_2$ at which the monetary and expenditure sectors are simultaneously in equilibrium at the full employment level of income $Y_f$. The rate of interest required for this overall equilibrium is $r_1$ and the equilibrium position is $E_1$ in the figure. At a lower price level $P_1$ the monetary sector curve intersects the expenditure sector curve at $E_2'$ and therefore at an income level above the full employment level and a rate of interest below the full employment rate. There is an excess of demand for goods and services over the full employment supply, and in an economy with a perfectly functioning price system this will raise the price level. As the price level increases the money wage rate will be bid up correspondingly to maintain the equilibrium real wage rate $(W/P)_f$. If this did not happen the real wage rate would fall and an excess demand for labour would appear. With the price level raised to $P_2$ overall equilibrium will be restored at the rate of interest $r_1$.

At a price level $P_3$, above $P_2$, the expenditure and monetary sectors are in simultaneous equilibrium at $E_1'$, that is at an income level below, and a rate of interest above, the full employment level. The aggregate demand for goods and services is less than the amount which would be supplied with the third sector in equilibrium. The price level falls to $P_2$ and the money wage rate is cut proportionately to maintain the full employment real wage rate.

The perfect functioning of the price system therefore guarantees *a stable equilibrium at full employment*. If any disturbance, that is any change in an exogenous variable, causes the expenditure and monetary sectors' equilibrium income level to diverge from the full employment level, then excess demand or supply in the commodity market will adjust the price level to the full employment level.

Having explained the characteristics of the overall equilibrium of the model, the analysis can now be extended to examine the impact on the endogenous variables, $Y$, $r$ and $P$, of changes in the exogenous variables $C_0$, $I_0$, $T_0$, $\bar{G}$, $\bar{M}$ and $L_0$. The comparative static approach here involves a comparison of the overall equilibrium before an exogenous change with the overall equilibrium achieved after it.

### 4.4.1 A change in expenditure

The point has been noted on more than one occasion that in the three-sector model with flexible prices and money wage rate the level of income in overall equilibrium cannot be changed. It should not surprise us to find, therefore, that a change in exogenous expenditure does not affect the level of income (or employment). From equation (4.17) we have the partial derivatives

$$\frac{\partial Y}{\partial C_0} = \frac{\partial Y}{\partial I_0} = \frac{\partial Y}{\partial T_0} = \frac{\partial Y}{\partial \bar{G}} = 0 \tag{4.21}$$

The multiplier is zero in all cases with the result that in this context a balanced-budget change also has a multiplier of zero. In Figure 4.3 the initial overall equilibrium is at $E_1$, with the income level $Y_f$, the rate of interest $r_1$, and the price level $P_1$. The effect of an increase in exogenous expenditure is shown by the shift from $IS/P$ to $IS'/P$ and the new equilibrium is $E_2$ which is characterized by the same income level as $E_1$ but a higher rate of interest $r_2$ and a higher price level $P_2$.

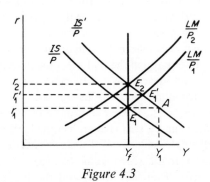

*Figure 4.3*

The effect on $r$ and $P$ is given by the following partial derivatives obtained from equations (4.18) and (4.19):

$$\frac{\partial r}{\partial C_0} = \frac{\partial r}{\partial I_0} = \frac{\partial r}{\partial G} = \frac{\left(\dfrac{\bar{M}}{P^2}\right)}{\varDelta} > 0 \tag{4.22}$$

$$\frac{\partial r}{\partial T_0} = \frac{-C_Y\left(\dfrac{\bar{M}}{P^2}\right)}{\varDelta} < 0 \tag{4.23}$$

$$\frac{\partial P}{\partial C_0} = \frac{\partial P}{\partial I_0} = \frac{\partial P}{\partial G} = \frac{-L_r}{\varDelta} > 0 \tag{4.24}$$

$$\frac{\partial P}{\partial T_0} = \frac{C_Y L_r}{\varDelta} < 0 \tag{4.25}$$

The reaction of both the rate of interest and the price level to an increase in exogenous expenditure can be explained by breaking the outcome into two parts, a movement from $E_1$ to $E_1'$ which would occur if the price level were fixed, and movement from $E_1'$ to $E_2$ which is the result of the increase in the price level. The increase in expenditure with the rate of interest remaining at $r_1$ would move us to position $A$ in Figure 4.3, but this point is associated with an excess demand for money which pushes up the rate of interest to $r_1'$. With the price level fixed the adjustment would end at $E_1'$, but in the model with flexible prices the excess demand for goods ($Y > Y_f$) at $E_1'$ raises the price level. This increase in the price level (accompanied by an equal proportional rise in the money wage rate) shifts the real $LM$ curve from $LM/P_1$ to $LM/P_2$. The real supply of money falls, thereby providing a secondary reason for the rate of interest to rise, and it will do so up to $r_2$. The adjustment in the price level and in the rate of interest ceases when the new overall equilibrium $E_2$ is reached, that is when the excess demands in the goods market and in the money market have both been eliminated.

### 4.4.2   A change in the supply of money (or in the liquidity preference)

Consider the effect of a reduction in the supply of money or an increase in liquidity preference. As with the shifts in the expenditure sector just examined the income effect of these changes is nil, the income level remaining at $Y_f$ in Figure 4.4. From equation (4.17) we have

$$\frac{\partial Y}{\partial \bar{M}} = \frac{\partial Y}{\partial L_0} = 0 \qquad (4.26)$$

When the impact on the rate of interest and the price level are considered the changes in the monetary sector do have different implications. Equations (4.18) and (4.19) yield the partial derivatives.

$$\frac{\partial r}{\partial \bar{M}} = \frac{\partial r}{\partial L_0} = 0 \qquad (4.27)$$

$$\frac{\partial P}{\partial \bar{M}} = \frac{-(C_r + I_r)\dfrac{1}{P}}{\varDelta} > 0 \qquad (4.28)$$

$$\frac{\partial P}{\partial L_0} = \frac{(C_r + I_r)}{\varDelta} < 0 \qquad (4.29)$$

These results will be explained in relation to Figure 4.4, where $E_1$ is the initial overall equilibrium position with the rate of interest $r_1$ and the price level $P_1$.

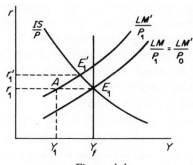

Figure 4.4

The effect of a fall in the supply of money is to shift the real $LM$ curve to the left from $LM/P_1$ to $LM'/P_1$. This signifies that the lower supply of money would be equal to the demand for money at rate of interest $r_1$ only if the level of income were as low as $Y_1$ (at point $A$). If the price level were fixed at $P_1$ the excess demand for money at the combination $r_1$, $Y_f$ would drive up the rate of interest to $r_1'$ and the position $E_1'$ would be attained. But at $E_1'$ there is excess supply of goods and services, and with flexible prices the price level falls to $P_0$. The fall in the price level is just sufficient to offset the fall in the nominal supply of money so that the real money supply is restored to its original level.† The new real $LM$ curve, $LM'/P_0$, is in the same position as the original curve, $LM/P_1$. The outcome is that the reduction in the nominal supply of money has an impact only on the price level. For the rate of interest to increase a fall in the supply of money in real terms would be necessary but this is prevented by the offsetting reduction in the price level. Consequently the rate of interest remains at $r_1$, and the partial derivatives (4.27) and (4.28) are respectively zero and positive.

An increase in liquidity preference similarly shifts the real $LM$ curve to the left but again the excess demand in the goods market restores overall equilibrium at $E_1$. The fall in the price level raises the real supply of money just sufficiently for the latter to equal the higher real demand for money at the original rate of interest $r_1$.

### 4.5   THE THREE-SECTOR MODEL WITH AN EXOGENOUS MONEY WAGE RATE

We have seen that in the absence of the limiting cases the perfect flexibility of all goods and factor prices will guarantee a full employment level of income, with the values of the other endogenous variables being determined by the values of the exogenous variables in the expenditure and monetary sectors.

The modifications to these conclusions required when some imperfections exist in the system will be explained, to begin with, by assuming that goods prices are flexible and that the limiting cases are absent. The imperfection postulated is a rigid money wage rate whose level is determined outside the system, by wage legislation or by trade union power for example. The restriction on the money wage rate, $\bar{W}$, gives rise to the possibility that the real wage rate, $\bar{W}/P$, is above or below the real wage rate which provides full employment, $(\bar{W}/P)_f$. The analysis is concerned, therefore, with the way in which the system reacts to disequilibrium in the labour market.

If the money wage rate is fixed at a level $\bar{W}$ the three-sector model, as set out in equations (3.50), (3.53) and (4.13) in the previous section, must be modified.

---

† In this case therefore, the percentage fall in the price level is the same as the percentage fall in the nominal money supply: for a different case see section 4.5.

The reason is that the equilibrium condition for the third sector, equation (4.13), was written on the assumption that the labour market would be automatically in equilibrium at $N_f$. It was therefore not necessary to include the labour market equilibrium condition, equation (4.11), explicitly in the model, although of course it was assumed to be satisfied. The third-sector equilibrium condition was simplified to the requirement that the level of income be consistent with the full employment of labour. Once disequilibrium in the labour market is possible it becomes necessary to add an equation which determines the level of employment, $N$, *whether or not* the labour market is in equilibrium.

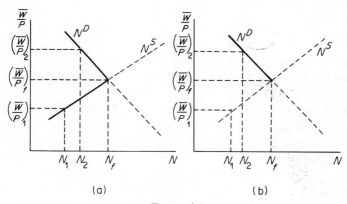

(a)                              (b)

*Figure 4.5*

If the labour market is in disequilibrium at a real wage rate above the equilibrium rate, such as $(\bar{W}/P)_2$ in Figure 4.5(a) the amount of labour employed will be determined by the demand curve for labour and the real wage rate, at $N_2$. Firms continue to employ workers up to the point at which their marginal product equals the real wage rate regardless of whether there is an excess supply of labour. At real wage rates below equilibrium, such as $(\bar{W}/P)_1$ in Figure 4.5(a), the supply determines the amount of employment, $N_1$. Consequently the solid line in Figure 4.5(a) indicates the level of employment at different real wage rates.

It is probably more realistic if, instead of assuming that the money wage rate is not determined by labour market forces, we postulate that the money wage rate is responsive to market pressures in an upwards direction but not in a downwards direction. This situation is depicted in Figure 4.5(b). When the current price level and money wage rate result in a real wage rate above $(\bar{W}/P)_f$, for example $(\bar{W}/P)_2$, the downward rigidity of the money wage rate prevents an adjustment in the real wage rate to $(\bar{W}/P)_f$ at the current price level. The solid line in Figure 4.5(b) shows the level of employment at the real wage rates above the equilibrium rate. If, on the other hand, the current price level and money wage rate result in a real wage rate below $(\bar{W}/P)_f$, for example $(\bar{W}/P)_1$, the excess demand for labour drives up the money wage rate to a level consistent with $(\bar{W}/P)_f$ at the current price level, and the level of employment is $N_f$.

In the modified model to be presented it will be assumed, for simplicity, that the money wage rate is inflexible in the downwards direction and is set at a level which, given the current price level, places the real wage rate above the equilibrium level $(\bar{W}/P)_f$. With the level of employment not fixed $N$ becomes an endogenous variable whose level is that which satisfies the demand side of the labour market equilibrium condition, equation (4.11), i.e. satisfies

$$Y_N' = \frac{\bar{W}}{P} \tag{4.30}$$

which is the condition (4.12) with $W$ exogenous. The level of employment $N_2$ in Figure 4.5, for example, satisfies the requirement that the marginal product of labour, $Y_N'$, be equal to the real wage rate $(\bar{W}/P)_2$.

Given the level of employment which, at a prevailing disequilibrium real wage rate satisfies equation (4.30), the level of income is found by substituting the level of $N$ into the production function (4.1). Since the level of employment need not be $N_f$ the third-sector equilibrium condition cannot be equation (4.13) as it was before. Instead both the equilibrium condition (4.30), to find $N$, and the production function to find the corresponding $Y$, must be included explicitly in the model. Consequently the three-sector model with the money wage rate exogenously determined is:

$$Y = C_0 + C(Y - T, r) + I_0 + I(Y, r) + \bar{G} \tag{3.50}$$

$$L_0 + L(Y, r) = \frac{\bar{M}}{P} \tag{3.53}$$

$$Y = Y(N) \tag{4.1}$$

$$Y_N' = \frac{\bar{W}}{P} \tag{4.30}$$

Taking the differentials of the four equations and rearranging terms we have:

$$(1 - C_Y(1 - T_Y) - I_Y)\,dY - (C_r + I_r)\,dr = dC_0 + dI_0 - C_Y\,dT_0 + d\bar{G} \tag{4.31}$$

$$L_Y\,dY + L_r\,dr + \frac{\bar{M}\,dP}{P^2} = \frac{d\bar{M}}{P} - dL_0 \tag{4.32}$$

$$dY = Y_N'\,dN \tag{4.33}$$

$$Y_N''\,dN = \frac{P\,d\bar{W} - \bar{W}\,dP}{P^2} \tag{4.34}$$

In matrix notation:

$$
\begin{bmatrix}
(1 - C_Y(1 - T_Y) - I_Y) & -(C_r + I_r) & 0 & 0 \\
L_Y & L_r & 0 & \dfrac{\bar{M}}{P^2} \\
1 & 0 & -Y'_N & 0 \\
0 & 0 & Y''_N & \dfrac{\bar{W}}{P^2}
\end{bmatrix}
\begin{bmatrix}
dY \\ dr \\ dN \\ dP
\end{bmatrix}
$$

$$
=
\begin{bmatrix}
dC_0 + dI_0 - C_Y dT_0 + d\bar{G} \\
\dfrac{d\bar{M}}{P} - dL_0 \\
0 \\
\dfrac{d\bar{W}}{P}
\end{bmatrix}
$$

The solutions for $dY$, $dr$, $dN$ and $dP$ are complicated and space-filling so they have been placed in an appendix at the end of this chapter. We will concentrate here on the implied partial derivatives and compare and contrast this model with the model where the money wage rate was flexible and determined endogenously (section 4.4).

### 4.5.1 A change in the money wage rate

The money wage rate is set, by assumption, at a level which yields a real wage rate above the equilibrium rate, $(\bar{W}/P)_f$, given the current price level. At this real wage rate there is unemployment. The fixed money wage rate acts as a constraint on the labour market and there are two questions to consider:

(a) can we confirm that the constraint is affecting the values of $Y$, $N$ and so on by finding out what happens to these variables if the constraint is relaxed, i.e. if the money wage rate is cut? and

(b) if the money wage rate remains fixed how will the system react to the resulting disequilibrium? Will there be any automatic adjustment to move the system to full employment equilibrium?

Answering question (a) first, the effect of a cut in $\bar{W}$ can be seen by obtaining from the solutions of the model for $dY$, $dr$, $dN$ and $dP$ (equations (A.1) to (A.4) in the appendix to this chapter) the following partial derivatives:

$$
\frac{\partial Y}{\partial \bar{W}} = \frac{Y'_N(C_r + I_r)\dfrac{\bar{M}}{P^2}\dfrac{1}{P}}{\Delta} < 0 \tag{4.35}
$$

$$
\frac{\partial r}{\partial \bar{W}} = \frac{Y'_N(1 - C_Y(1 - T_Y) - I_Y)\dfrac{\bar{M}}{P^2}\dfrac{1}{P}}{\Delta} > 0 \tag{4.36}
$$

$$\frac{\partial N}{\partial \bar{W}} = \frac{(C_r + I_r)\dfrac{\bar{M}}{P^2}\dfrac{1}{P}}{\Delta} < 0 \tag{4.37}$$

$$\frac{\partial P}{\partial \bar{W}} = -Y'_N \frac{\dfrac{1}{P}[(1 - C_Y(1 - T_Y) - I_Y)L_r + (C_r + I_r)L_Y]}{\Delta} > 0 \tag{4.38}$$

A cut in the exogenous money wage rate raises income and employment and reduces the rate of interest and the price level. The reasons for these reactions of the endogenous variables can be most easily understood if we refer to Figure 4.6. Take as the starting point a level of money wage rate $\bar{W}_0$ which, at the prevailing price level $P_0$, produces the real wage rate $(\bar{W}/P)_0$. At this real

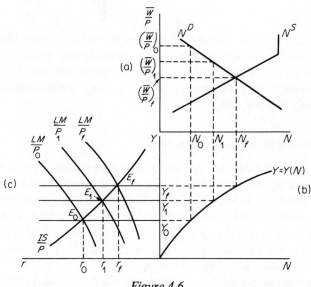

*Figure 4.6*

wage rate $N_0$ men are employed and they produce an output level $Y_0$ which we assume to be equated to the level of demand associated with the $IS/P$ curve, the $LM$ curve $LM/P_0$ and the rate of interest $r_0$ in Figure 4.6(c). That is, the starting point is two-sector equilibrium at $E_0$, where $Y_0$ is consistent with the initial real wage rate $(\bar{W}/P)_0$. Now let the money wage rate be cut from $\bar{W}_0$ to $\bar{W}_1$. The first question which arises is whether this will lead to a decline in the real wage rate in Figure 4.6(a). Let us assume, for a moment, that it will. The decline in the real wage rate then raises the demand for labour from $N_0$ to $N_1$; employment rises by this amount and the increment to output is $Y_1$ minus $Y_0$. If the real expenditure and real demand for and supply of money were unaffected, the original two-sector equilibrium position of $E_0$ would be associated with a level of demand, $Y_0$, which is less than the level of supply $Y_1$. The result is a fall in the price level from $P_0$ to $P_1$ which by raising the real supply of money (reflected in a shift from $LM/P_0$ to $LM/P_1$) restores two-sector equilibrium at $E_1$. The decline in the rate of interest, from $r_0$ to $r_1$, is sufficient to stimulate demand to equal the new level of supply $Y_1$.

This reasoning explains the signs of the partial derivatives (4.35) to (4.38). But it has been said that the money wage rate and the price level *both* fall. Is it possible, therefore, that the real wage rate could remain constant, with the price fall negating the cut in the money wage rate?

Imagine a cut in $\bar{W}$ accompanied by an equi-proportionate fall in the price level leaving the real wage rate at $(\bar{W}/P)_0$ in the figure. Employment would remain at $N_0$ and output supplied at $Y_0$. But the price level has fallen, shifting the real $LM$ curve to the right, so that demand in the two-sector equilibrium would necessarily be above the level $Y_0$ in Figure 4.6(c). There would consequently be excess demand if the price level had fallen so much as to negate the cut in $\bar{W}$. It is not therefore possible in two-sector equilibrium to have a reduction in the money wage rate which does not (given the values of $L_0$, $\bar{M}$ etc. fixed) lead to a cut in the real wage rate.

We have seen that a cut in the money wage rate from $\bar{W}_0$ to $\bar{W}_1$ reduced the real wage rate from $(\bar{W}/P)_0$ to $(\bar{W}/P)_1$ and increased the level of income from $Y_0$ to $Y_1$. But the increase in income was not sufficient to move the economy to full employment equilibrium at $Y_f$. It would seem therefore, that the answer to question (b) is that the system will not move automatically to full employment in the presence of a rigid money wage rate. This point may be made more clearly by viewing the matter from a slightly different angle. Imagine that, in Figure 4.6, the system is initially in overall equilibrium at $E_f$ with the endogenous variables having the values $Y_f$, $N_f$, $r_f$ and $P_f$. Now increase the money wage rate sufficiently for the real wage rate to rise from $(\bar{W}/P)_f$ to $(\bar{W}/P)_0$. With the equilibrium income level for the expenditure and monetary sectors at $Y_f$ there would be an excess demand for goods if the level of output $Y_0$, which is implied by the real wage rate $(\bar{W}/P)_0$, were produced. The resulting increase in the price level reduces the real wage rate but at the same time the real $LM$ curve moves from $LM/P_f$ to $LM/P_1$ and the process of adjustment towards $Y_f$ is halted. The decline in the real supply of money curtails the level of real demand by forcing up the rate of interest, and the new equilibrium position for the expenditure and monetary sectors is at $Y_1$, consistent with a real wage rate $(\bar{W}/P)_1$ which is below the real wage rate $(\bar{W}/P)_0$ but above $(W/P)_f$. With a given supply of money in nominal terms the automatic equilibrating process is prevented from restoring overall equilibrium, and therefore eliminating unemployment, even with perfectly flexible prices other than the money wage rate. The constraint imposed by the fixed nominal supply of money may be overcome by expansionary monetary policy, which is considered in section 4.5.3.

### 4.5.2　A change in expenditure

In the model with no restriction on the money wage rate we found (in equation (4.21)) that changes in exogenous expenditure do not affect the equilibrium level of income which is determined in the production and employment sector, but that an increase in expenditure does raise both the rate of interest and the price level. In the model with an exogenous wage rate, on the other hand, the fixed nominal money supply prevents two-sector underemployment equilibrium from being converted automatically, through changes in the price level, into full employment (overall) equilibrium. It is to be expected, therefore, that if the level of income which provides equilibrium in the expenditure and monetary sectors can be increased by some means then a movement of $Y$ towards $Y_f$ can be achieved. The effects on $Y$, $r$, $N$ and $P$ of an increase in exogenous expenditure are given by the following partial derivatives, obtained from the solutions of the model (in the appendix to this chapter):

$$\frac{\partial Y}{\partial C_0} = \frac{\partial Y}{\partial I_0} = \frac{\partial Y}{\partial \bar{G}} = \frac{-Y'_N L_r \dfrac{\bar{W}}{P^2}}{\Delta} > 0 \tag{4.39}$$

$$\frac{\partial r}{\partial C_0} = \frac{\partial r}{\partial I_0} = \frac{\partial r}{\partial \bar{G}} = \frac{Y'_N L_Y \dfrac{\bar{W}}{P^2} - Y''_N \dfrac{\bar{M}}{P^2}}{\Delta} > 0 \tag{4.40}$$

$$\frac{\partial N}{\partial C_0} = \frac{\partial N}{\partial I_0} = \frac{\partial N}{\partial \bar{G}} = \frac{-L_r \dfrac{\bar{W}}{P^2}}{\Delta} > 0 \tag{4.41}$$

$$\frac{\partial P}{\partial C_0} = \frac{\partial P}{\partial I_0} = \frac{\partial P}{\partial \bar{G}} = \frac{Y''_N L_r}{\Delta} > 0 \tag{4.42}$$

The impact of $dT_0$ can be found by multiplying the results for $dC_0$, $dI_0$, $d\bar{G}$ by $(-C_Y)$. Again the results can be explained in terms of a diagram. In Figure 4.7 the system is at less than full employment at $Y_1$ and the two-sector equilibrium position $E_1$ corresponds with the position $E_1$ in Figure 4.6(c). An increase in expenditure, shown by the shift from $(IS/P)$ to $(IS/P)'$, initially creates demand in excess of the supply, $Y_1$. The price level and rate of interest increase, the real wage rate falls and supply is stimulated. The overall equilibrium is achieved at $E_2$ on a new real $LM$ curve $LM/P_f$ corresponding to the full employment price level $P_f$ which is higher than $P_1$. The injection of expenditure, as shown by the shift to $(IS/P)'$ in the figure, is sufficient to more than offset the dampening effect on demand of the decline in the real supply of money. If the real supply of money had not declined a smaller injection, and an $IS$ curve to the left of $(IS/P)'$, would have sufficed to achieve overall equilibrium at point A on the original real $LM$ curve $(LM/P_1)$. The expenditure increase has therefore raised $Y$, $r$, $N$ and $P$, and eliminated the unemployment which characterized the system in the absence of policy.

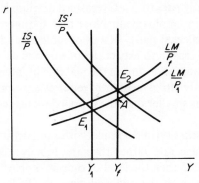

*Figure 4.7*

### 4.5.3 A change in the supply of money

An alternative way of overcoming the obstacle to full employment is to expand sufficiently the nominal supply of money. The effect of this policy on the endogenous variables is shown by the following partial derivatives obtained from the solutions in the appendix. In the interest of brevity the results for a change in liquidity preference are omitted but these can easily be obtained for $dL_0$ by multiplying the partial derivatives (4.43) to (4.46) by $(-P)$. The reasoning is similar to that for changes in the supply of money.

$$\frac{\partial Y}{\partial \bar{M}} = \frac{-Y'_N(C_r + I_r)\frac{1}{P}\frac{\bar{W}}{P^2}}{\Delta} > 0 \tag{4.43}$$

$$\frac{\partial r}{\partial \bar{M}} = \frac{-Y'_N(1 - C_Y(1 - T_Y) - I_Y)\frac{1}{P}}{\Delta} < 0 \tag{4.44}$$

$$\frac{\partial N}{\partial \bar{M}} = \frac{-(C_r + I_r)\frac{1}{P}\frac{\bar{W}}{P^2}}{\Delta} > 0 \tag{4.45}$$

$$\frac{\partial P}{\partial \bar{M}} = \frac{Y''_N(C_r + I_r)\frac{1}{P}}{\Delta} > 0 \tag{4.46}$$

Referring back to Figure 4.6 it may be remembered that the system was, in the absence of policy, stuck in two-sector equilibrium at $E_1$. If the money supply is now increased sufficiently in nominal terms to raise the supply of money in *real* terms then the obstacle to full employment is overcome. The price level increases, the real $LM$ curve shifts from $LM/P_1$ to $LM/P_f$ and as the rate of interest falls demand is stimulated to equal $Y_f$. At the same time the real wage rate declines and supply rises to $Y_f$. Overall equilibrium is attained at $E_f$, with an implied increase in employment. Note that the increase in the nominal supply of money is reflected partly in a price increase and partly in an output increase. There is no reason to expect the proportionate change in $\bar{M}$ and in $P$ to be the same. In fact the decline in the real rate of interest which stimulates expenditure to the full employment level requires a proportionate increase in the price level which is smaller than the proportionate increase in the nominal supply of money.

To conclude the discussion of the model with a restriction on wage flexibility, if it were the *real* wage rate rather than the money wage rate which were exogenously determined then the level of output supplied, $Y$, would be fixed from outside the system. If the rate were fixed at $(W/P)_0 > (W/P)_f$ then the labour market would be in disequilibrium, with unemployment, and no changes in the expenditure or monetary sectors could alter the income and employment levels. This result could be confirmed by solving the model again with the labour market equilibrium condition (4.30) replaced by

$$Y'_N = \left(\frac{W}{P}\right)_0 \tag{4.47}$$

—that is the condition that the marginal product of labour be equal to the fixed real wage rate $(W/P)_0$. From the solution it would be found that the partial derivatives for $Y$ and $N$ with respect to changes in the supply of money and changes in exogenous expenditure are all zero. With output fixed the system reacts to an increase in planned expenditure, whether originating from a shift in an expenditure function or from an increase in the supply of money, by an increase in the price level alone. Expansionary policy in the context of unions' monopoly power in controlling the *real* wage rate is therefore necessarily inflationary and unsuccessful in raising employment.

## 4.6   THE THREE-SECTOR MODEL IN LIMITING CASES

To conclude the analysis of the operation of the three-sector model we shall examine the significance of the two limiting cases for the possibility of achieving overall equilibrium.† To begin with, in each case it will be assumed that the government exerts no control over exogenous expenditure and the supply of money. This will tell us whether overall equilibrium can be expected in the

† On the theoretical implications of the third (the monetarist) limiting case see section 8.2.2.

freely operating market system. Then we will turn to the effect of the manipulation of $\bar{G}$, $T_0$ and $\bar{M}$ by a government aiming to bring the system into equilibrium at full employment. Apart from the limiting cases the system will be assumed to be operating perfectly, so that the model of section 4.4 with flexible goods and factor prices is used.

Consider first the case of interest-insensitive expenditure decisions, $(C_r + I_r) \to 0$. If the positions of the $IS$ and $LM$ curves and the full employment level of income are as illustrated in Figure 4.8, the three curves in pairs have

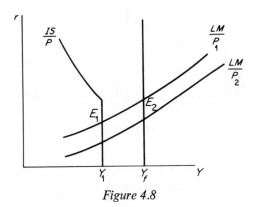

*Figure 4.8*

intersection points but there is no *common* point of intersection to provide overall equilibrium. At $E_1$ there is two-sector equilibrium but the level of demand $Y_1$ falls short of full employment supply. If $Y_f$ were produced excess supply would force down the price level with the result that the real $LM$ curve would shift to the right, as from $LM/P_1$ to $LM/P_2$. But this cannot overcome the inconsistency between the expenditure-monetary equilibrium and the full employment level of income, since there is no $r, Y$ combination which yields equilibrium in the expenditure sector at full employment. The system, even with perfectly flexible prices, is doomed in this extremity to two-sector equilibrium at less than full employment.

This inconsistency in the system is the result of a peculiarity in the expenditure sector. It should not surprise us, therefore, to find that monetary policy cannot overcome the problem. A change in the supply of money merely shifts the position of the real $LM$ curve, as previously shown by equation (3.41). This changes the equilibrium rate of interest but expenditure is unresponsive and the deficiency of demand is unresolved however low the rate of interest falls.

Fiscal policy, on the other hand, has a better chance of success because it operates directly on the expenditure sector, through the multiplier given by equation (3.34), and can be used to alter the position of the expenditure sector equilibrium curve. In the model where exogenous expenditure cannot be controlled, if expenditure is interest insensitive there is no guarantee of avoiding the situation depicted in Figure 4.8. But the use of fiscal policy to shift the real *IS* curve, for example to the position shown in Figure 4.9, can overcome the inconsistency.

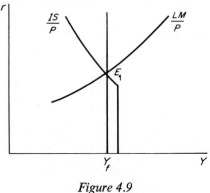

*Figure 4.9*

The situation in the liquidity trap case, $L_r \to -\infty$, is shown in Figure 4.10 where, given the positions of the curves as drawn, all of the curves in pairs have

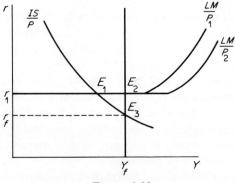

*Figure 4.10*

points of intersection but there is no common intersection which represents overall equilibrium. A fall in the price level due to a deficiency of total demand will shift the real *LM* curve, for example from $LM/P_1$ to $LM/P_2$, but the section of the curve in which the intersections with the real *IS* curve and full employment income occur does not shift. There is, therefore, no automatic adjustment in the system which can bring about full employment. It is clear from the figure that, given the real *IS* curve, a rate of interest as low as $r_f$ is necessary if the level of demand is to be raised to $Y_f$. But the liquidity trap prevents the rate of interest from falling below $r_1$.

Adjustments in the supply of money shift the real $LM$ curve, just as changes in the price level do, but this has no impact on the liquidity trap situation. The rate of interest $r_1$ remains the floor so that monetary policy cannot stimulate demand to the full employment level.

The aim of fiscal policy in this context is to increase the level of demand, at the rate of interest $r_1$, to the full employment level. Conceptually this is possible if fiscal policy is sufficiently expansionary to shift the real $IS$ curve from $(IS/P_1)$ to $(IS/P_2)$ in Figure 4.11. In this case the floor rate of interest $r_1$ becomes the full employment rate.

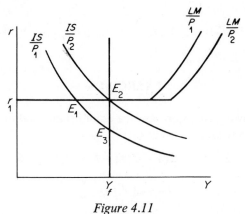

Figure 4.11

## APPENDIX: SOLUTION OF THE THREE-SECTOR MODEL WITH AN EXOGENOUS MONEY WAGE RATE

$$dY = \frac{-Y'_N \left[ (dC_0 + dI_0 - C_Y dT_0 + d\bar{G}) L_r \frac{\bar{W}}{P^2} - (C_r + I_r) \frac{\bar{M}}{P^2} \frac{d\bar{W}}{P} + (C_r + I_r) \left( \frac{d\bar{M}}{P} - dL_0 \right) \frac{\bar{W}}{P^2} \right]}{\Delta} \tag{A.1}$$

$$dr = \frac{-Y'_N \left[ (1 - C_Y(1 - T_Y) - I_Y) \left( \frac{d\bar{M}}{P} - dL_0 \right) \frac{\bar{W}}{P^2} - (1 - C_Y(1 - T_Y) - I_Y) \times \frac{\bar{M}}{P^2} \frac{d\bar{W}}{P} - (dC_0 + dI_0 - C_Y dT_0 + d\bar{G}) L_Y \frac{\bar{W}}{P^2} \right]}{\Delta}$$

$$- \frac{Y''_N (dC_0 + dI_0 - C_Y dT_0 + d\bar{G}) \frac{\bar{M}}{P^2}}{\Delta} \tag{A.2}$$

$$dN = \frac{(C_r + I_r)\left[\dfrac{\bar{M}}{P^2}\dfrac{d\bar{W}}{P} - \left(\dfrac{d\bar{M}}{P} - dL_0\right)\dfrac{\bar{W}}{P^2}\right] - L_r\dfrac{\bar{W}}{P^2}(dC_0 + dI_0 - C_Y\,dT_0 + d\bar{G})}{\Delta}$$

(A.3)

$$dP = \frac{-Y'_N\left[(1 - C_Y(1 - T_Y) - I_Y)L_r\dfrac{d\bar{W}}{P} + (C_r + I_r)L_Y\dfrac{d\bar{W}}{P}\right] + Y''_N\left[(C_r + I_r)\right.}{\Delta}$$
$$\times\left.\left(\dfrac{d\bar{M}}{P} - dL_0\right) + L_r(dC_0 + dI_0 - C_Y\,dT_0 + d\bar{G})\right]$$

(A.4)

where

$$\Delta = -[1 - C_Y(1 - T_Y) - I_Y]\,Y'_N L_r\frac{\bar{W}}{P^2} - (C_r + I_r)\frac{1}{P^2}(L_Y\,Y'_N\bar{W} - Y''_N\,\bar{M}) > 0$$

## EXERCISES

**4.1** The following equations are the equilibrium conditions of the three-sector model with the money wage rate exogenous:

$$Y = C_0 + C(Y - T, r) + I_0 + I(Y, r) + \bar{G} \tag{3.50}$$

$$L_0 + L(Y, r) = \frac{\bar{M}}{P} \tag{3.53}$$

$$Y = Y(N) \tag{4.1}$$

$$Y'_N = \frac{\bar{W}}{P} \tag{4.30}$$

Without referring to section 4.5:

(a) Derive the multipliers $\partial Y/\partial \bar{M}$, $\partial Y/\partial \bar{G}$ and $\partial Y/\partial T_0$.

(b) Explain the impact on each of these multipliers of an increase in the size of the parameter $I_r$, *ceteris paribus*.

**4.2** In the three-sector model with an endogenous money wage rate each of the multipliers $\partial Y/\partial \bar{M}$, $\partial Y/\partial \bar{G}$, $\partial Y/\partial T_0$ equals zero. Can we conclude from this that fiscal and monetary policy have no role to play within the model?

# CHAPTER V

# Aggregate Supply and Aggregate Demand

The analysis in this and the next chapter consists of some refinements and extensions of the three-sector model completed in Chapter IV. It will become apparent as we proceed that there is no analytical innovation in this chapter before the real balance effect ('Pigou effect') is introduced in section 5.2. Rather there will be a change of emphasis, in interpreting the three-sector model, to the relationship between aggregate income and the price level. To this end two useful relationships will be derived from the model. These are the *aggregate demand function* (AD) which shows the quantity of output demanded at different price levels, and the *aggregate supply function* (AS) which indicates the quantity of output which producers are willing to sell at different price levels. In effect we shall be collecting together into two relationships all of the factors which affect the decisions to spend (demand) and to produce (supply) goods and services. The derivation of these two functions is desirable because it shifts the analysis to the relationship between two endogenous variables, $Y$ and $P$, which are generally regarded as target variables for government policy. This change of emphasis helps, for example, in the study of inflation in section 5.3.

The main analytical development in this chapter, therefore, will be the introduction of the real balance effect into the theory of the expenditure sector, and the exploration of its implications for the operation of the three-sector model. This will be undertaken at first in terms of the *IS–LM* analysis (section 5.2.1) and then using aggregate demand and supply functions (sections 5.2.2 and 5.2.3).

## 5.1 AGGREGATE SUPPLY AND DEMAND

### 5.1.1 Aggregate supply

In the analysis of the three-sector model a number of references were made to the causal links between the endogenous variables $Y$, $r$, $N$ and $P$. In section

4.5.2 for example it was argued that an increase in exogenous expenditure (in the model with an exogenous money wage rate) raises the price level, thereby reducing the real wage rate and stimulating supply. It is clear that the reasoning relied on an implicit relationship between prices and output (via the real wage rate, given that the money wage rate is constant). It is time now to make this relationship explicit by solving the equations of the production and employment sector in terms of a *Y–P* function.

The production and employment sector with an exogenous money wage rate consists of the two equations (from section 4.5)

$$Y = Y(N) \tag{4.1}$$

$$Y'_N = \frac{\bar{W}}{P} \tag{4.30}$$

Firms take on the number of workers which, at the prevailing price level, equates the marginal product of labour to the real wage rate, and this level of employment determines the level of output given the production function (4.1). This now familiar system contains three endogenous variables $Y$, $P$ and $N$. In order to obtain a relationship between $Y$ and $P$ alone it is necessary to eliminate $N$. Taking the differentials of equations (4.1) and (4.30) we have respectively

$$dY = Y'_N \, dN \tag{4.33}$$

$$Y''_N \, dN = \frac{P \, d\bar{W} - \bar{W} \, dP}{P^2} \tag{4.34}$$

From equation (4.34) the expression for $dN$ is

$$dN = \frac{P \, d\bar{W} - \bar{W} \, dP}{P^2 \, Y''_N} \tag{5.1}$$

Substituting this expression for $dN$ into equation (4.33) we have a function for $dY$ in terms of $dP$ alone:

$$dY = Y'_N \frac{(P \, d\bar{W} - \bar{W} \, dP)}{P^2 \, Y''_N} \tag{5.2}$$

This is the *aggregate supply function* which tells us the change in the level of output supplied which is associated with any change in the price level. The slope of the function is, from equation (5.2)

$$\frac{\partial Y}{\partial P} = \frac{-Y'_N \, \bar{W}}{P^2 \, Y''_N} > 0 \tag{5.3}$$

Therefore in Figure 5.1 with the price level on the vertical axis and the level of output $Y$ on the horizontal axis, the aggregate supply curve AS is upward sloping. As the price level increases the real wage rate (with $\bar{W}$ fixed) declines, as we argued before, planned supply increases and we move along the aggregate supply curve.

If, on the other hand, there is an increase in the exogenous money wage rate at any given price level the real wage rate is increased and supply *at the given price level* is reduced. This is represented diagrammatically by a shift of the AS curve to the left, as from $AS_1$ to $AS_2$ in Figure 5.1, with aggregate supply at

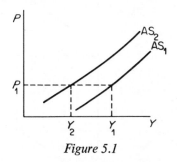

*Figure 5.1*

the price level $P_1$ falling from $Y_1$ to $Y_2$. This result is formally given by the partial derivative (from equation (5.2)):

$$\frac{\partial Y}{\partial \overline{W}} = \frac{Y_N' P}{P^2 Y_N''} < 0 \qquad (5.4)$$

It is necessary now to consider more carefully the shape of the aggregate supply curve. The shape depends on the particular assumption which the model makes about the flexibility of the money wage rate. Three cases can be distinguished.

(1) *A price inelastic aggregate supply curve.* In the model with the endogenously determined money wage rate and perfect flexibility of all prices, the real wage rate produced is the one which leads to full employment, as we have seen. The aggregate supply curve in this 'classical' case is completely price inelastic ($\partial Y/\partial P = 0$ from equation (4.17)) so that supply is fixed at the level $Y_f$. The function is shown in Figure 5.2(c) by the line $Y_f A$, corresponding to $\overline{W}/P_f$ and $Y_f$ in parts (a) and (b) of the figure.

(2) *A price elastic aggregate supply curve.* We have seen that when the money wage rate is exogenous, and therefore does not respond in *either direction* to labour market forces, and the real wage rate is at or above $\overline{W}/P_f$ in Figure 5.2(a), the aggregate supply curve is price elastic with a positive slope. This is shown in Figure 5.1 and as the curve $F_1 F_2$ in Figure 5.2(c). But what if the real wage rate falls below $\overline{W}/P_f$? Referring back to Figure 4.5(a) it will be remembered that as the real wage rate continues to decline below $\overline{W}/P_f$ employment *falls* as the amount of labour supplied imposes a maximum which is lower than the amount demanded by firms. As employment declines the increase in the price level $P_f$ is associated with a decline in output and the aggregate supply

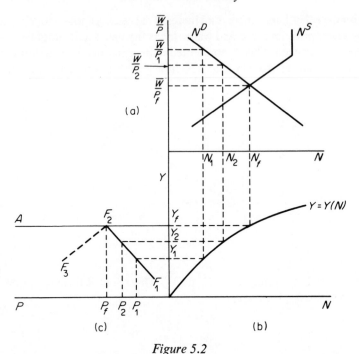

*Figure 5.2*

curve bends 'backwards' at full employment, so that the whole curve in Figure 5.2(c) is $F_1 F_2 F_3$.

(3) *A hybrid aggregate supply curve.* If the money wage rate is responsive to market pressures in an upwards direction but not downwards, then the aggregate supply curve has two distinct sections. As prices rise from a low level towards $P_f$ the real wage rate falls towards $(\bar{W}/P)_f$ in Figure 5.2(a) and output increases. Consequently at price levels below $P_f$ the aggregate supply curve is price elastic and has a positive slope. But once $P_f$ is reached further increases in the price level would reduce the real wage rate below $W/P_f$. By the assumption of upward flexibility of the money wage rate, the excess demand for labour which would result prevents increases in the price level reducing the real wage rate below $W/P_f$. At price levels above $P_f$, therefore the real wage rate is constant at $W/P_f$ and output constant at $Y_f$. The aggregate supply curve in this case is price inelastic and the hybrid curve, which results with the money wage rate flexible only upwards, is shown by $F_1 F_2 A$ in Figure 5.2(c).

### 5.1.2  Aggregate demand

When the two-sector model was re-stated, in section 3.8, to allow for the effect of changes in the price level on equilibrium income in the expenditure and monetary sectors, a relationship was obtained (equation 3.56) between

$dY$ and several exogenous variables including the changes in the price level $dP$. The reasoning behind this relationship between $dY$ and $dP$ was that an increase in the price level reduces the real supply of money, raises the rate of interest and cuts back planned expenditure. It is clear that this link between prices and planned expenditure is in fact an *aggregate demand function*. The function is

$$dY = \frac{\left(\dfrac{d\bar{M}}{P} - \dfrac{\bar{M}\,dP}{P^2} - dL_0\right)(C_r + I_r) + (dC_0 + dI_0 - C_Y dT_0 + d\bar{G})L_r}{(1 - C_Y(1 - T_Y) - I_Y)L_r + (C_r + I_r)L_Y} \tag{3.56}$$

where the denominator is negative. The slope of the function is:

$$\frac{\partial Y}{\partial P} = \frac{-(C_r + I_r)\dfrac{\bar{M}}{P^2}}{(1 - C_Y(1 - T_Y) - I_Y)L_r + (C_r + I_r)L_Y} < 0 \tag{3.58}$$

This aggregate demand function is shown in Figure 5.3(b). Figure 5.3 also illustrates the construction of an aggregate demand curve from the *IS* and *LM* curves. In Figure 5.3(a) we have the familiar determination of equilibrium

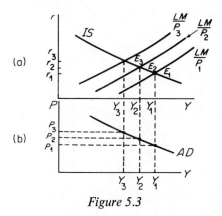

*Figure 5.3*

income (and rate of interest) for different price levels. At price level $P_1$ equilibrium income in the two sectors, and therefore the level of demand, is $Y_1$ associated with $E_1$. Higher price levels $P_2$ and $P_3$ produce real *LM* curves to the left of $LM/P_1$ and therefore different equilibrium levels of demand. The price-demand combinations which result, $P_1 Y_1$, $P_2 Y_2$ and $P_3 Y_3$, are shown in Figure 5.3(b) as points on the aggregate demand curve.

The position of the aggregate demand curve is determined by the size of the exogenous variables of the two-sector model, $C_0$, $I_0$, $T_0$, $\bar{G}$, $L_0$ and $\bar{M}$. While a change in the price level, *ceteris paribus*, causes a movement along a given aggregate demand curve, a change in any of these exogenous variables alters the level of demand at any price level, that is shifts the aggregate demand curve.

The following partial derivatives (from section 3.6) indicate that an increase in $C_0$, $I_0$, $\bar{G}$ and $\bar{M}$, and a decrease in $T_0$ and $L_0$, raise demand at any price level:

$$\frac{\partial Y}{\partial C_0} = \frac{\partial Y}{\partial I_0} = \frac{\partial Y}{\partial \bar{G}} > 0 \quad (3.22), \qquad \frac{\partial Y}{\partial T_0} < 0 \qquad (3.23)$$

$$\frac{\partial Y}{\partial \bar{M}} > 0 \quad (3.31), \qquad \frac{\partial Y}{\partial L_0} < 0 \qquad (3.30)$$

It is important to realize that, since we are now considering shifts in the real *IS* and *LM* curves *at any price level*, in the case of changes in the exogenous monetary variables the shift in the real *LM* is a shift at a given price level. This is to be kept distinct from a shift in the real *LM* curve resulting from a price level change which causes a movement *along* the demand curve. In Figure 5.3 the movement was *along* the demand curve as prices rose. In Figure 5.4,

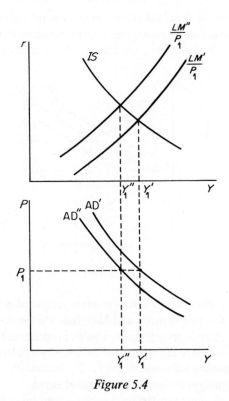

*Figure 5.4*

on the other hand, as (say) the nominal supply of money is reduced the real *LM* curve at the price level $P_1$ shifts to the left from $LM'/P_1$ to $LM''/P_1$, and a new aggregate demand curve AD″ is created to the left of the original one AD′.

The relationships between changes in the price level and changes in demand in the limiting cases of interest-insensitive expenditure and the liquidity trap, are given by the partial derivatives (3.60) and (3.62) respectively:

$$\frac{\partial Y}{\partial P} = 0 \tag{3.60}$$

$$\frac{\partial Y}{\partial P} \to 0 \tag{3.62}$$

The construction of the aggregate demand curve in each case is shown in Figure 5.5.

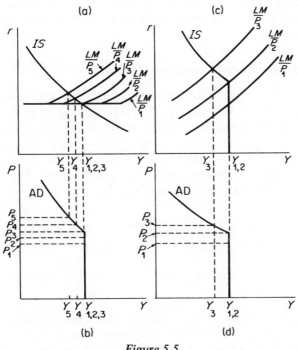

*Figure 5.5*

Taking the liquidity trap case first, Figures 5.5(a) and (b) show that, as the price level rises from $P_1$ to $P_2$, the shift in the real $LM$ curve from $LM/P_1$ to $LM/P_2$ does not produce any change in the rate of interest since the $IS$ curve still intersects the horizontal section of the $LM$ curve. The same is true for the further price rise from $P_2$ to $P_3$, and both of these price rises consequently fail to cut back demand, which remains at $Y_1 = Y_2 = Y_3$. In the price range $P_1$ to $P_3$, therefore, the aggregate demand curve is completely inelastic. However, once price level $P_3$ is reached further price increases shift the real $LM$ curve to the left to positions $LM/P_4$ and $LM/P_5$, which results in equilibrium rates of interest above the floor level. Above $P_3$, therefore, the aggregate demand curve is price elastic as price increases raise the rate of interest. It is clear that if the liquidity trap exists deflation does not stimulate demand because the rate of interest cannot be driven down.

Figure 5.5(c) and (d) show that as the price level rises from $P_1$ to $P_2$ the rate of interest increases, but because expenditure is unresponsive to changes in the rate of interest (in this range of interest rate) demand does not respond. Below $P_2$ the aggregate demand curve is price inelastic. At still higher price levels such as $P_3$, however, the rate of interest is driven up to levels at which expenditure does respond and the demand curve becomes price elastic.

The conclusion is that the existence of either of the limiting cases at some rate of interest results in an aggregate demand curve which is price inelastic for some of its length.

### 5.1.3    Aggregate supply and aggregate demand

The three-sector model with an exogenous money wage rate has been reduced, in this chapter, to two relationships. The aggregate supply relationship is the solution of the third sector in terms of $Y$ and $P$; and the aggregate demand curve is the solution of the other two sectors for $Y$ and $P$. The solution of the model in this two-equation form for the two endogenous variables $Y$ and $P$ produces the same comparative static results as the solution of the three sectors simultaneously. The new matrix for the model is

$$\begin{bmatrix} [1 - C_Y(1 - T_Y) - I_Y]L_r + (C_r + I_r)L_Y & \dfrac{\bar{M}(C_r + I_r)}{P^2} \\ Y_N'' P^2 & Y_N' \bar{W} \end{bmatrix} \begin{bmatrix} dY \\ dP \end{bmatrix}$$

$$= \begin{bmatrix} (dC_0 + dI_0 - C_Y dT_0 + d\bar{G})L_r + \left( \dfrac{d\bar{M}}{P} - dL_0 \right)(C_r + I_r) \\ Y_N' P d\bar{W} \end{bmatrix}$$

This can be solved to produce the same partial derivatives as were obtained in Section 4.5 for $dY$ and $dP$. Rather than repeat them we will summarize the conclusions and then show the results diagrammatically using aggregate demand and supply curves.

The comparative static results indicate that:

(a) an increase in $C_0$, $I_0$, $\bar{G}$ or $\bar{M}$ raises the equilibrium levels of income (equations (4.39) and (4.43)) and the price level (equations (4.42) and (4.46));

(b) an increase in $T_0$ or $L_0$ decreases the levels of income and the price level (see sections 4.5.2 and 4.5.3);

(c) an increase in the money wage rate $\bar{W}$ decreases the level of income (equation (4.35)) and raises the price level (equation (4.38)).

Referring to Figure 5.6(a), a shift of the aggregate demand curve from AD′ to AD″ results from an increase in $C_0$, $I_0$, $\bar{G}$ or $\bar{M}$, or a decrease in $T_0$ or $L_0$. None of these changes affects the aggregate supply curve so that the demand shift brings about a movement along the supply curve from $E_1$ to $E_2$. Higher income and price levels result as long as the demand curves intersect the upward sloping section of the supply curve assumed in the figure.

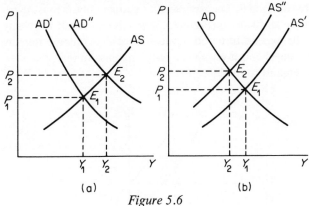

*Figure 5.6*

An increase in the money wage rate, on the other hand, shifts the aggregate supply curve to the left from AS′ to AS″ in Figure 5.6(b) causing a movement along the aggregate demand curve from $E_1$ to $E_2$. The consequence is a reduction in $Y$ and a rise in the price level. The impact on the price level of these shifts in the aggregate demand and supply curves will be looked at in more detail in section 5.3.

Turning to the situation in the model where the money wage rate is endogenous, and therefore to the case of the price inelastic aggregate supply curve, the model in matrix notation is

$$
\begin{bmatrix} [1 - C_Y(1 - T_Y) - I_Y]L_r & \dfrac{\bar{M}(C_r + I_r)}{P^2} \\ 1 & 0 \end{bmatrix} \begin{bmatrix} dY \\ dP \end{bmatrix}
$$
$$
= \begin{bmatrix} (dC_0 + dI_0 - C_Y\,dT_0 + d\bar{G})L_r + \left(\dfrac{d\bar{M}}{P} - dL_0\right)(C_r + I_r) \\ 0 \end{bmatrix}
$$

which yields the same solutions for $dY$ and $dP$ as obtained in section 4.4:

$$dY = 0 \tag{4.17}$$

$$dP = \frac{\left(\dfrac{d\bar{M}}{P} - dL_0\right)(C_r + I_r) + (dC_0 + dI_0 - C_Y\,dT_0 + d\bar{G})L_r}{(C_r + I_r)\dfrac{\bar{M}}{P^2}} \tag{4.19}$$

The results of the comparative static analysis are therefore the same as in Chapter IV, and they can be shown using aggregate demand and supply curves. The first point to remember is that with the money wage rate being endogenous there is no exogenous change on the supply side which can shift the aggregate supply curve. The curve is therefore in a fixed position determined by the labour market and the production conditions which are assumed unchangeable in the short-run model. The comparative static analysis must therefore rely on demand curve shifts, as in Figure 5.7, which can result from any exogenous change in the expenditure and monetary sectors. Income remains at the full employment level and it requires a large increase in the price level to restrain aggregate demand to the level $Y_f$.

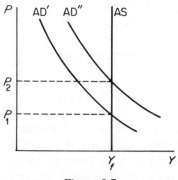

*Figure 5.7*

As we found in section 4.6, even if the aggregate supply curve is inelastic, full employment may be prevented by the existence of the limiting cases. With part of the aggregate demand curve inelastic as a result, the model becomes inconsistent. There is no point of intersection between AD and AS to provide

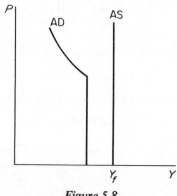

*Figure 5.8*

overall equilibrium (Figure 5.8). The same is true also in the case of the exogenous money wage rate, the only difference in Figure 5.8 being that AS would have a positive slope which does not guarantee an intersection.

## 5.2 THE PIGOU EFFECT

### 5.2.1 Introduction: cash balances and consumption

In this section the *IS–LM* framework will be used to examine the consequences of introducing real cash balances as a variable in the consumption function. The implications of the new function for the aggregate demand and supply analysis will be considered in section 5.2.2.

We start from the rationale for including real cash balances as one of the variables affecting the level of desired consumption. Pigou argued† that in deciding on the proportion of his income to use for consumption the typical consumer will take into account the real value of his stock of possessions. Patinkin suggested‡ that the marginal propensity to spend out of real balances will be greater than zero but less than unity, so that any increase in real balances will shift the aggregate consumption function upwards. The rationale at the level of the individual consumer is that he holds real cash balances, which yield a stream of utility as a result of their convenience for transactions purposes, up to the point at which the marginal utility from holding an extra pound of balances just equals the marginal utility derived from other uses of the money, such as from consumption. If the real value of his cash balances increases, then assuming that all uses of money are subject to diminishing marginal utility, he will switch some funds out of cash balances into alternative uses, including consumption. This is known as the Pigou effect. In the formal analysis to follow it will be assumed that an increase in real cash balances does have this effect on consumers. But it is important to note that considerable controversy surrounds the proposition. A number of writers have argued§ that in practice money enters the economic system (through open market operations) only in exchange for another asset of the private sector, government bonds. The implication drawn is that when prices, including the price of bonds, fall by a given percentage, the asset-holders will find that the increase in the real value of their cash is accompanied by an equal decrease in the real value of their holdings of government bonds, leaving their *net* wealth unaltered. A reply to this argument is that asset-holders may more readily recognize the increased purchasing power of their cash-holdings than the reduced real value of their bonds, and

---

† Pigou (1943).
‡ Patinkin (1950), Ch. IX.
§ These views are surveyed by Johnson (1971), Ch. 14 and 15. But see also Pesek and Saving (1967), especially the summary Ch. 9, 12 and 20, for a defence of the 'wealth effect' which encompasses adjustments via changes in real cash balances.

regard their net wealth as having been raised by a price cut as a result of this (partial) money illusion.

Let us trace formally, using to begin with the expenditure sector alone, the implications of introducing this new influence on consumption decisions. Adding the real cash balances $\bar{M}/P$ the consumption function, equation (2.75), becomes:

$$C = C_0 + C\left(Y^d, r, \frac{\bar{M}}{P}\right) \tag{5.5}$$

where $\partial C/[\partial(\bar{M}/P)] = C_M > 0$, the marginal response of consumption to changes in real cash balances.

The equilibrium condition for the expenditure sector, the equation of the *IS* curve, becomes

$$Y = C_0 + C\left(Y^d, r, \frac{\bar{M}}{P}\right) + I_0 + I(Y, r) + \bar{G} \tag{5.6}$$

Taking differentials and rearranging terms we have

$$dY = \frac{dC_0 - C_Y dT_0 + dI_0 + d\bar{G} + \dfrac{C_M \, d\bar{M}}{P} - \dfrac{C_M \bar{M} \, dP}{P^2} + (C_r + I_r)\, dr}{1 - C_Y(1 - T_Y) - I_Y} \tag{5.7}$$

from which we obtain the partial derivative indicating the effect on expenditure of a change in price

$$\frac{\partial Y}{\partial P} = \frac{-\dfrac{C_M \bar{M}}{P^2}}{1 - C_Y(1 - T_Y) - I_Y} < 0 \tag{5.8}$$

Once real balances enter the consumption function and the *IS* function an increase in the price level reduces the equilibrium level of income in the expenditure sector. This is because, *ceteris paribus*, a rise in the price level, which reduces the real value of available cash balances, shifts the real consumption function downwards and therefore shifts the real *IS* curve to the left.

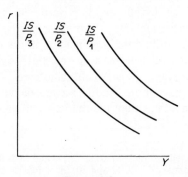

*Figure 5.9*

Since they are (or think they are) less wealthy in real terms consumers spend a lower proportion of their income and thereby reduce the average propensity to spend out of income in the economy as a whole. Instead of a single real *IS* curve we now have a family of curves, as shown in Figure 5.9 where $P_1 < P_2 < P_3$.

Introducing the new expenditure sector equilibrium condition, equation (5.6), into the three-sector model with the money wage rate endogenous, the model in matrix notation becomes:

$$
\begin{bmatrix}
[1 - C_Y(1 - T_Y) - I_Y] & -(C_r + I_r) & \dfrac{C_M \bar{M}}{P^2} \\[2ex]
L_Y & L_r & \dfrac{\bar{M}}{P} \\[2ex]
1 & 0 & 0
\end{bmatrix}
\begin{bmatrix}
dY \\[2ex] dr \\[2ex] dP
\end{bmatrix}
$$

$$
=
\begin{bmatrix}
dC_0 - C_Y \, dT_0 + dI_0 + d\bar{G} + \dfrac{C_M \, d\bar{M}}{P} \\[2ex]
\dfrac{d\bar{M}}{P} - dL_0 \\[2ex]
0
\end{bmatrix}
$$

It can be shown by solving for $dY$, $dr$ and $dP$ that the comparative static qualities of this model are substantially the same as those of the model studied in section 4.4. But the significance of the Pigou effect becomes clear when the limiting cases are considered. It was found in section 4.6 that the limiting cases created inconsistencies in the system. As Figures 4.8 and 4.10 showed there need be no intersection of the real *IS* and *LM* curves at full employment in the limiting cases. With the real balance effect on consumption there is an added means of adjustment in the system which may overcome the inconsistency. Whether it does do so depends on the *size* of the effect. The following discussion assumes the real balance effect to overcome the inconsistency.

In the case of interest-insensitive expenditure, with $(C_r + I_r) \to 0$ and a real cash balances variable in the consumption function the system becomes consistent and a solution exists. In Figure 5.10 the initial point of two-sector equilibrium is $E_2$, with the price level $P_2$ and demand lower than the full employment supply. Downward adjustments of product prices raise the real value of consumers' cash balances and stimulate consumption plans so that an overall equilibrium becomes possible, with the lower price level $P_1$, at $E_1$ on the new real *IS* and *LM* curves. Theoretically, therefore, as long as the price level can fall without limit overall equilibrium can be restored automatically.

The problem posed by the liquidity trap is disposed of in a similar fashion by the real balance effect. Again the system becomes consistent even though

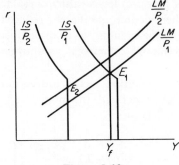

*Figure 5.10*

$L_r \rightarrow -\infty$. From the starting point $E_2$ in Figure 5.11 a fall in the price level shifts the real *IS* curve to the right so that overall equilibrium is achieved at $E_1$. Note that the effect of the price fall on expenditure overcomes the problem by stimulating expenditure at the minimum rate of interest $r_1$.

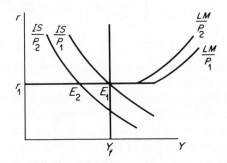

*Figure 5.11*

The *theoretical* significance of the Pigou effect is clear. As long as all prices are flexible and as long as expenditure decisions are sufficiently sensitive to changes in real cash balances, full employment is guaranteed, at some price level, by the automatic response of the market system. In the real world the two requirements may not be satisfied. Certainly in recent experience the required downward flexibility of prices, even when unemployment is relatively high, has not been observed. Even if there were no institutional constraints on price flexibility the repercussions of serious deflation may be sufficiently adverse in other respects (for example on investment plans) for governments to use policy instruments in preference to a reliance on market adjustments. In addition the evidence on the sensitivity of the consumption decision to changes in real balances is not clear cut, with some studies having denied that it is significantly greater than zero and others having implied a relatively strong real balance effect.†

### 5.2.2 The Pigou effect and the aggregate demand function

The main results of the previous section can be re-stated in terms of the aggregate demand and supply functions developed in this chapter. The first task is to derive the new aggregate demand function from the expenditure and monetary sector equations (5.7) and (3.54). In matrix notation the model is

$$
\begin{bmatrix} 1 - C_Y(1 - T_Y) - I_Y & -(C_r + I_r) \\ \\ L_Y & L_r \end{bmatrix} \begin{bmatrix} dY \\ \\ dr \end{bmatrix}
$$

$$
= \begin{bmatrix} dC_0 + dI_0 - C_Y\,dT_0 + d\bar{G} + \dfrac{C_M\,d\bar{M}}{P} - \dfrac{C_M\,\bar{M}\,dP}{P^2} \\ \\ \dfrac{d\bar{M}}{P} - \dfrac{\bar{M}\,dP}{P^2} - dL_0 \end{bmatrix}
$$

which yields the solution for $dY$, the new aggregate demand function:

$$
dY = \frac{\left(\dfrac{d\bar{M}}{P} - \dfrac{\bar{M}\,dP}{P^2} - dL_0\right)(C_r + I_r) + \left(dC_0 + dI_0 - C_Y\,dT_0 + d\bar{G} + \dfrac{C_M\,d\bar{M}}{P} - \dfrac{C_M\,\bar{M}\,dP}{P^2}\right)L_r}{[1 - C_Y(1 - T_Y) - I_Y]L_r + (C_r + I_r)L_Y} \tag{5.9}
$$

where the denominator is negative.

Comparing equation (5.9) with equation (3.56) it is clear that the new aggregate demand function contains two more terms than the original one. The first of these extra terms, $C_M\,d\bar{M}/P$, represents the impact on planned consumption of a change in real cash balances, resulting from a change in the nominal supply of money $\bar{M}$. The term is positive since an increase in $M$ raises $\bar{M}/P$ and shifts the consumption function upwards. The second term $C_M\,\bar{M}\,dP/P^2$ introduces the impact on consumption of a change in real cash balances caused by a change in the price level when $\bar{M}$ is constant. The sign of this term is negative as an increase in the price level reduces $\bar{M}/P$ and shifts the consumption function downwards.

From equation (5.9) we have the partial derivative:

$$
\frac{\partial Y}{\partial P} = \frac{-[(C_r + I_r) + C_M L_r]\dfrac{\bar{M}}{P^2}}{[1 - C_Y(1 - T_Y) - I_Y]\,L_r + (C_r + I_r)\,L_Y} < 0 \tag{5.10}
$$

† The empirical evidence of a real balance effect is surveyed by Simkin (1968), pp. 54–8. One paper not reviewed by Simkin argues that the effect has been strong, Liu (1963).

which means that the aggregate demand curve is downward sloping. Comparing equation (5.10) with equation (3.58), it is apparent that the slope of the curve is negative with or without the real balance effect. It is not surprising, therefore, that the comparative static qualities of the Pigovian aggregate demand curve prove to be similar to those displayed in equations (3.22), (3.23), (3.30) and (3.31) in section 5.1.2 for the demand curve without the Pigou effect.

The more interesting properties of the Pigovian aggregate demand curve appear in the limiting cases. Setting $(C_r + I_r) \to 0$ in equation (5.10) for the case of interest-insensitive expenditure, we have the partial derivative

$$\frac{\partial Y}{\partial P} = \frac{\dfrac{-C_M \bar{M}}{P^2}}{1 - C_Y(1 - T_Y) - I_Y} < 0 \tag{5.11}$$

And with the liquidity trap dividing equation (5.10) through by $L_r$ we have:

$$\frac{\partial Y}{\partial P} \to \frac{\dfrac{-C_M \bar{M}}{P^2}}{1 - C_Y(1 - T_Y) - I_Y} < 0 \tag{5.12}$$

as $L_r \to -\infty$.

Comparing equations (5.11) and (5.12) with equations (3.60) and (3.62) indicates that in a model which incorporates the real balance effect the significance of the two limiting cases for the *qualitative* characteristics of aggregate demand disappears. There is no vertical section in the Pigovian aggregate demand curve.

### 5.2.3 Aggregate supply and Pigovian aggregate demand

Introducing the Pigovian aggregate demand function into the three-sector model (with the money wage rate exogenous) in the two-equation form, we have the system of equations (5.2) and (5.9) which in matrix notation is

$$
\begin{bmatrix}
[1 - C_Y(1 - T_Y) - I_Y]L_r + (C_r + I_r)L_Y & \dfrac{C_M \bar{M} L_r + \bar{M}(C_r + I_r)}{P^2} \\
Y_N'' P^2 & Y_N' \bar{W}
\end{bmatrix}
\begin{bmatrix}
dY \\
dP
\end{bmatrix}
$$
$$
=
\begin{bmatrix}
dC_0 + dI_0 - C_Y dT_0 + d\bar{G} + \dfrac{C_M d\bar{M}}{P}L_r + (C_r + I_r)\left(\dfrac{d\bar{M}}{P} - dL_0\right) \\
Y_N' P d\bar{W}
\end{bmatrix}
$$

The solutions for $dY$ and $dP$ are qualitatively similar to the model without the real balance effect. The comparative static qualities are similar to those summarized in section 5.1.3, but now in the limiting cases the inconsistencies which led to the situation shown in Figure 5.8 no longer occur because there is no vertical section of the aggregate demand curve.

## 5.3  THE COMPARATIVE STATICS OF INFLATION

It should be apparent, from much of the discussion in Chapter IV and the previous section that an increase in the price level in the three-sector model can result from either an increase in demand, at any price, or a reduction in supply, at any price (or both). The former gives rise to 'demand pull' inflation, the latter to 'cost push' inflation.

It will be assumed in the discussion to follow that an increase in the price level, *ceteris paribus*, imposes a cost on society. The usual reasoning behind this assumption is that an increase in the price level results in a redistribution of real income which may conflict with the government's distribution objective, and that, in an open economy, if the prices of domestically produced goods rise relative to those of foreign goods, a deterioration in the balance of trade may occur.

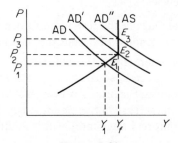

*Figure 5.12*

It will not be necessary to repeat the mathematics behind the theory used. Rather the purpose of this section is to bring out several points on price level effects not mentioned hitherto and also to indicate some of the limitations of the comparative static framework for analysing inflation.

An increase in demand in the three-sector model raises the price level whether the starting position is at or below full employment. There is, however, an important difference between the two cases. If demand is increased when the economy is below full employment, as, for example, from AD to AD' in Figure 5.12, the increase in the price level stimulates an increase in income from $Y_1$ to $Y_f$. The cost to society of the increase in the price level from $P_1$ to $P_2$ must be weighed against the increase in real income. While society's income increases the combination of inflation and increased returns to owners of factor inputs (except that labour which is already employed and suffers a cut in real wages) means that there will be a redistribution of aggregate income. Clearly the case for expansionary policy must rest on consideration of both the output and the distribution effects of the policy.

If demand is increased when the economy is already at full employment, as from AD′ to AD″ in Figure 5.12, there are no favourable output and employment effects to include in the cost-benefit balance sheet, and the distributional and balance of payments effects of inflation (from $P_2$ to $P_3$) are paramount.

Turning to cost push inflation, as illustrated in Figure 5.6(b), the increase in the money wage rate raises the real wage rate, curtails the demand for labour and reduces the level of employment and income (from $Y_1$ to $Y_2$). The cost incurred by society as a result of the inflation is now compounded by an *output* loss. The gainers from such an occurrence are those who retain their employment at a higher real wage rate, and their incomes are raised relative to other groups (such as profit earners and those who lose employment).

The analysis of inflation in terms of comparative static models inevitably limits attention to the generation of once-and-for-all increases in the equilibrium price level. It gives us no idea of the time path of the price level in disequilibrium or of the path of equilibrium price in the context of continuing inflation. As a description of inflation in the real world the static model suffers from three main deficiencies:

(a) it cannot incorporate lags in the response of price to changes in demand and supply, or in the response of output supplied to changes in prices;

(b) it cannot allow for interactions through time between variables in the price determination process, such as the possibility that an increase in exogenous demand raises the price level which shifts the aggregate supply curve by inducing an increase in the money wage rate (as unions attempt to maintain a constant real wage rate), which in turn raises the price level further;

(c) expectations of future price increases, since they are generated by experience through time, cannot convincingly be handled within the static context.

It will not be possible in this book to discuss comprehensively the recent theory of inflation, which is in a state of considerable controversy, but to illustrate the development of dynamic models of price determination a simple example will be presented in the last section of Chapter VII.

## EXERCISES

**5.1**　Consider the theoretical grounds for including a real cash balances variable in

(a) the investment function
(b) the production function.

What would such real balance effects imply for the three-sector model of income determination?

**5.2** Under what conditions might a high rate of employment accompany a sustained cost-push inflation?

**5.3** Examine carefully the causal relationships between the endogenous variables in the three-sector model which enable us to derive relationships between $P$ and $Y$ on both the demand and the supply side.

# CHAPTER VI

# The External Sector

The analysis of income determination has so far been concerned with purely domestic affairs as if the economy were operating in isolation, closed to the outside world. In this chapter an attempt will be made to remedy this deficiency of the theory by introducing a foreign trade or external sector into the model of income determination. In order to keep the theory reasonably manageable the external sector will be added to the two-sector model with constant prices, and no account will be taken of production and employment considerations in the analysis.

## 6.1 IMPORTS, EXPORTS AND THE BALANCE OF PAYMENTS

The first task is to consider the determinants of the components of the balance of payments, that is to say the planned level of imports and exports on current account and the planned net flow of capital to or from the country concerned. Two simplifying assumptions will be adopted:

(1) that there are only two trading areas, the domestic country and a foreign country (or group of countries);
(2) that there are no impediments to free trade such as tariffs and quotas.

Imports are an expenditure on goods and services similar to domestic expenditure by consumers, investors and the government, except that they do not constitute a demand for the resources of the domestic economy. Just as it was argued, in Chapter II, that consumption and investment decisions are affected by changes in consumers' and investors' incomes, we will accept here the hypothesis that the demand for imported goods is a function of aggregate income. But the desire to import may well also be affected by price. The price variable which is expected to influence import decisions is the 'relative price' of the imports, i.e. the ratio of the price of foreign goods $P_F$ to the price of domestically produced goods $P_D$ *in terms of the domestic currency*. If we consider the decisions of potential United States importers of British goods, for example, the relevant price variable is $P_F^\$/P_D^\$$. The relative price of foreign and domestic goods in terms of the domestic currency is defined as:

$$\frac{P_F^\$}{P_D^\$} = \frac{P_F^\pounds}{P_D^\$} \cdot \gamma$$

where $\gamma$, the exchange rate, is defined as the number of units of domestic currency required to buy one unit of foreign currency. For the United States importer, $\gamma$ is the number of dollars required to buy one pound (and for the British importer the exchange rate is $1/\gamma$, the number of pounds required to buy one dollar). The definition above indicates that the relative price $P_F^\$/P_D^\$$ is determined by two factors: (a) the ratio of the prices of imports and domestic goods in terms of the currency of the producing countries, i.e. $P_F^\pounds/P_D^\$$, which will be assumed constant throughout the analysis—and (b) by the rate of exchange $\gamma$. The impact of changes in $\gamma$ is summarized in Table 6.1. A United States importer converts the British price of £100 into an equivalent dollar price given the existing rate of exchange. The dollar price is raised from $250 to $300 when the exchange rate changes from $2·50 to the £1 to $3·00 to the £1, i.e. when the dollar is devalued. Devaluation of the US dollar therefore raises the price of British products to the importers in the United States.

TABLE 6.1    Prices of a representative product X produced in Britain and exported to the United States

|  | Britain | United States |
|---|---|---|
| Price of X in terms of currency of producing country | £100 | £100 |
| Price of X in each country in terms of the two domestic currencies. | | |
| exchange rate $2·50 to £1 | £100 | $250 |
| exchange rate $3·00 to £1 | £100 | $300 |

The analysis will assume that an increase in the exchange rate $\gamma$, i.e. a devaluation of the domestic currency (such as the increase in the number of dollars required to buy £1 in the United States, as in the example above), reduces the value of imports demanded ($F$) in terms of the domestic currency. This means that devaluation will reduce the import bill in the balance of trade, and it requires the assumption that the elasticity of demand for imports with respect to the exchange rate is (in absolute value) greater than unity. This assumption is stronger than we really need but it helps to simplify the analysis. The weaker assumption which actually will be necessary is known as the Marshall–Lerner condition and will be explained below.

In line with the above reasoning and assumptions we can write the import function as:

$$F = F(Y, \gamma) \tag{6.1}$$

where

$$F_Y = \frac{\partial F}{\partial Y} > 0 \quad \text{and} \quad F_\gamma = \frac{\partial F}{\partial \gamma} < 0$$

Analogously to the consumption function, $F_Y$ is called the marginal propensity to import, and $F/Y$ is the average propensity to import.

Turning to the export side of the current account, it will be assumed that the amount (valued in terms of the domestic currency) which a country exports at any rate of exchange is dependent not on its own income level but on the income level of the importing country. From the point of view of the economy of the exporter, therefore, exports are exogenous. However, if the exchange rate changes, the value of exports $X$ will be affected, so that

$$X = X(\gamma) \tag{6.2}$$

where $X_\gamma = dX/d\gamma > 0$. It should be realized that this export function is a demand function of the countries which import from the dómestic country, and is *not* a supply function of the domestic country. Consequently equation (6.2) resembles relationship (6.1), and the restriction $dX/d\gamma > 0$ implies that we are assuming that the elasticity of other countries' demand for the domestic country's exports, with respect to the exchange rate is (ignoring signs) greater than unity. Devaluation of the domestic currency will increase the value of the country's exports. Again this is a stronger assumption than is required for the Marshall–Lerner condition to hold, but it will be adopted for simplicity.

The algebraic sum of imports and exports on current account is known as the *balance of trade B*. Therefore we can write

$$B = X - F$$

or

$$B = X(\gamma) - F(Y, \gamma) \tag{6.3}$$

where $B$ is measured in units of the domestic currency. The balance of trade depends on both the rate of exchange and the domestic income level. In general form this balance of trade function will be written as:

$$B = B(Y, \gamma) \tag{6.4}$$

where

$$B_Y = \frac{\partial B}{\partial Y} < 0 \quad \text{and} \quad B_\gamma = \frac{\partial B}{\partial \gamma} > 0$$

An increase in income affects only the import side and this adversely, so that the balance of trade deteriorates. An increase in the exchange rate, $\partial \gamma > 0$

which means devaluation of the domestic currency, improves the balance of trade. This follows from the assumptions made concerning the slopes of the import and export functions with respect to changes in the exchange rate, i.e. $\partial F/\partial\gamma$ and $\partial X/\partial\gamma$. The assumed slopes are as shown in Figure 6.1. The import function drawn is one of a family of such curves for different levels of income. Devaluation, an increase in $\gamma$, increases the value of exports and reduces the import bill and therefore *necessarily* improves the balance of trade. Similarly

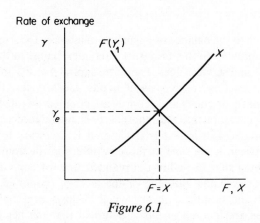

*Figure 6.1*

a revaluation necessarily leads to a deterioration of the balance of trade on these assumptions. It has been mentioned that the assumptions $\partial F/\partial\gamma < 0$ and $\partial X/\partial\gamma > 0$ are stronger than required. What will in fact be necessary for the later theory is that $\partial B/\partial\gamma > 0$. It can be shown that $\partial B/\partial\gamma$ can still be positive even if, say, $\partial F/\partial\gamma > 0$, that is if a devaluation raises the value of imports (which would imply an upward sloping $F$ curve in Figure 6.1). Whether devaluation would improve the balance of trade in this case would depend on whether the adverse import effect were outweighed by the favourable export effect. In diagrammatic terms it would depend on the relative slopes of the two upward sloping curves. But since we have ruled out this possibility by our strong assumptions we will not pursue it further here. An upward sloping import curve, or a downward sloping export curve, is, however, permitted by the *Marshall–Lerner condition* for a favourable effect of devaluation on the balance of trade. This condition states that the *sum* of the elasticities of the two demands (domestic demand for imports and foreign demand for the country's exports) must exceed unity.†

Given the import and export functions as shown in Figure 6.1 there is (for any level of income, say $Y_1$) only one rate of exchange, $\gamma_e$, which exactly balances planned imports and exports, and leads to equilibrium in the balance of trade where $B = X - F = 0$.

† For more on this condition and on devaluation generally see Vanek (1962), Ch. 5, sections 5.3 to 5.5.

In order to extend the analysis from the balance of trade to the whole *balance of payments*, account must be taken of the imports and exports of financial capital. By financial capital we shall mean short-term financial assets and not real capital or long-term investments, both of which will be ignored. The net flow of financial capital into (or out of) a country $K$ is the sum of the positive inflow, which is capital imports $K^F$, and the outflow (negative inflow), which is capital exports $K^X$. The net inflow is therefore:

$$K = K^F - K^X \tag{6.5}$$

It is favourable to the balance of payments to increase the size of the positive net inflow of capital since this brings in foreign exchange in the same way as exporting goods and services does. Therefore capital *imports* are a credit in the balance of payments as are exports of goods and services; likewise capital *exports* and imports of goods and services are counted on the debit side.

If the net flow of capital into the country is to be introduced as an endogenous variable in a model with an external sector it is necessary to hypothesize a relationship between $K$ and one or more variables in the domestic economy. It can be accepted that in reality the planned flow of capital is affected by variations in the exchange rate and/or the level of economic activity in the country. But in the simplified theory which follows expectations of capital gains and losses are ignored and it is assumed that the net flow of capital responds to changes in the domestic rate of interest $r$ relative to foreign rates of interest.† If foreign rates of interest do not change then the capital flow depends only on the domestic rate of interest, so that:

$$K = K(r) \tag{6.6}$$

where $K_r = dK/dr > 0$. An increase in the domestic rate of interest attracts capital from abroad and therefore raises the level of net inflow (or reduces net outflow).

Pulling together the statements which have been made about the determinants of the balance of trade and the net flow of capital we have an implied balance of payments function. The balance of payments $H$ is the sum of credits and debits in the balance of trade (current account) and the credits and debits in the capital account (i.e. $B + K$). The balance of payments is said to be in equilibrium if the balance of trade and the net capital flow sum to zero. It is important to realize that by balance of trade we mean the net level of *planned* exports minus *planned* imports, and by the net capital flow we mean the net level of *planned* monetary movements. Consequently the balance of trade and capital flow functions (6.4) and (6.6) are behavioural equations explaining planned magnitudes.

† On the complications introduced by making $K$ a function of the rate of exchange as well see Takayama (1969), p. 168.

The above condition for balance of payments equilibrium can be written as

$$H = B(Y, \gamma) + K(r) = 0 \tag{6.7}$$

If this is satisfied there will be no loss or gain of foreign reserve holdings since changes in these holdings occur only to offset any imbalance between the sum of credits and of debits of the balance of trade and capital flow together.

Changes in the overall balance of payments derive from changes in the two components so that we can write:

$$\frac{\partial H}{\partial Y} = B_Y < 0, \qquad \frac{\partial H}{\partial_\gamma} = B_\gamma > 0$$

and

$$\frac{\partial H}{\partial r} = K_r > 0 \tag{6.8}$$

A reduction in income or an increase in the rate of exchange has a favourable effect on the balance of trade and therefore on the balance of payments, while an increase in the domestic rate of interest increases the net inflow of capital and improves the balance of payments.

## 6.2 THE BALANCE OF TRADE AND THE MODEL OF INCOME DETERMINATION

As a first step in extending the model of income determination to incorporate the balance of payments, let us concentrate in this section on the balance of trade first in the expenditure sector alone and then in the model with expenditure and monetary sectors. In this and the next section attention will be limited to the case of a fixed exchange rate, and flexible exchange rates will be considered in section 6.4.

Since it is assumed to be fixed the exchange rate does not enter the import function, so the function (6.1), with an exogenous element $F_0$ added, can be written as

$$F = F_0 + F(Y) \tag{6.9}$$

where $F_0 \lesseqgtr 0$ and $F_Y > 0$. In addition exports become exogenous, $\bar{X}$, since the functional relationship (6.2) no longer applies.

With foreign demand for the country's exports and domestic demand for imports included the expenditure sector equilibrium condition becomes

$$Y = C + I + \bar{G} + \bar{X} - F \tag{6.10}$$

because planned exports constitute a demand for domestic output and planned imports constitute part of income *not* used to demand domestic output.

Substituting in equation (6.10) for $C$, $I$ and $\bar{G}$ as in section 2.7, for $F$ from equation (6.9) and for exogenous exports, the new equilibrium condition for the expenditure sector is

$$Y = C_0 + C(Y - T, r) + I_0 + I(Y, r) + \bar{G} + \bar{X} - F_0 - F(Y) \qquad (6.11)$$

Differentiating equation (6.11) and rearranging terms we find that

$$\frac{\partial Y}{\partial C_0} = \frac{\partial Y}{\partial I_0} = \frac{\partial Y}{\partial \bar{G}} = \frac{\partial Y}{\partial \bar{X}} = -\frac{\partial Y}{\partial F_0} = \frac{1}{1 - C_Y(1 - T_Y) - I_Y + F_Y} > 0 \qquad (6.12)$$

which is the multiplier for the 'open' economy. This is smaller than the corresponding multiplier for the closed economy (equation (2.79)), and the *IS* curve in the open economy is therefore steeper than that for the closed economy.

The multiplier is reduced because imports (like savings and taxes) constitute a leakage, expenditure in this case being directed abroad rather than to the domestic economy. At each 'round' of the multiplier a proportion, $F_Y$, of income fails to be spent on domestic goods, so that the larger is the marginal propensity to import the smaller is the reaction of the system to a change in exogenous expenditure. In this sense a large propensity to import, at the margin, is stabilizing for the domestic economy because the country 'exports' part of the response to the exogenous change to foreign economies by way of the import leakage.

On the other hand the introduction of exports and imports means that there are two further possible sources of exogenous change, $dF_0$ and $d\bar{X}$, to disturb the domestic economy. In particular a fluctuation in foreign demand for the country's exports alters the equilibrium income level in the expenditure sector by an amount greater than the fluctuation itself, as shown by the multiplier (6.12). Consequently introducing the balance of trade provides a combination of a reduced multiplier and an increase in disturbances from outside the system.

This conclusion could be confirmed by solving the two-sector model with the new expenditure function. But it is more interesting to ask now what are the effects in the opposite direction: that is, how do changes in the domestic economy affect the balance of trade in the model with a monetary sector? To answer this question the balance of trade must be added to the model separately so that we can solve for $dB$. Consequently the model used will consist of the expenditure and monetary sector equilibrium conditions (6.11) and (3.3) and the balance of trade function, (6.13):

$$B = \bar{X} - (F_0 + F(Y)) \qquad (6.13)$$

Taking the differentials of the three equations the model is

$$(1 - C_Y(1 - T_Y) - I_Y + F_Y)\,dY - (C_r + I_r)\,dr =$$
$$dC_0 + dI_0 - C_Y\,dT_0 + d\bar{G} + d\bar{X} - dF_0 \qquad (6.14)$$

$$L_Y\,dY + L_r\,dr = d\bar{M} - dL_0 \qquad (3.18)$$

$$dB = d\bar{X} - dF_0 - F_Y\,dY \qquad (6.15)$$

or, in matrix notation

$$\begin{bmatrix} [1 - C_Y(1 - T_Y) - I_Y + F_Y] & -(C_r + I_r) & 0 \\ F_Y & 0 & 1 \\ L_Y & L_r & 0 \end{bmatrix}\begin{bmatrix} dY \\ dr \\ dB \end{bmatrix}$$
$$= \begin{bmatrix} dC_0 + dI_0 - C_Y dT_0 + d\bar{G} + d\bar{X} - dF_0 \\ d\bar{X} - dF_0 \\ d\bar{M} - dL_0 \end{bmatrix}$$

The solutions for $dY$ and $dr$ are similar to those given before (Chapter III), but in addition we now have

$$dB =$$
$$\frac{\begin{aligned}-(C_r + I_r)(d\bar{X} - dF_0)L_Y + F_Y L_r(dC_0 + dI_0 - C_Y dT_0 + d\bar{G} + d\bar{X} - dF_0) \\ - [1 - C_Y(1 - T_Y) - I_Y + F_Y](d\bar{X} - dF_0)L_r + F_Y(C_r + I_r)(d\bar{M} - dL_0)\end{aligned}}{\Delta_1}$$

(6.16)

where

$$\Delta_1 = -(C_r + I_r)L_Y - [1 - C_Y(1 - T_Y) - I_Y + F_Y]L_r > 0 \qquad (6.17)$$

This solution for $dB$ provides us with the partial derivatives showing the impact on the balance of trade of changes in domestic expenditure and monetary variables:

$$\frac{\partial B}{dC_0} = \frac{\partial B}{\partial I_0} = \frac{\partial B}{\partial \bar{G}} = \frac{F_Y L_r}{\Delta_1} < 0 \qquad (6.18)$$

$$\frac{\partial B}{\partial \bar{M}} = \frac{-\partial B}{\partial L_0} = \frac{F_Y(C_r + I_r)}{\Delta_1} < 0 \qquad (6.19)$$

The result for $dT_0$ is not included but is simply equation (6.18) times $(-C_Y)$. These results can be explained by relating them to Figure 6.2. The balance of trade is in equilibrium when $B = 0$ and at only one level of income is this equilibrium achieved. In the figure this is income level $Y_1$ at which $\bar{X} = F_0 + F(Y_1)$. The balance of trade equilibrium is shown as a vertical line at $Y_1$, indicating that in this model the equilibrium is not affected by changes in the rate of interest ($\partial B/\partial r = 0$). Two-sector equilibrium in the domestic economy and equilibrium in the balance of trade can be achieved only if the $IS$ and $LM$ curves happen to intersect on the $B$ curve, i.e. if $Y_1$ happens to be the internal equilibrium income level. Starting from internal and external equilibrium at $E_1$ (with $r_1$ the rate of interest associated with internal equilibrium), the effect of an increase in domestic expenditure is shown by the shift from $IS$ to $IS'$ in the figure with the new internal equilibrium levels of income and the rate of interest being $Y_2$ and $r_2$ at $E_2$, a point to the right of the balance of trade equilibrium curve. At points to the right of the $B$ curve income exceeds $Y_1$ and since $B = \bar{X} - [F_0 + F(Y)]$, the level of imports is greater than that which just matches the

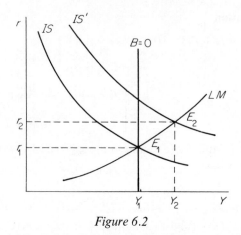

*Figure 6.2*

given level of exports $\bar{X}$. Consequently the increase in expenditure causing a move from $Y_1$ to $Y_2$ creates a balance of trade deficit equal to $\bar{X} - (F_0 + F(Y_2))$. This conclusion is confirmed by equation (6.18) where an increase in expenditure brings about a decline in $B$ from zero which means a balance of trade deficit.

Using similar reasoning it is clear that an increase in the money supply or reduction in demand for money, which shift the *LM* curve to the right will also create a balance of trade deficit by raising the income level above $Y_1$. Equation (6.19) confirms this result.

Changes in expenditure which shift the *IS* curve to the left and changes in monetary variables which shift the *LM* curve to the left have the opposite impact on the balance of trade. The income level which provides internal equilibrium falls below $Y_1$ so that imports now are cut to a level below $\bar{X}$ and a surplus in the balance of trade results. All points to the left of the $B$ curve are associated with balance of trade surplus.

Having established that there are links between the domestic economy and the balance of trade it can now be noted that, as we would expect, the balance of trade is responsive also to changes in the exogenous domestic demand for imports and in foreign demand for the country's exports. From equation (6.16) we have:

$$\frac{\partial B}{\partial \bar{X}} = -\frac{\partial B}{\partial F_0} = \frac{-L_Y(C_r + I_r) - L_r[1 - C_Y(1 - T_Y) - I_Y]}{\Delta_1} > 0 \qquad (6.20)$$

Some care is needed in interpreting this result, and it is necessary to keep clear two effects of an increase in foreigners' demand or a decrease in the exogenous component of the domestic demand for imports. These are:

(a) an increase in the level of income (and therefore of the income-induced component of imports) which is consistent with balance of trade equi-

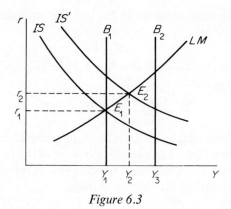

*Figure 6.3*

librium. This is shown in Figure 6.3 by a shift in the $B$ curve to the right from $B_1$ to $B_2$;

(b) an increase in the internal equilibrium level of income (and therefore an increase in the level of the income-induced component of imports) which is consistent with *internal* equilibrium. In Figure 6.3 this is shown by the movement from $IS$ to $IS'$ and from $Y_1$ to $Y_2$, as the internal equilibrium position $E_2$ replaces $E_1$.

The combined effect of these two elements is to create a balance of trade surplus, as shown by the fact that $E_2$ lies to the left of the new $B$ curve and that equation (6.20) is positive. In this model the initial favourable impact of the increase in exports or cut in import demand outweighs the induced increase in imports. But is this *necessarily* the case? Can we establish the condition required for an increase in $\bar{X}$ (or a decrease in $F_0$) to improve the balance of trade, that is for

$$\frac{\partial B}{\partial \bar{X}} > 0$$

For this to hold the increase in exports must exceed the induced rise in imports, that is

$$d\bar{X} > dF$$

or

$$d\bar{X} > d[F(Y)]$$

or

$$d\bar{X} > F_Y \, dY \qquad (6.21)$$

Now the increase in income in this expression is equal to $d\bar{X}$ times the multiplier, that is

$$dY = d\bar{X} \cdot \frac{L_r}{[1 - C_Y(1 - T_Y) - I_Y + F_Y]L_r + (C_r + I_r)L_Y} \qquad (6.22)$$

Substituting for $dY$ from equation (6.22) into the inequality (6.21) we have that $d\bar{X} > dF$ if

$$d\bar{X} > \frac{F_Y \, d\bar{X} L_r}{[1 - C_Y(1 - T_Y) - I_Y + F_Y]L_r + (C_r + I_r)L_Y}$$

which can be written as

$$\frac{1 - C_Y(1 - T_Y) - I_Y}{(C_r + I_r)} < -\frac{L_Y}{L_r} \qquad (6.23)$$

The left-hand side of inequality (6.23) is the slope of the *IS* curve and the right-hand side is the slope of the *LM* curve. If the slope of the *IS* curve is negative, as normally assumed, the condition is satisfied and an increase in $\bar{X}$ (or a fall in $F_0$) necessarily improves the balance of trade.

### 6.3   THE BALANCE OF PAYMENTS AND THE MODEL OF INCOME DETERMINATION: FIXED EXCHANGE RATE

The analysis will now be extended to include the capital account so that the effect of changes in the domestic economy on the overall balance of payments can be examined. For simplicity we will use the balance of payments function with the sum of the exogenous components $F_0$ and $\bar{X}$ assumed to be zero and omitted. Since the exchange rate is fixed ($d\gamma = 0$) the balance of payments function is the modified form of equation (6.7):

$$H = B(Y) + K(r) \qquad (6.24)$$

The model consists of this equation plus the expenditure sector and monetary sector equilibrium conditions (6.11) and (3.3), and is similar to the model on page 126 except that now $F_0 + \bar{X} = 0$ by assumption, and imports and exports are consolidated into a balance of trade, so that $B_Y$ replaces $F_Y$ (but remember that $B_Y = -F_Y$ anyway); also the capital flow component is now included. Taking the differentials of the three equilibrium conditions we have

$$[1 - C_Y(1 - T_Y) - I_Y - B_Y]dY - (C_r + I_r)\,dr = dC_0 + dI_0 - C_Y\,dT_0 + d\bar{G}$$
$$(6.25)$$

$$L_Y\,dY + L_r\,dr = d\bar{M} - dL_0 \qquad (3.18)$$

$$dH = B_Y\,dY + K_r\,dr \qquad (6.26)$$

or, in matrix notation:

$$\begin{bmatrix} [1 - C_Y(1 - T_Y) - I_Y - B_Y] & -(C_r + I_r) & 0 \\ -B_Y & -K_r & 1 \\ L_Y & L_r & 0 \end{bmatrix} \begin{bmatrix} dY \\ dr \\ dH \end{bmatrix}$$

$$= \begin{bmatrix} dC_0 + dI_0 + -C_Y\,dT_0 + d\bar{G} \\ 0 \\ d\bar{M} - dL_0 \end{bmatrix}$$

The solutions of the model for $dY$ and $dr$ do not affect our earlier conclusions concerning the effect of changes in exogenous factors on these variables, but the solution for $dH$ does introduce some new considerations. We have

$$dH = \frac{-[K_r(1 - C_Y(1 - T_Y) - I_Y - B_Y) + B_Y(C_r + I_r)][d\bar{M} - dL_0]}{\Delta_1}$$
$$+ \frac{[L_Y K_r - B_Y L_r][dC_0 + dI_0 - C_Y dT_0 + d\bar{G}]}{\Delta_1} \quad (6.27)$$

where

$$\Delta_1 = -[(C_r + I_r)L_Y + (1 - C_Y(1 - T_Y) - I_Y - B_Y)L_r] > 0 \quad (6.28)$$

From equation (6.27) we have the following partial derivatives:

$$\frac{\partial H}{\partial C_0} = \frac{\partial H}{\partial I_0} = \frac{\partial H}{\partial \bar{G}} = \frac{L_Y K_r - B_Y L_r}{\Delta_1} \gtrless 0 \quad (6.29)$$

$$\frac{\partial H}{\partial \bar{M}} = -\frac{\partial H}{\partial L_0} = \frac{-[K_r(1 - C_Y(1 - T_Y) - I_Y - B_Y) + B_Y(C_r + I_r)]}{\Delta_1} < 0 \quad (6.30)$$

It is apparent from these results that an expansionary monetary policy (or a fall in the demand for money) will necessarily have a detrimental effect on the balance of payments, whereas expansionary fiscal policy (or an increase in $C_0$ or $I_0$) may have either an adverse or a beneficial effect. The explanation of these conclusions will be simplified if we first recognize that changes in the domestic economy can affect the balance of payments *either* through changes in the level of income, which affect imports of goods and services, *or* through changes in the rate of interest, which affect the net flow of capital to (or from) the country, or both. In the case of expansionary monetary policy both the 'income effect' *and* the 'rate of interest effect' damage the balance of payments. An increase in the money supply raises the equilibrium level of income and the value of imports, making the balance of trade deteriorate. It also reduces the rate of interest, thereby reducing the net inflow of capital from abroad and causing the capital account to deteriorate. The sum of these two effects is to create a

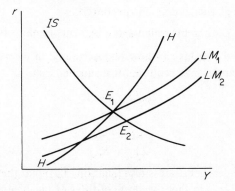

*Figure 6.4*

balance of payments deficit if expansionary monetary policy is used from a starting point characterized by internal equilibrium as well as balance of payments equilibrium. Such a starting point is $E_1$ in Figure 6.4, which is one point on the $HH$ curve representing combinations of $r$ and $Y$ which result in balance of payments equilibrium. The slope of the $HH$ curve is positive since an increase in income, which worsens the balance of trade, must be compensated for by an increase in the rate of interest to attract capital, if balance of payments equilibrium is to be maintained $(dH = 0)$. Formally, from equation (6.26) we have the equation of the $HH$ curve:

$$dr = \frac{-B_Y \, dY + dH}{K_r} \tag{6.31}$$

and from (6.31), the slope of the $HH$ curve is

$$\frac{\partial r}{\partial Y} = \frac{-B_Y}{K_r} > 0 \tag{6.32}$$

where $B_Y < 0$ and $K_r > 0$.

An increase in the money supply shifts the $LM$ curve from $LM_1$ to $LM_2$ and internal equilibrium from $E_1$ to $E_2$. But points to the right of the $HH$ curve, such as $E_2$, are associated with deficits in the balance of payments, so that monetary policy creates such a deficit.

With fiscal policy the situation is complicated by the fact that the 'income effect' and the 'rate of interest effect' work *against* each other. The increase in income accompanying an increase in government spending raises imports; but it also raises the demand for money so that, with the supply of money fixed, the rate of interest is pushed up and more capital is attracted. Clearly the net balance of payments effect (starting from a point of balance of payments equilibrium) must depend on the strengths of these two opposing forces. Using equation (6.29) we can say that:

if        $L_Y K_r > B_Y L_r$ then a surplus is produced,

if        $L_Y K_r < B_Y L_r$ then a deficit is produced,

if        $L_Y K_r = B_Y L_r$ then the balance of payments remains in equilibrium.

The condition for a surplus can now be interpreted in terms of the slopes of the $LM$ and $HH$ curves. We require, for a surplus, that

$$L_Y K_r > B_Y L_r \tag{6.33}$$

or

$$\frac{-L_Y}{L_r} > \frac{-B_Y}{K_r} \tag{6.34}$$

But we know, from earlier discussion (equation (3.7)) that the left-hand side of the inequality (6.34) is in fact the slope of the $LM$ curve, and the right-hand side is the slope of the *HH* curve, equation (6.32). Therefore expansionary fiscal policy will create a surplus *only if* the slope of the *LM* curve is greater than the slope of the *HH* curve, where both slopes are positive. In this case, the shift in the *IS* curve produces a rate of interest effect on the balance of payments which is strong relative to the adverse income effect. The result is a movement to the left away from the *HH* curve, which implies a surplus, as from $E_1$ to $E_2$ in Figure 6.5(a). If on the other hand we have

$$\frac{-L_Y}{L_r} < \frac{-B_Y}{K_r} \tag{6.35}$$

the slope of the *HH* curve is the greater of the two, and expansionary fiscal policy moves the balance of payments into deficit, as at $E_2$ in Figure 6.5(b).

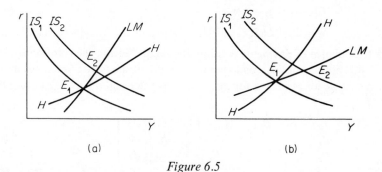

(a)                        (b)

*Figure 6.5*

Here the favourable rate of interest effect on capital account is weaker than the adverse income effect on current account. The intermediate case is where

$$\frac{-L_Y}{L_r} = \frac{-B_Y}{K_r} \tag{6.36}$$

the *HH* and *LM* curves are identical if there is any point at which they coincide to take as an initial equilibrium. The interest rate effect and the income effect are of equal strength and fiscal policy brings about a movement along the *HH* curve so that the balance of payments remains in equilibrium.

## 6.4 THE BALANCE OF PAYMENTS AND THE MODEL OF INCOME DETERMINATION: FLEXIBLE EXCHANGE RATE

We have seen how the balance of payments is affected by changes in the domestic economy given the assumption that the occurrence of surpluses and deficits does not bring about changes in the foreign exchange rate. By contrast it will now be assumed that the exchange rate responds immediately to disequilibrium in the balance of payments so that the equilibrating rate $\gamma_e$ is guaranteed and deficits and surpluses are eliminated.† Formally the exchange rate which prevails is that which sets changes in the balance of payments equal to zero, i.e. $dH = 0$. Therefore, with the balance of payments function

$$H = B(Y, \gamma) + K(r) \tag{6.7}$$

the change in the equilibrium exchange rate is obtained by solving, for $\gamma$, the differential

$$dH = B_Y \, dY + B_\gamma \, d\gamma + K_r \, dr = 0 \tag{6.37}$$

The model now consists of the equations for the fixed exchange rate system ($d\gamma = 0$) with $\gamma$ added as a determinant of the balance of trade in both the expenditure sector and balance of payments equilibrium conditions:

$$Y = C_0 + C(Y - T, r) + I_0 + I(Y, r) + \bar{G} + B(Y, \gamma) \tag{6.38}$$

$$H = B(Y, \gamma) + K(r) \tag{6.7}$$

$$\bar{M} = L_0 + L(Y, r) \tag{3.3}$$

With the balance of payments continually in equilibrium the solution for $dH$ drops out, but $\gamma$ is now an endogenous variable responsive to changes in the system so that we can solve for $d\gamma$ (as well as the usual $dY$ and $dr$) using the matrix

$$\begin{bmatrix} [1 - C_Y(1 - T_Y) - I_Y - B_Y] & -(C_r + I_r) & -B_\gamma \\ B_Y & K_r & B_\gamma \\ L_Y & L_r & 0 \end{bmatrix} \begin{bmatrix} dY \\ dr \\ d\gamma \end{bmatrix}$$

$$= \begin{bmatrix} dC_0 + dI_0 - C_Y \, dT_0 + d\bar{G} \\ 0 \\ d\bar{M} - dL_0 \end{bmatrix}$$

In addition to the solutions for $dY$ and $dr$, which again are not substantially different from earlier results and will not be discussed, we have

$$d\gamma = \frac{\begin{aligned} &(d\bar{M} - dL_0)(B_Y(C_r + I_r)) + K_r[1 - C_Y(1 - T_Y) - I_Y - B_Y] \\ &\quad + (dC_0 + dI_0 - C_Y \, dT_0 + d\bar{G})(B_Y L_r - L_Y K_r) \end{aligned}}{\Delta_2} \tag{6.39}$$

where

$$\Delta_2 = B_\gamma L_Y[K_r - (C_r + I_r)] - B_\gamma L_r[1 - C_Y(1 - T_Y) - I_Y - B_Y] > 0 \tag{6.40}$$

From equation (6.39) we have the partial derivatives:

$$\frac{\partial \gamma}{\partial C_0} = \frac{\partial \gamma}{\partial I_0} = \frac{\partial \gamma}{\partial \bar{G}} = \frac{B_Y L_r - L_Y K_r}{\Delta_2} \gtreqless 0 \tag{6.41}$$

$$\frac{\partial \gamma}{\partial \bar{M}} = -\frac{\partial \gamma}{\partial L_0} = \frac{B_Y(C_r + I_r) + K_r(1 - C_Y(1 - T_Y) - I_Y - B_Y)}{\Delta_2} > 0 \tag{6.42}$$

† This assumption implies that the foreign exchange market is stable. See Vanek (1962), p. 70–2.

If equations (6.41) and (6.42) are compared with (6.29) and (6.30) it should immediately be clear that the results in the two cases are similar. In fact the condition for a surplus is *qualitatively* the same as the condition for a reduction in $\gamma$, that is an appreciation of the domestic currency. Consequently an increase in the money supply, which resulted in a deficit in the fixed exchange rate system, now necessarily results instead in an increase in $\gamma$, a depreciation of the currency, as equations (6.30) and (6.42) show.

In the case of fiscal policy, as we have seen, in the fixed exchange rate model a surplus resulted from expansionary policy if $L_Y K_r > B_Y L_r$. From equation (6.41) we see that this is also the condition for a reduction in $\gamma$, that is for an appreciation of the currency when the exchange rate is flexible. Again the result depends on the relative strengths of the income effect and the interest rate effect of fiscal policy on the balance of payments.

The condition for an appreciation of the currency can be interpreted, as was the condition for surplus, in terms of the slopes of the $LM$ curve and an external sector equilibrium curve. If equation (6.37) is solved for $\partial r / \partial Y$ we have a locus of $Y, r$ points providing a constant rate of exchange. This is, in fact, the same as the $HH$ curve with a slope equal to

$$\frac{\partial r}{\partial Y} = \frac{-B_Y}{K_r} > 0 \tag{6.32}$$

The points on this curve now provide balance of payments equilibrium *and* a constant exchange rate. Any policy which moves us to the right of the curve leads to a deficit in the fixed exchange rate case and to depreciation in the flexible exchange rate model. Movements to the left of the curve result in surplus or appreciation. Consequently the effects of policy changes in the flexible exchange rate case are identical to the effects with the fixed exchange rate *except that* for surplus we substitute appreciation and for deficit depreciation of the currency.

## 6.5  TARGETS AND INSTRUMENTS: INTERNAL AND EXTERNAL EQUILIBRIUM

### 6.5.1  Reinterpretation of the model with a fixed exchange rate

We have, throughout the book, followed a common procedure of examining the impact of changes in known exogenous variables, including policy instruments $\bar{G}$ and $\bar{M}$, on unknown endogenous variables, including policy targets $Y, P$ and $H$. There is an alternative way of viewing models of the type that have been presented, which is to assume that there is a set of changes in *target variables* which it is desired to achieve, and to obtain from the model the changes in the policy instruments which could do so. In this case the changes in the target variables become the knowns and we wish to solve the system to obtain the required changes in instruments which are the unknowns. This constitutes an inversion of the previous procedure with known instruments and unknown targets.

In this section the alternative procedure is illustrated using the example of attempts to achieve internal and external targets by means of fiscal and monetary policy instruments. The exchange rate will be assumed fixed because the problems of balancing internal and external stability have usually been discussed in this context. If the exchange rate were flexible the external sector would be self equilibrating, and the possibility of a conflict between the requirements of internal equilibrium and of balance of payments equilibrium would be avoided unless the government wished to stabilize the exchange rate.

The model is the same as in section 6.3, that is equations (6.11), (3.3) and (6.24), which in differential form are as we have seen previously:

$$[1 - C_Y(1 - T_Y) - I_Y - B_Y] dY - (C_r + I_r) dr = dC_0 + dI_0 - C_Y dT_0 + d\bar{G} \tag{6.25}$$

$$L_Y dY + L_r dr = d\bar{M} - dL_0 \tag{3.18}$$

$$dH = B_Y dY + K_r dr \tag{6.26}$$

For the present analysis we shall concentrate on the exogenous variables $\bar{G}$ and $\bar{M}$ which are policy instruments and set changes in the remaining exogenous variables (including the instrument $T_0$) equal to zero, i.e. $dC_0 = dI_0 = dT_0 = dL_0 = dP = 0$. In the inversion procedure to be used, $dY$ and $dH$ are the two exogenously determined targets, $d\bar{G}$ and $d\bar{M}$ are the two unknowns used as instruments and $dr$ is an unknown determined by the system.† The matrix of the model in inverted form is:

$$\begin{bmatrix} 1 & (C_r + I_r) & 0 \\ 0 & K_r & 0 \\ 0 & -L_r & 1 \end{bmatrix} \begin{bmatrix} d\bar{G} \\ dr \\ d\bar{M} \end{bmatrix} = \begin{bmatrix} [1 - C_Y(1 - T_Y) - I_Y - B_Y] dY \\ dH - B_Y dY \\ L_Y dY \end{bmatrix}$$

Comparing the inverted matrix with the original one in section 6.3 it will be seen that $dY$ and $dH$ have replaced $dC_0$, $d\bar{G}$ etc. as the knowns in the right-hand determinant, while $d\bar{G}$ and $d\bar{M}$ replace $dY$ and $dH$ as the unknowns and $dr$ remains as an unknown.

Solving for the instruments $d\bar{G}$ and $d\bar{M}$ we have:

$$d\bar{G} = \left( \frac{K_r[1 - C_Y(1 - T_Y) - I_Y - B_Y] + B_Y(C_r + I_r)}{K_r} \right) dY - \left( \frac{C_r + I_r}{K_r} \right) dH \tag{6.43}$$

$$d\bar{M} = \left( \frac{L_Y K_r - B_Y L_r}{K_r} \right) dY + \left( \frac{L_r}{K_r} \right) dH \tag{6.44}$$

The sign of the partial derivative of an instrument with respect to a target will tell us the *direction* in which the instrument must change if the target variable

---

† On the relationship between the number of instruments and targets see Tinbergen (1952).

is to be moved in the desired direction while the other target variable remains unchanged.

Consider, as the first case, that the government wishes to raise the level of income *while leaving the balance of payments in equilibrium* (so that $dH = 0$). From equations (6.43) and (6.44) we find

$$\frac{\partial \bar{G}}{\partial Y} > 0 \tag{6.45}$$

$$\frac{\partial \bar{M}}{\partial Y} \gtrless 0 \tag{6.46}$$

The required fiscal policy is expansionary, but whether this should be accompanied by an increase or a decrease in the supply of money depends on whether the fiscal policy has a favourable or adverse effect on the balance of payments. If $L_Y K_r > B_Y L_r$ as we have seen (in section 6.3) expansionary fiscal policy *alone* would create a surplus because the favourable interest rate effect on the balance of payments outweighs the unfavourable income effect. Consequently the money supply must be increased to weaken the interest rate effect which attracts capital from abroad. Thus if $L_Y K_r > B_Y L_r$ then (6.46) is positive, and the increase in the income target with no balance of payments effect is achieved by expansionary fiscal policy plus expansionary monetary policy. If on the other hand $L_Y K_r < B_Y L_r$, then the expansionary fiscal policy alone would create a deficit and a contraction in the money supply is needed to raise the rate of interest and increase the inflow of capital. In this case (6.46) would be negative.

A second example is an attempt by the government to improve the balance of payments *while leaving income in equilibrium* ($dY = 0$). From equations (6.43) and (6.44) we have:

$$\frac{\partial \bar{G}}{\partial H} > 0 \tag{6.47}$$

$$\frac{\partial \bar{M}}{\partial H} < 0 \tag{6.48}$$

In order to improve the balance of payments the money supply is reduced (equation (6.48)) to raise the rate of interest and improve the capital account. However, the contractionary monetary policy *alone* would reduce the equilibrium income level and this tendency must be offset by an increase in government spending (equation (6.47)). The fiscal policy in addition raises the rate of interest but this merely reinforces the effect of monetary policy as far as the capital account is concerned. Since the two instruments are used to keep the equilibrium income level constant the balance of *trade* is unaffected, and the impact of the coordinated monetary and fiscal policy on the overall balance of payments is therefore necessarily favourable.

### 6.5.2　The assignment of instruments to targets

In recent years much has been written on the problem of achieving simultaneously both full employment and balance of payments equilibrium. The discussion has centred on the question of the appropriate policy instrument for each of the targets: does it matter whether fiscal policy is used for internal stability and monetary policy to control the balance of payments, or vice versa? We will not attempt to survey the vast literature but will be content rather to illustrate the argument used by Mundell, which initiated the debate, using a simple model with a fixed exchange rate.†

The model consists of only two sectors, an expenditure sector and an external sector. The rate of interest affects both expenditure decisions and the balance of payments capital account but it is not determined within the system. Since the monetary sector is excluded and the rate of interest is exogenous we can use $\bar{G}$ and $r$, instead of $\bar{G}$ and $\bar{M}$, as the instruments of fiscal and monetary policy. The system in differential form is that presented in section 6.3 but with the monetary sector equation omitted and, in order to concentrate on the effect of changes in the two instruments, with $dC_0 = dI_0 = dT_0 = 0$:

$$[1 - C_Y(1 - T_Y) - I_Y - B_Y]\,dY - (C_r + I_r)\,dr = d\bar{G} \qquad (6.49)$$

$$dH = B_Y\,dY + K_r\,dr \qquad (6.50)$$

or in matrix form:

$$\begin{bmatrix} [1 - C_Y(1 - T_Y) - I_Y - B_Y] & 0 \\ -B_Y & 1 \end{bmatrix} \begin{bmatrix} dY \\ dH \end{bmatrix} = \begin{bmatrix} d\bar{G} + (C_r + I_r)\,dr \\ K_r\,dr \end{bmatrix}$$

The solutions for $dY$ and $dH$ are

$$dY = \frac{d\bar{G} + (C_r + I_r)\,dr}{[1 - C_Y(1 - T_Y) - I_Y - B_Y]} \qquad (6.51)$$

$$dH = \frac{B_Y\,d\bar{G} + [(1 - C_Y(1 - T_Y) - I_Y - B_Y)\,K_r + (C_r + I_r)\,B_Y]\,dr}{[1 - C_Y(1 - T_Y) - I_Y - B_Y]} \qquad (6.52)$$

The analysis will be based on the assumption that there is some equilibrium level of income which provides full employment equilibrium and that, once this is arrived at, the internal stability objective is henceforth to avoid changes in income. This means that the target is to set $dY = 0$. In addition, the external stability objective is to avoid disturbances from balance of payments equilibrium once this has been achieved, that is to set $dH = 0$.

It is clear from earlier discussion and from equations (6.51) and (6.52) that a change in either policy instrument will affect *both* of the target variables $Y$ and $H$. An increase in $\bar{G}$, or a reduction in $r$, raises the equilibrium level of

† See Mundell (1962). For a lucid survey of the literature and extensive references see Whitman (1970).

income, and if we wish to avoid such changes there must be an offsetting variation in the other instrument. This is demonstrated by setting equation (6.51) equal to zero and solving the equation for $d\bar{G}/dr$ which tells us the change in one instrument which must accompany a change in the other for internal equilibrium to be maintained. The solution is

$$\frac{d\bar{G}}{dr} = -(C_r + I_r) > 0 \qquad (6.53)$$

This relationship is the slope of the *internal balance curve* II shown in Figure 6.6, which is the locus of combinations of the two instruments which maintains internal stability. The positive slope indicates that expansionary fiscal policy $(d\bar{G} > 0)$ must be compensated for by contractionary monetary policy $(dr > 0)$ if internal equilibrium is to be maintained.

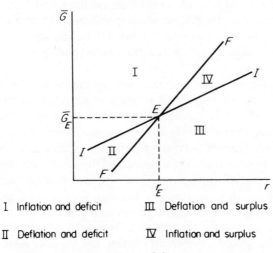

I  Inflation and deficit      III  Deflation and surplus

II  Deflation and deficit      IV  Inflation and surplus

*Figure 6.6*

Following similar reasoning an *external balance* curve, *FF* in Figure 6.6, can be obtained by setting the balance of payments equation (6.52) equal to zero, and solving the equation to find the change in the rate of interest which must accompany a change in government spending for the balance of payments to remain in equilibrium:

$$\frac{d\bar{G}}{dr} = \frac{-[(1 - C_Y(1 - T_Y) - I_Y - B_Y) K_r + (C_r + I_r) B_Y]}{B_Y}$$

or

$$\frac{d\bar{G}}{dr} = \frac{-[1 - C_Y(1 - T_Y) - I_Y - B_Y] K_r}{B_Y} - (C_r + I_r) > 0 \qquad (6.54)$$

The positive slope of the *FF* curve indicates that expansionary fiscal policy must be accompanied by contractionary monetary policy to keep the balance of payments in equilibrium.

It will be important in the discussion to follow to determine whether the slope of the external balance curve is greater or smaller than that of the internal balance curve. In fact a comparison of equations (6.53) and (6.54) shows that the *FF* curve is the steeper of the two, as drawn in Figure 6.6. This is so because the right-hand term in (6.54) is common to both slopes and the left-hand term is additional and positive in the external equilibrium curve. The explanation of the difference in slopes hinges on the interest sensitivity of the flow of capital $K_r$. The *II* slope is the ratio of the responsiveness of equilibrium expenditure to changes in the rate of interest to the responsiveness of equilibrium expenditure to changes in government spending. If there is no interest sensitivity of capital flows ($K_r = 0$) the balance of payments depends *only* on the balance of trade and hence on the level of domestic expenditure. The *FF* slope in this case must therefore also be the ratio of the responsiveness of domestic expenditure to $r$ and $\bar{G}$. Consequently the two slopes will be the same, a result which is confirmed by setting $K_r = 0$ in equation (6.54) and finding that (6.54) and (6.53) are then equal.

Now introduce a positive responsiveness of capital flows to changes in the rate of interest ($K_r > 0$). If *FF* and *II* had the same slopes a movement to the right on $FF = II$ would maintain constant income and balance of *trade* equilibrium. But the rising rate of interest would attract more capital from abroad, and to maintain balance of *payments* equilibrium there must be a greater offsetting increase in $\bar{G}$ (to make the balance of trade deteriorate) than is required for internal equilibrium. The *FF* curve must be steeper than *II*.

As a final word of explanation of the nature of the internal and external stability curves we can identify four zones in Figure 6.6. To the left of *FF* the interest rate is too low for external equilibrium, at any level of income, and the balance of payments is in deficit; to the right we have surplus. To the left of the *II* curve the level of government spending is too high for internal equilibrium, at any rate of interest, and inflationary pressure results; to the right there is deflationary pressure. The outcome of this twofold classification is the four zones I to IV identified beneath Figure 6.6. The only point at which there is simultaneous internal and external equilibrium is at $E$ where government spending is $\bar{G}_E$ and the rate of interest $r_E$.

The internal and external balance curves can now be used to demonstrate the problem of assigning instruments to targets *à la* Mundell. This requires an examination of the characteristics of points other than $E_1$ in Figure 6.7 and of the effect of trying to use the two instruments to move us to $E_1$. If the economy is initially at point $C$, with internal equilibrium achieved but the balance of payments in deficit, consider the outcome if the government assigns monetary policy to the maintenance of internal balance and fiscal policy to the attainment

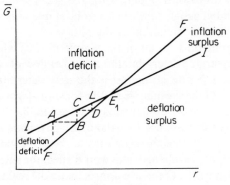

*Figure 6.7*

of external balance. In an attempt to correct the balance of payments deficit the fiscal authority must reduce its level of spending, a movement say from *C* to *B*. But this action creates recession, requiring the monetary authority to reduce the rate of interest to stimulate demand, as with the movement from *B* to *A*. Clearly the assignment of fiscal policy to the control of the balance of payments and monetary policy to controlling the domestic economy in this context is destabilizing, causing a movement away from $E_1$.

The alternative assignment, fiscal policy to domestic problems and monetary policy to external control is, by contrast, stabilizing. Starting again from point *C* the monetary authority attempts to reduce the balance of payments deficit by raising the rate of interest to attract capital and dampen the demand for imports. The movement to point *D* which results introduces a recession but this can be controlled in a stabilizing manner by expansionary fiscal policy (movement from *D* to *L*). The assignment moves the system towards $E_1$.

It should be noted that the system is not always sensitive to the assignment of instruments to targets in this way. If we are in quadrant I or III (Figure 6.6) the two targets require changes in either instrument in the same direction. The argument above does, however, suggest the *possibility* that incorrectly assigned instruments may produce instability, and the need for the careful coordination of policies in a world of multiple policy targets.†

The simple analysis of instrument assignment must be qualified in the light of the drastic simplifications assumed by the model. In the first place no account was taken of the monetary sector. Consequently the monetary feedback effects of fiscal policy were ignored, and the complication of the condition required for *FF* to be steeper than *II* to include parameters of the monetary sector was avoided. In a model with a monetary sector the possibility is introduced of an

† More recent work than Mundell's has attempted to extend the analysis to systems with more than two instruments and targets. The theory tends to become complicated when this is done. See, for example, Artoni (1970).

*FF* curve which is downward sloping while the *II* curve is upward sloping. In this case the Mundell assignment proves to be stable only if the absolute size of the *FF* slope is greater than that of the *II* slope.†

Secondly, in common with all of the simple models which have been discussed in this chapter, the determination of the net flow of capital from abroad is over-simplified. The rate of interest is the only determinant and therefore no account is taken of the speculative motive for short-term capital movements. In the real world, where the exchange rate is fixed in the short run but subject to periodic changes in response to balance of payments disequilibrium the holder of capital in a foreign currency runs the risk of capital losses (or gains) and expected changes in exchange rates would affect the decisions to send funds to foreign capital markets. Clearly to approximate the real world more closely, models with more complicated behavioural equations (investment functions etc.) are needed.‡

Thirdly, again in common with all of the theory of the external sector in this chapter, no attempt has been made to include flows of interest payments in the capital account of the balance of payments. But an increase in the rate of interest, while it may attract more capital from abroad, also increases the outflow of interest payments to foreign lenders. The difference between the *FF* and *II* slopes will be determined by the *net* effect on the inflow of funds from abroad which is not *necessarily* positive for a rise in the rate of interest.§

Finally, the model assumed by the Mundell type of assignment of instruments to targets is couched in terms of adjustments in the *flow* of capital between countries rather than in terms of a worldwide balancing of the portfolios of international asset-holders. In particular, equation (6.6), the crucial equation of the capital account, postulates that the level of the *flow* of capital is a function of the level of the rate of interest. Consequently a *change* in the domestic rate of interest is assumed to cause a permanent change in the level of the capital flow ($K_r = dK/dr > 0$). The opposing view is that this formulation is applicable only to a (short-run) adjustment period in which the holders of assets are adjusting their portfolios.‖ Thus, an increase in the domestic rate of interest relative to foreign rates increases the optimal holding of the domestic currency by foreign asset-holders. Consequently the demand for the currency increases causing capital inflow, *until* the optimal holding is reached. At that point the inflow of capital will cease, so that the increase in the interest rate has resulted only in a temporary, disequilibrium inflow of capital. There is a permanent

---

† Cf. Whitman (1970), pp. 17–18 (but notice that her reference to slopes there is for curves in a $\bar{G}$–$\bar{M}$ and not a $\bar{G}$–$r$ plane). Part III of the monograph contains a useful discussion of qualifications of the simpler targets and instruments theory.

‡ Krueger (1965), has developed broader models in this area.

§ On this point see Willett and Forte (1969). If the *II* curve were in fact steeper than *FF* the assignment of monetary policy to internal balance and fiscal policy to external balance would be *stable* and the reverse assignment unstable!

‖ See, for example, Floyd (1969).

increase in the *stock* of domestic assets held abroad, and an increase in the country's reserves of foreign exchange. The impact on the balance of payments, however, is quite different with this alternative stock-adjustment interpretation. The temporary inflow of capital creates a surplus but once the adjustment period is over a further surplus can be achieved only by *further* increases in the domestic interest rate. What is more, when the adjustment period is over and the inflow of capital ceases, the increased outflow of interest payments to the foreign asset-holders continues. The long-run effect on the capital account of an increase in the domestic rate of interest is therefore expected to be unfavourable, so that $K_r = dK/dr < 0$. This opposing interpretation is clearly significant for a long-run analysis of the balance of payments effects of fiscal and monetary policy. We found before that in the (short-run) model with a monetary sector the impact of fiscal policy on the balance was ambiguous (equation (6.29)), but now both the income effect *and* the interest rate effect of expansionary fiscal policy are detrimental to the balance of payments in the long run, $\partial H/\partial \bar{G} < 0$. By contrast, with monetary policy the situation was previously unambiguous (equation (6.30)); now the income effect of expansionary monetary policy is unfavourable while the accompanying interest rate effect is favourable, so that $\partial H/\partial \bar{M} \gtreqless 0$ in the long run.

In the model without a monetary sector used in section 6.5.2 the situation is affected by the reversal of the capital *flow* effect of a change in the exogenous rate of interest. The result is that the *II* curve becomes steeper than the *FF* curve and the reader can verify that the Mundellian instrument assignment is reversed.

The resolution of these conflicting views of the impact of policies depends on the time horizon of the policy-maker. The models in this chapter are essentially applicable to the short run. The stock-adjustment model emphasizes the long-run equilibrium situation, but if in the real world policies for external balance are dominated by rapid changes in international money movements the long-run equilibrium may well be of minor interest. The policy-maker is concerned with the causes, and possible ways of controlling, the capital *flows* associated with exchange rate speculation. Undoubtedly the short-run models will have to be improved.† An attempt must be made to incorporate an explanation of changes in exchange rate expectations, and particularly to discuss the impact of policy instruments on the expectation of exchange rate variations. Relating capital flows to relative interest rates, as the flow models usually do, is insufficient for the expectation-dominated money markets, but nevertheless it is perhaps with developments of the *short-run* analysis that our knowledge of the problems of policy for external balance will be enhanced. The importance of the stock-adjustment view lies in showing us that *permanent* changes in capital flows do not result from a change in interest rates; such a

---

† See for example Williamson (1971) on the development of normative models of policies for internal and external balance.

permanent improvement of the balance of payments capital account requires continuous increases in the domestic interest rate relative to foreign rates.

## EXERCISES

**6.1** Consider the following model

$$F = \bar{F}$$
$$X = \bar{X}$$
$$C = C(Y, r)$$
$$I = I(Y, r)$$
$$M = \bar{M}$$
$$L = L(Y, r)$$
$$K = K(Y, r)$$

(a) Write the expenditure sector, monetary sector and balance of payments functions.

(b) Assuming that imports, $F$, are determined by an import quota, consider the effects of changes in the quota on the balance of payments.

(c) Under what conditions can expansionary monetary policy create a surplus in the balance of payments? Would fiscal policy be more successful?

**6.2** Construct and solve a numerical model comprising an expenditure sector, a monetary sector and an external sector. Use the model to demonstrate the sensitivity of the size of the policy multipliers $\partial Y/\partial \bar{M}$ and $\partial Y/\partial \bar{G}$ to adopting or dropping the assumption of a closed economy.

# CHAPTER VII

# An Introduction to Dynamic Models of Income and Price Determination

The theory of macroeconomic models developed in previous chapters has been entirely static with no account being taken of the interaction between variables through time. Comparative static analysis is limited to a comparison of equilibrium situations before and after some disturbance affects the economic system. The analysis does not establish the time path followed by particular variables during the adjustment from one equilibrium to another. Dynamic analysis on the other hand does allow variables to react to each other through time and it describes the implications of the adjustment process for the time path of the endogenous variables. The reactions between variables typically include a causal chain of events which includes time lags. The model in the next section for example is basically different from the static one-sector income determination model only in that consumption is affected by a change in income after a time lag of one period.

Much of dynamic macroeconomic theory is complex and requires more advanced mathematics than has been assumed for this book. We will limit attention, therefore, to two of the simpler dynamic models of income determination and the exercise is worth undertaking because it gives one an idea of the limitations of the conventional static theory.† The second of the two models will be used in the next chapter to illustrate the problems confronting a policy-maker who is concerned with stabilization in a dynamic economy.

The final section of the chapter, which as regards content but not method is largely independent of the previous sections, outlines a simple dynamic model of price determination. This is intended to illustrate the types of problem which dynamic models can help us to handle, and complements the comparative-static theory of price changes discussed in Chapter V.

† Even the simpler dynamic models require a knowledge of difference equations and this can be obtained from Chiang (1967), Ch. 16 and 17.

## 7.1 DYNAMIC CONSUMPTION FUNCTION

We begin with a one-sector model of income determination with a constant price level, in which consumers' spending plans are based on the level of aggregate income in the previous period, that is:

$$C_t = c_0 + c_Y Y_{t-1} \qquad (7.1)$$

Investment and government spending plans, $I$ and $G$, are assumed to be exogenous and unvarying through time.

It is necessary at this point to clarify the nature of equilibrium in the model. It is possible to distinguish between equilibrium in the sense of the compatibility of spending plans *within* a time period $t$, and equilibrium in the sense of unchanging plans from one period to the next, that is a *stationary state*. It will be convenient for the subsequent analysis if we assume that spending plans are compatible and realized in each period, and concentrate on the condition for a stationary state. Indeed we shall refer to the stationary state as the equilibrium of the dynamic model and to other situations as disequilibrium. But the reader would do well to remember the restricted sense in which these other situations are disequilibrium: plans are realized *within* a period but are changing *between* periods.

Since in any period $t$ planned and realized spending are the same we can write as the sum of realized, equals planned, spending:

$$Y_t = C_t + \bar{I} + \bar{G} \qquad (7.2)$$

and the model consists of the two equations (7.1) and (7.2). The stationary state requires that consumption plans are constant, $C_t = C_{t-1}$. But it is clear from equation (7.1) that this can only be the case if income is constant, $Y_{t-1} = Y_{t-2}$. Consequently the condition for the stationary state, equilibrium in the model, is that $Y_{t-1} = Y_{t-2}$.

In solving the model for $Y_t$ we will effectively be asking two questions:

(a) what is the equilibrium level of income, stationary state, towards which a stable system will adjust if a disturbance causes an initial disequilibrium?
(b) what will be the time path of income during the period of adjustment to equilibrium?

It is necessary first to find a general expression for $Y_t$ from the model, and then to obtain from this two components, one to tell us the equilibrium income and the other to describe the time path of income when it deviates from equilibrium.

Substituting for $C_t$ from equation (7.1) into the income equation (7.2), the expression for $Y_t$ is

$$Y_t = c_Y Y_{t-1} + (c_0 + \bar{I} + \bar{G}) \qquad (7.3)$$

Rearranging terms we have a *first-order difference equation*:

$$Y_t - c_Y Y_{t-1} - (c_0 + \bar{I} + \bar{G}) = 0 \qquad (7.4)$$

This can be solved for $Y_t$ by using a standard procedure for such equations,† the solution being divided into two components. The first component, called the *particular integral*, is an expression for the equilibrium level of income $Y^e$. The second, the *complementary function* $Y^c$, is the solution for the deviations of the income time path from equilibrium. The sum of the equilibrium income and the deviations from it of actual income yield the time path of income, that is

$$Y_t = Y^e + Y^c \qquad (7.5)$$

Setting $Y_t = Y_{t-1}$ in equation (7.4) to find the equilibrium, we have

$$Y^e = \frac{c_0 + \bar{I} + \bar{G}}{1 - c_Y} \qquad (7.6)$$

The equilibrium income level, for all time periods $(t = 1 \ldots n)$, is the product of exogenous expenditure and the multiplier as in the simple static model of income determination.

Once the system is disturbed by a change in exogenous expenditure the new equilibrium income level will be different from income in the previous period. The income path following the disturbance will depend on the deviation from equilibrium as determined by the complementary function. This is found by setting exogenous expenditure equal to zero (so that the deviations will be from a level of zero) and obtaining the reduced form of equation (7.4):

$$Y_t - c_Y Y_{t-1} = 0 \qquad (7.7)$$

Following the normal procedure for the solution of the complementary function we try a solution of the form $Y_t = Ab^t$, where $Ab \neq 0$ and $A$ is an arbitrary constant. If the solution *were* of this form it would follow that $Y_{t-1} = Ab^{t-1}$. Substituting $Ab^t$ for $Y_t$ and $Ab^{t-1}$ for $Y_{t-1}$ in equation (7.7) we have:

$$Ab^t - c_Y Ab^{t-1} = 0 \qquad (7.8)$$

But $Ab^t = (Ab^{t-1})b$ by definition, so that equation (7.8) can be rewritten as

$$(Ab^{t-1})b - (Ab^{t-1})c_Y = 0$$

or

$$b - c_Y = 0 \qquad (7.9)$$

From equation (7.9) we know that the complementary function is

$$Y^c = Ab^t = Ac_Y{}^t \qquad (7.10)$$

and it is apparent that the deviations of actual from equilibrium income are going to depend critically upon the value of the marginal propensity to consume.

† See Chiang (1967), pp. 507–10.

Combining the two components of the solution for $Y_t$ we have

$$Y_t = Y^c + Y^e = Ac_Y{}^t + \frac{(c_0 + \bar{I} + \bar{G})}{1 - c_Y} \qquad (7.11)$$

In order to eliminate the arbitrary constant $A$ from the solution we set $t = 0$ in equation (7.11) so that

$$Y_0 = A + \frac{(c_0 + \bar{I} + \bar{G})}{1 - c_Y}$$

or

$$A = Y_0 - \frac{(c_0 + \bar{I} + \bar{G})}{1 - c_Y} \qquad (7.12)$$

The general solution for $Y_t$ is, from equations (7.11) and (7.12):

$$Y_t = \left( Y_0 - \frac{(c_0 + \bar{I} + \bar{G})}{1 - c_Y} \right) c_Y{}^t + \frac{(c_0 + \bar{I} + \bar{G})}{1 - c_Y} \qquad (7.13)$$

By way of interpretation of this solution we can return to the two questions posed at the outset. In answer to question (a), if $t$ approaches infinity the first term in equation (7.13) will approach zero *as long as* $c_Y < 1$, as it is assumed to be. That is

$$Y_t \to \frac{(c_0 + \bar{I} + \bar{G})}{1 - c_Y} \qquad \text{as } t \to \infty \qquad (7.14)$$

As long as $c_Y < 1$ the system is stable and converges on the equilibrium level of income given by equation (7.6). It is to be noted that a change in exogenous expenditure affects the equilibrium income level (equation (7.6)) but does not alter the character of the time path by which equilibrium is reached (i.e. does not enter equation (7.10)).

As regards question (b), the time path to equilibrium depends on the value of $c_Y$. We have seen that given the usual restriction that $0 < c_Y < 1$ the system

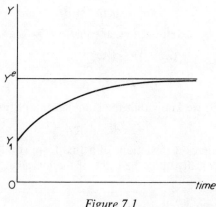

*Figure 7.1*

converges on $Y^e$. In addition the restriction also means that the adjustment to equilibrium will be a smooth one since the condition for the absence of oscillations (cycles)[†] is that $c_Y \geqslant 0$. The time path of income, starting from a disequilibrium income $Y_1$ will be as illustrated in Figure 7.1, a smooth curve approaching $Y^e$ as the multiplier works itself out.

## 7.2  A MULTIPLIER–ACCELERATOR INTERACTION MODEL

We have seen that, given the usual restriction on the sign and size of the marginal propensity to consume, the simple model with a dynamic consumption function produces smooth time paths of income. It is necessary therefore to look to more complicated dynamic models if we are to find cyclical time paths produced while the restrictions on parameters are satisfied.

The model which will be used to illustrate the construction and interpretation of the more complex models is the Samuelson multiplier–accelerator model.[‡] This is a one-sector model with both consumption and investment endogenous and with both functions taking a dynamic form. The equations of the model are

$$C_t = c_0 + c_Y Y_{t-1}, \qquad 0 < c_Y < 1 \tag{7.1}$$

$$I_t = a(C_t - C_{t-1}), \qquad a > 0 \tag{7.15}$$

$$Y_t = C_t + I_t + \bar{G} \tag{7.16}$$

As in the previous section consumption is a linear function of income of the previous period. Investment is proportional to the change in the level of consumption between the previous and the current period. The ratio of investment to the change in consumption is the accelerator, $a$, assumed to be positive as we saw in Chapter II. It will also be assumed that spending plans in period $t$ are realized, so that the income definition is (7.16). In this model, which we may call the no-policy model, government expenditure is exogenous and constant. No attempt is made to use $G$ as an instrument for controlling the time path of income.

Substituting for $C_t$ and $I_t$ from equations (7.1) and (7.15) in the income equation (7.16) we have the expression for $Y_t$:

$$Y_t = c_0 + \bar{G} + c_Y Y_{t-1} + a(C_t - C_{t-1})$$

or

$$Y_t = c_Y(1 + a) Y_{t-1} - ac_Y Y_{t-2} + (c_0 + \bar{G}) \tag{7.17}$$

This is a *second-order difference equation* which can be solved using a method similar to that followed for the first-order equation in the previous section.

[†] See Chiang (1967), pp. 512 and 514.
[‡] Samuelson (1939), reprinted in Mueller (1967).

Once again the solution for $Y_t$ is the sum of the particular integral and the complementary function (equation (7.5)). The former component, $Y^e$, is found by setting for equilibrium $Y_t = Y_{t-1} = Y_{t-2}$ in equation (7.17), so that

$$Y^e = \frac{c_0 + \bar{G}}{1 - c_Y} \tag{7.18}$$

Comparing equations (7.6) and (7.18) it is clear that the equilibrium characteristics of this model and the previous one are essentially the same. Investment is now entirely endogenous so that there is no $\bar{I}$ in equation (7.18) but this is the only difference: equilibrium income in both cases is the product of exogenous expenditure and the multiplier. The reason for the equivalence is that in equilibrium $Y_t = Y_{t-1} = Y_{t-2}$ which means (from equation (7.1)) that $C_t = C_{t-1}$. With consumption constant there is no *induced* investment (from equation (7.15)) and the two models are the same.

In disequilibrium, however, consumption plans change as the multiplier effect of a change in exogenous expenditure works itself out. With $C_t \neq C_{t-1}$, the multiplier–accelerator model displays different characteristics from the simple dynamic consumption function model. Investment reacts to the change in consumption, and the change in investment expenditure in turn feeds back, via income, to consumption. There is an interaction between induced consumption changes and induced investment changes which gives rise to the *possibility* of cycles in the time path of income. In order to establish the conditions under which cycles will occur we need to find the complementary function which determines the disequilibrium income path.

The required reduced form of equation (7.17) is:

$$Y_t - c_Y(1 + a) \, Y_{t-1} + ac_Y \, Y_{t-2} = 0 \tag{7.19}$$

As before we try a solution of the form $Y_{t-j} = Ab^{t-j}$, for $j = 0, 1, 2$, where $Ab^{t-j} \neq 0$. Thus, substituting $Ab^t$ for $Y_t$, $Ab^{t-1}$ for $Y_{t-1}$ and $Ab^{t-2}$ for $Y_{t-2}$ in equation (7.19) we have:

$$Ab^t - c_Y(1 + a) \, Ab^{t-1} + ac_Y \, Ab^{t-2} = 0 \tag{7.20}$$

But since $Ab^t = (Ab^{t-1})b = (Ab^{t-2})b^2$ by definition, we can rewrite equation (7.20) as

$$Ab^{t-2}[b^2 - c_Y(1 + a) \, b + ac_Y] = 0 \tag{7.21}$$

Therefore, with $Ab^{t-2} \neq 0$, we find

$$b^2 - c_Y(1 + a) \, b + ac_Y = 0 \tag{7.22}$$

This expression is similar to equation (7.9) for the simpler model and in fact if investment were exogenous we could set $a = 0$ in equation (7.22) which would then reduce to equation (7.9). In the case of the simpler model, since $b = c_Y$ it was easy to obtain the complementary function as in equation (7.10), and we found that the sign and size of $b$, and therefore of $c_Y$, determined the dis-equilibrium income path. In the multiplier–accelerator model $b$ is again important, but here it is dependent on both $c_Y$ and $a$, as equation (7.22) shows. It will be found, therefore, that the income path varies with different combinations of the parameters $c_Y$ and $a$.

Because equation (7.22) is quadratic there is not a simple solution for $b$ to put in the complementary function ($Y^c = Ab^t$). There are two roots $b_1$ and $b_2$ of equation (7.22), *both* of which enter the complementary function and which are found from

$$b_1, b_2 = \frac{c_Y(1 + a) \pm \sqrt{[c_Y(1 + a)]^2 - 4ac_Y}}{2} \tag{7.23}$$

The values of $b_1$ and $b_2$ determine whether the system is stable and converges on $Y^e$, and whether the path towards, or away from, equilibrium will be smooth or

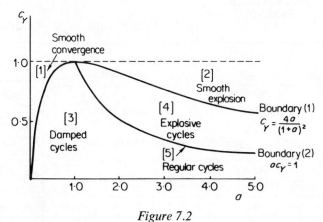

*Figure 7.2*

cyclical.† Since $b_1$ and $b_2$ depend on $c_Y$ and $a$, the conditions for convergence and for cycles can be expressed in terms of $c_Y$ and $a$. The outcome is a classification of all possible combinations of $c_Y$ and $a$, first into those producing cycles and those yielding smooth income paths; and second into combinations leading to convergence on equilibrium and those which produce explosive (divergent) income paths.

The requirement for cycles to occur is that

$$c_Y < \frac{4a}{(1 + a)^2}$$

In Figure 7.2 all combinations of $a$ and $c_Y$ which are below boundary (1) meet this requirement and produce cycles. Those on or above this boundary represent smooth growth or smooth decline of income.

† See Chiang (1967), pp. 534–6 and 542 *et seq.*

The condition for the system to be convergent is that

$$ac_Y < 1$$

In the figure the combinations above boundary (2) do not satisfy this requirement and yield explosive income paths. Those falling on boundary (2) yield regular cycles and those below it yield damped (convergent) income paths.

These two divisions create four areas of combinations of $a$ and $c_Y$, plus the special case of a fifth 'area' on the boundary (2). The characteristics of the resulting income paths following a disturbance from equilibrium $Y^e$ are summarized by means of Figure 7.2 and Table 7.1. In Table 7.1 the first column

TABLE 7.1

| | Parameter values | | | |
|---|---|---|---|---|
| Area no. | Boundary (1) | Boundary (2) | Description | Illustration |
| [1] | $c_Y > \dfrac{4a}{(1+a)^2}$ | $ac_Y < 1$ | smooth convergence | |
| [2] | $c_Y > \dfrac{4a}{(1+a)^2}$ | $ac_Y > 1$ | smooth explosion | |
| [3] | $c_Y < \dfrac{4a}{(1+a)^2}$ | $ac_Y < 1$ | damped cycles | |
| [4] | $c_Y < \dfrac{4a}{(1+a)^2}$ | $ac_Y > 1$ | explosive cycles | |
| [5] | $c_Y < \dfrac{4a}{(1+a)^2}$ | $ac_Y = 1$ | regular cycles | |

† Figure after Samuelson (1939).

gives the number of the corresponding area in Figure 7.2. The second and third columns show the relationship of each area to the two boundary conditions. In the case of area [3], for example, both the condition for convergence and that for cycles is met, and the result is damped (convergent) cycles as shown in words in the fourth column and diagrammatically in the fifth column. In these illustrative figures $Y^e$ is the equilibrium income level and $Y_1$ an initial disequilibrium income.

The classification of the $a$ and $c_Y$ combinations into these areas is dependent on the fundamental structure of the multiplier–accelerator model. As we shall see in section 8.3 any changes in this structure which alter the coefficients for $Y_{t-1}$ and $Y_{t-2}$ in the basic difference equation (for example by introducing parameters other than $a$ and $c_Y$) will alter the boundaries, and therefore the areas. This would result in the income path for some combinations of $a$ and $c_Y$ being changed in character. But given the model as it has been specified in this section, with only the two parameters entering, the income time path is determined by the values of $a$ and $c_Y$ alone. Changes in exogenous expenditure alter the equilibrium income level, but they do not affect the time path which income takes from a disequilibrium situation, or indeed whether income does approach equilibrium at all.

## 7.3  SOME DEVELOPMENTS OF DYNAMIC MODELS OF INCOME

To complete this introduction to macrodynamics some of the limitations of the multiplier–accelerator model will be considered in this section, and mention will be made of a few of the developments from the version we have discussed.

There are at least four important limitations of the multiplier–accelerator model as an explanation of the business cycle:

(1) It is built on a very simple explanation of the determinants of aggregate demand since the expenditure sector used contains no monetary factors.
(2) It does not impose any restrictions on variations in income and therefore in output. The combination of $a$ and $c_Y$ determines the time path of aggregate demand, and the model assumes that none of the resulting demand levels exceeds full employment output.
(3) It produces symmetrical cycles, that is cycles with upswings and downswings of similar duration.
(4) It does not explain the *trend* of equilibrium income about which cycles may occur in practice because the equilibrium level of income is exogenous to the model.

The first of these limitations is not difficult to overcome and in section 8.3 some problems of stabilization policy will be analysed using a multiplier–accelerator model in which aggregate demand is determined by an expenditure *and* a monetary sector. It turns out that, although the boundaries between areas discussed above are to some extent affected by the introduction of the monetary sector, the basic character of the classification of $a$ and $c_Y$ combinations is not substantially altered.

The second of the limitations has been tackled by the introduction of a ceiling on output set by the full employment of labour and capital. Hicks suggested that the business cycle in the real world is inherently explosive but that the potential explosions are prevented by the constraint imposed by the output ceiling.[†] The effect of this constraint on the time path of income can be explained in terms of Figure 7.3. As the figure is drawn the equilibrium level of income, $Y^e$, is growing through time due to investment (in Hicks' model)

[†] Hicks (1950).

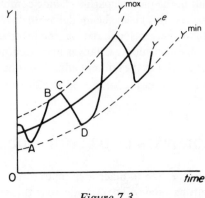

*Figure 7.3*

having an exogenous component which is growing through time. The $Y^{\max}$ curve represents the output ceiling which is also assumed to be growing. In addition, a floor income level $Y^{\min}$ is introduced, though this is not strictly necessary. The impact of the ceiling can be seen by considering the expansionary phase A–B in the figure. After the upturn at point A the interaction between the multiplier and the accelerator pushes up the level of income, with induced investment building on consumption changes and induced increases in consumption resulting from the consequent increases in income. At point B the output ceiling is reached and the subsequent increase in income is constrained by the rate of change of $Y^{\max}$. Hicks postulated an investment function of the form

$$I_t = a(Y_{t-1} - Y_{t-2}) \tag{7.24}$$

rather than the Samuelson form, equation (7.15), so that in his theory the ceiling results directly in a reduction (with a lag) in the level of investment. Income and consumption follow and the downward path is taken after point C. The plateau B–C represents the delay in the down turn due to the lag in the investment function. If the Samuelson investment function is used the same argument holds, since by substituting in equation (7.15) for $C_t$ and $C_{t-1}$ from equation (7.1) we have

$$I_t = ac_Y(Y_{t-1} - Y_{t-2}) \tag{7.25}$$

and the slow-down of the income change still reduces investment. Analogous reasoning explains an increase in investment which produces an upturn after point D has been reached.

Turning to the third limitation, there are a number of ways in which the multiplier–accelerator model can be modified to introduce a lack of symmetry in the cycles, for example to permit longer upswings than downswings.† The

† Evans (1969), Ch. 14, surveys these developments.

modifications generally involve non-linearities such as a variable accelerator. Goodwin, for example, argued that the size of the accelerator varies with the size of the change in income.† This amounts to replacing the linear investment function $I_1$ in Figure 7.4, with the non-linear function $I_2$, where $a$ is constant but $\alpha$ is not. One reason for expecting the accelerator to be variable is that as income accelerates, i.e. $(Y_{t-1} - Y_{t-2})$ rises, the greater is the change in investment from one period to the next which would be implied by a constant accelerator. The faster the change in investment the higher will be the adjustment costs

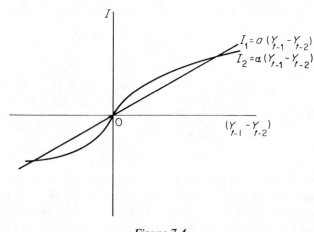

*Figure 7.4*

of planning and undertaking new investment projects and the more likely that investors will be constrained by a shortage of funds for expansion. The result of the variable accelerator in the Goodwin model is to produce a cyclical income time path characterized by upswings which last longer than downswings.

The final limitation is that equilibrium in the model is a stationary state. It is easy to introduce into the model growth in the equilibrium level of income simply by assuming a steady rate of growth of exogenous expenditure. The particular integral then is a function of time and the result is cyclical growth. However, the growth element would not be *explained* by the model in this case and what is needed is to make the growth rate itself endogenous. A number of attempts have been made in this direction, for example by incorporating the growth of output as a function of the saving/income ratio and the capital/output ratio, but they involve complex models beyond the scope of this introduction to dynamics.‡

† Goodwin (1951).
‡ Two models of this kind are explained in Allen (1967), Ch. 20.

## 7.4   A SIMPLE DYNAMIC MODEL OF PRICE DETERMINATION

The comparative static theory of the price level identifies the causes of changes in equilibrium price. A dynamic model of price determination, on the other hand, attempts to trace the *time path* of the price level during the adjustment from one equilibrium to another. In so doing it may remedy *some* of the deficiencies of the comparative static analysis mentioned in section 5.3.

In the three-sector static model the changes in price level were implicitly determined by the level of excess demand (or supply) in the goods market. We can now make the price function explicit by postulating that starting from an equilibrium price level in period $t - 1$, the change in the price level is

$$dP_t = \beta_1[D_t - Q_t - (D_{t-1} - Q_{t-1})]$$

or

$$dP_t = \beta_1(dD_t - dQ_t) \qquad (7.26)$$

where $dP_t = P_t - P_{t-1}$, $dD_t = D_t - D_{t-1}$ and $dQ_t = Q_t - Q_{t-1}$; $P$ is the price level, $D$ aggregate demand, $Q$ aggregate output supplied and $\beta_1$ the response of the price level to a change in excess demand. Since $D_{t-1} = Q_{t-1}$ in the initial equilibrium, equation (7.26) can be rewritten as

$$dP_t = \beta_1(D_t - Q_t) \qquad (7.27)$$

so that the absolute change in the price level is proportional to the absolute level of excess demand (or supply). However, the emphasis in the dynamic theory of inflation is placed upon the determinants of the *percentage rate of inflation*. For this reason we will substitute for equation (7.27) the assumption that the percentage rate of inflation in period $t$ is proportional to the percentage level of excess demand (or supply) in the same period:

$$\frac{dP_t}{P_{t-1}} = \beta_2\left(\frac{dD_t - dQ_t}{Q_{t-1}}\right) \qquad (7.28)$$

where $\beta_2$ is the elasticity of the price level with respect to changes in excess demand or supply.

The variables $dD_t$ and $dQ_t$ in equations (7.26) and (7.28) are the changes in aggregate demand and supply at the price prevailing at the beginning of period $t$. A change in demand can result from a change in any of the exogenous variables of the expenditure and monetary sectors. If $\bar{X}$ represents these exogenous influences† we can write the shift in the aggregate demand curve as:

$$\frac{dD_t}{D_{t-1}} = \delta\left(\frac{d\bar{X}}{\bar{X}}\right) \qquad (7.29)$$

where $\delta$ is the elasticity of aggregate demand with respect to changes in exogenous expenditure.

† The letter $X$ is used for the exogenous variables as a group only in this section. Elsewhere $X$ has been used for the value of exports.

A change in the quantity of goods supplied at any price level can result from a change in production costs which, in the three-sector model, means labour cost. If unions are able to exert an independent influence on the money wage rate at a given price level then firms are assumed to react by reducing supply proportionately:

$$\frac{dQ_t}{Q_{t-1}} = -\sigma\left(\frac{d\bar{W}_t}{\bar{W}_{t-1}}\right) \tag{7.30}$$

where $\sigma$ is the elasticity of aggregate supply with respect to changes in wage cost. If unions pursue the objective of maintaining their real wage levels then the rate of change of the union-determined money wage rate will be

$$\frac{d\bar{W}_t}{\bar{W}_{t-1}} = \frac{dP_t^*}{P_{t-1}^*} \tag{7.31}$$

where $dP_t^*/P_{t-1}^*$ is the rate of inflation *expected* by unions in period $t$.

Substituting $dP_t^*/P_{t-1}^*$ for $d\bar{W}_t/\bar{W}_{t-1}$ in equation (7.30) we have

$$\frac{dQ_t}{Q_{t-1}} = -\sigma\left(\frac{dP_t^*}{P_{t-1}^*}\right) \tag{7.32}$$

so that the rate of change of supply depends on the rate of inflation expected by unions. This assumes that firms are price-takers and do not expect to be able to pass on the higher cost in higher prices while maintaining the period $t-1$ level of output.

Clearly the next step is to explain how unions form their expectations of inflation. It is possible to imagine various ways in which unions make their forecast but most of the hypotheses make $dP_t^*/P_{t-1}^*$ a function of some past actual rates of inflation. A commonly used formulation is to assume that *all* past rates of inflation affect the expectation but with weights attached to past experience which decline geometrically the further back in time the experience occurred. We will adopt a special case, which is that the weight attached to the previous period's actual rate of inflation is positive, and the weight attached to experience before that is zero. The expected rate of inflation for period $t$ is then

$$\frac{dP_t^*}{P_{t-1}^*} = \rho\left(\frac{dP_{t-1}}{P_{t-2}}\right) \tag{7.33}$$

where $\rho$ is the elasticity of price expectations with respect to changes in the actual price level in the previous period. If $\rho = 1$, last period's rate of inflation is expected to continue. From equations (7.32) and (7.33) we find that

$$\frac{dQ_t}{Q_{t-1}} = -\sigma\rho\left(\frac{dP_{t-1}}{P_{t-2}}\right) \tag{7.34}$$

We are now in a position to obtain an expression for the rate of inflation. Substituting in equation (7.28) for $dQ_t/Q_{t-1}$ from equation (7.34) and for $dD_t/D_{t-1} (=dD_t/Q_{t-1})$ from equation (7.29) yields:

$$\frac{dP_t}{P_{t-1}} = \beta_2 \delta \frac{d\bar{X}}{\bar{X}} + \beta_2 \sigma\rho \frac{dP_{t-1}}{P_{t-2}} \tag{7.35}$$

This is a first-order difference equation which can be interpreted using the standard method used in section 7.1 for the dynamic consumption function. The method need not be repeated but the results obtained are:

*Particular integral:* (equilibrium $dP_t/P_{t-1}$)

$$\left(\frac{dP_t}{P_{t-1}}\right)^e = \frac{\beta_2 \delta\, d\bar{X}/\bar{X}}{1 - \beta_2 \sigma\rho} \tag{7.36}$$

which would be zero if the rate of change of demand, $d\bar{X}/\bar{X}$, were zero. Given the values of parameters $\beta_2$, $\sigma$ and $\rho$ only changes in demand can disturb the equilibrium rate of inflation.

*Complementary function:* (deviations of $dP_t/P_{t-1}$ from $(dP_t/P_{t-1})^e$.

Following the usual procedure for finding the complementary function we have:†

$$b - \beta_2 \sigma\rho = 0$$

so that

$$\left(\frac{dP_t}{P_{t-1}}\right)^c = A(\beta_2 \sigma\rho)^t \tag{7.37}$$

If exogenous expenditure remains constant the price level will be constant in equilibrium, as equation (7.36) shows, but if expenditure plans continually expand (contract) there will be a positive rate of inflation (deflation) in equilibrium. But will the rate of inflation tend to the equilibrium rate once the system has been disturbed? This depends on the complementary function (7.37) and therefore on the three parameters $\beta_2$, $\sigma$ and $\rho$. If

$$\beta_2 \sigma\rho < 1 \tag{7.38}$$

then

$$\frac{dP_t}{P_{t-1}} \to \left(\frac{dP_t}{P_{t-1}}\right)^e \qquad \text{as } t \to \infty$$

If condition (7.38) is satisfied the rate of inflation will adjust smoothly to the equilibrium rate, as in Figure 7.5. If not, it will explode monotonically. With $\rho = 1$, the larger is $\beta_2$, the elasticity of prices with respect to changes in excess demand, and the larger is $\sigma$, the elasticity of supply with respect to changes in wage cost, the greater is the risk of an unstable system, a monotonic explosion of the rate of inflation.

† This is the equivalent of equation (7.9) for the dynamic multiplier model.

Even if $\beta_2 \sigma < 1$, expectations of inflation can be such that $\rho > 1$ and $\beta_2 \sigma \rho > 1$ so that a potentially stable situation is converted into an accelerating inflation by the very existence of the *expectation* that inflation will become more rapid than previously.

In this simple model the path followed by the rate of inflation during the adjustment to equilibrium is a smooth one (as long as $\beta_2 \sigma \rho > 0$). It is easy, however, to extend the model to introduce the possibility of cyclical adjustment paths. All that is required is that, due to a lag in response in the system

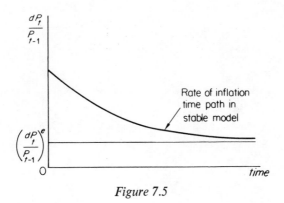

*Figure 7.5*

such as expectations of forthcoming inflation being based on the actual rate in both $t-1$ *and* $t-2$, the expression for $dP_t/P_{t-1}$ contains the dependent variable lagged one and two periods. The price equation then becomes a second-order difference equation and it is possible to classify the time paths of inflation-adjustment into the categories 'smooth convergence', 'damped cycles' etc. which were obtained for income in the multiplier–accelerator model.

The simple model in this section has been presented for illustrative purposes and is not intended as a penetrating analysis of the causes of the current inflation. The model contains some serious naivities, such as the assumption that producers are price takers who offer goods for sale at a market determined price and are satisfied to adjust output to the quantity demanded at that price. No mention has been made of the likelihood that producers will hedge against cost increases by building a normal rate of increase into their price setting. Despite these and other deficiencies the model shows how relatively conventional theory can be extended, dynamized, to allow interactions between variables through time and to admit the possibility that continuing rates of inflation may replace the once-and-for-all increases in the equilibrium price level which are analysed by the static macroeconomic theory.

## EXERCISES

**7.1**  Explain the main difference between the model of income determination with a dynamic consumption function (but investment exogenous) and the multiplier–accelerator interaction model. Does this explain the possibility of cycles in the latter model?

**7.2**  Outline the main difficulties inherent in an attempt to construct a dynamic model of inflation.

# CHAPTER VIII

## The Business Cycle and Stabilization Policy

If no attempt is made to control the economy the values of many economic variables will fluctuate through the business cycle. Attempts by the government to use its policy instruments to control such short term, cyclical variations are called stabilization policy. In reality the government is only concerned about the variations in *some* of the numerous endogenous variables, the target variables. A realistic evaluation of the success of stabilization attempts would require us to identify the impact of instrument changes on several target variables, such as the unemployment rate, the price level, *per capita* real income and the balance of payments. Although economists are currently in the process of judging past policy in the context of multiple instrument and target models using econometric estimation,† in this chapter we shall keep the theory relatively simple by assuming real income to be the only target variable, and government spending on goods and services $\bar{G}$, the real level of exogenous direct tax yield $T_0$ and the nominal supply of money $\bar{M}$ to be the only instruments.

In the first part of the chapter it is assumed that the aim of policy is to offset changes in income which are produced by the system. The analysis proceeds to compare the income multipliers, and hence the change in equilibrium income, associated with changes in different instruments to see if their impact on the target variable differs.

In section 8.3 there is a change of emphasis because the income change which creates the need for policy intervention is not taken as given. Instead a simple dynamic model of the business cycle is employed in which policy changes are built into the process of income determination. The aim of policy in this context is to offset deviations of income from some target income level.

† An explanation of how econometric models can be used for this purpose is given by Suits (1962).

161

While the main purpose of the chapter is to analyse the role of fiscal and monetary policy in formal static and dynamic models, it is difficult to discuss stabilization policy at the present time without some reference to the current debate on the effectiveness of these two instruments. Consequently a slight digression from the formal theory will be made in section 8.2 to consider the main points at issue in this debate.

## 8.1 COMPARATIVE STATIC ANALYSIS: A SUMMARY AND AN EXTENSION

If the government wishes to offset a change in income which it expects to occur in the absence of stabilization policy it must have an idea of the size of the multiplier effect of any change in expenditure. From previous chapters we know that the multiplier associated with any policy-induced expenditure change depends on

(a) the structure of the model used,
    and
(b) the particular instrument used.

To summarize the earlier results and assist a comparison of them, Table 8.1 shows the income multipliers for the monetary and fiscal instruments in the one-, two- and three-sector models.

The multipliers in Table 8.1 have all been derived in earlier chapters and need not be explained individually again. But a comparison of the three multipliers, e.g. for $d\bar{G}$, emphasizes the severe *ceteris paribus* assumptions of the simple one-sector model of income determination. The comparison also shows that fiscal and monetary policies cannot be interpreted as if they were independent of each other. The impact of fiscal policy depends on the control of the money supply. If the money supply is held constant (in nominal terms, i.e. $d\bar{M} = 0$), we have the government expenditure multipliers in the second row, columns 2 and 4, of Table 8.1. These can be rewritten respectively as:

$$\frac{\partial Y}{\partial \bar{G}} = \frac{1}{[1 - C_Y(1 - T_Y) - I_Y] + (C_r + I_r)\dfrac{L_Y}{L_r}} \tag{8.1}$$

for the two-sector model, and

$$\frac{\partial Y}{\partial \bar{G}} = \frac{1}{[1 - C_Y(1 - T_Y) - I_Y] + (C_r + I_r)(L_Y Y_N' \bar{W} - Y_N'' \bar{M})\dfrac{1}{Y_N' \bar{W} L_r}} \tag{8.2}$$

for the three-sector model. Because the second terms in the denominators of both (8.1) and (8.2) are positive, these multipliers are smaller than the corresponding simple (one-sector) multiplier in the second row, column 1, of

TABLE 8.1   Monetary and fiscal multipliers

| | One-sector model | Two-sector model | Three-sector model | |
| --- | --- | --- | --- | --- |
| | | | Endogenous money wage rate (full employment) | Exogenous money wage rate† |
| $\dfrac{\partial Y}{\partial M}$ | — | $\dfrac{(C_r+I_r)\frac{1}{P}}{[1-C_Y(1-T_Y)-I_Y]L_r+(C_r+I_r)L_Y}>0$ | 0 | $\dfrac{-Y_N'(C_r+I_r)\frac{W}{P^2}\frac{1}{P}}{\Delta}>0$ |
| $\dfrac{\partial Y}{\partial G}$ | $\dfrac{1}{1-C_Y(1-T_Y)-I_Y}>0$ | $\dfrac{L_r}{[1-C_Y(1-T_Y)-I_Y]L_r+(C_r+I_r)L_Y}>0$ | 0 | $\dfrac{-Y_N'L_r\frac{W}{P^2}}{\Delta}>0$ |
| $\dfrac{\partial Y}{\partial T_0}$ | $-\dfrac{C_Y}{1-C_Y(1-T_Y)-I_Y}<0$ | $-\dfrac{C_YL_r}{[1-C_Y(1-T_Y)-I_Y]L_r+(C_r+I_r)L_Y}<0$ | 0 | $\dfrac{Y_N'L_r\frac{W}{P^2}C_Y}{\Delta}<0$ |

† In this column

$$\Delta = -[1-C_Y(1-T_Y)-I_Y]Y_N'L_r\frac{W}{P^2}-(C_r+I_r)\frac{1}{P^2}(L_Y Y_N'W-Y_N''M)>0$$

Table 8.1. This is due, as we have seen (e.g. in section 3.6) to the monetary feedback effect of expansionary fiscal policy.

This matter of the relationship between fiscal and monetary policy can be pursued further by assuming that the government is bound by a *budget constraint* which requires that any increase in government expenditure be matched by an equivalent (or greater) increase in government revenue from some source.† For the sake of simplicity we shall assume that neither the amount of government debt outstanding nor the revenue from taxation can be increased, so that the additional revenue required to finance $d\bar{G} > 0$ must come from an equivalent increase in the supply of money.

We have seen, in section 2.7, that a change in the size of a budget which is balanced initially (*ex ante*) will become unbalanced due to induced tax revenue changes ($T_Y > 0$). An increase in the size of the budget which is balanced *ex ante* creates a budget surplus as income increases. Now a government which is bound by a budget constraint can avoid running a surplus by *reducing* average tax rates as income increases in order to offset the induced increase in revenue ('fiscal drag'). This reduction in tax rates is formally equivalent to setting $T_Y = 0$ in our models, and consequently the balanced budget multipliers (such as equation (2.82)) can be interpreted as the impact of a budget which is balanced *ex post* if $T_Y$ is set equal to zero in them.

Returning to an increase in government spending financed by an increase in the money supply above, the multiplier effect can be found by:

(a) summing the multipliers for the two instruments, $d\bar{G}$ and $d\bar{M}$, just as we summed the multipliers for $d\bar{G}$ and $dT_0$ in the balanced budget case; and

(b) offsetting any induced increase in tax revenue by reducing average tax rates, setting $T_Y = 0$ in the multipliers.

The result of these two operations for the two-sector model is:

$$\frac{\partial Y}{\partial \bar{G}} d\bar{G} + \frac{\partial Y}{\partial \bar{M}} d\bar{M} = \frac{1 + (C_r + I_r)\dfrac{1}{L_r P}}{(1 - C_Y - I_Y) + (C_r + I_r)\dfrac{L_Y}{L_r}} d\bar{G} \qquad (8.3)$$

and for the three-sector model:

$$\frac{\partial Y}{\partial \bar{G}} d\bar{G} + \frac{\partial Y}{\partial \bar{M}} d\bar{M} = \frac{1 + (C_r + I_r)\dfrac{1}{L_r P}}{(1 - C_Y - I_Y) + (C_r + I_r)(L_Y Y_N' \bar{W} - Y_N'' \bar{M})\dfrac{1}{Y_N' \bar{W} L_r}} d\bar{G} \qquad (8.4)$$

These multipliers are greater than the fiscal multipliers (8.1) and (8.2) for two reasons which result from the operations (a) and (b) just undertaken. Firstly,

† Christ (1968), presents a two-sector model with a budget constraint formally introduced.

the budget constraint is met by raising the money supply so that the expansionary impact of $d\bar{G}$ is necessarily combined with the expansionary money effect. This is represented by the additional positive term $(C_r + I_r)(1/L_rP)$ in the numerators of (8.3) and (8.4). Secondly, the multiplier is increased in the presence of the budget constraint because tax rates are reduced to offset the fiscal drag: the elimination of $T_Y$ makes the denominators smaller in (8.3) and (8.4) than in (8.1) and (8.2). The inclusion of a budget constraint forces one to recognize that government spending must be financed by some means, and that fiscal instruments cannot be manipulated independently of monetary instruments unless the budget is balanced. Different multipliers are produced by different methods of financing, as we have found with the balanced budget multiplier which is smaller than the expenditure multiplier alone due to the depressing effect of the withdrawal of funds from the private sector through increased taxation.

In a similar fashion we cannot talk about the multiplier effect of monetary policy independently of fiscal operations. Firstly, in the two- and three-sector models the size of the monetary policy multiplier depends on the size of the income tax rate, $T_Y$. If the government reduces the supply of money there will be a reduction in income and the yield of income tax will decline. With government spending at a constant level there will be a conflict with the government budget constraint and contractionary spending or taxation policy will be required. Even in the absence of a budget constraint, the presence of the income tax in the monetary policy multiplier reduces the size of the multiplier compared with the 'no-tax' multiplier ($T_Y = 0$). The income tax is a built-in stabilizer providing negative feedback just as the real supply of money does in the fiscal multipliers. Secondly, if the government aims to inject extra money into the economic system without an equivalent reduction in other assets (such as bills and bonds) held by the private sector, then it must print money and use a fiscal deficit to achieve the injection. In this case the change in the monetary instrument must be accompanied by a change in the fiscal instrument. In general we can conclude that in many cases the fiscal and monetary instruments cannot be manipulated independently of each other.

## 8.2 THE RECENT MONETARY–FISCAL POLICY DEBATE

### 8.2.1 Main points at issue

Most students who have reached this stage of the book will be aware of, and perhaps familiar with, the recent stream of articles and books on the subject of the relative significance of monetary and fiscal instruments for the control of the economy. Perhaps even more than the earlier great debate over Keynes and the Classics the present dispute puts one's sanity to the test as argument and counter argument are presented. The purpose of this section is to outline the main points at issue in the light of the comparative static analysis of fiscal and monetary policy.

The question which needs to be tackled at the outset is whether the disagreement between 'Keynesians' and 'monetarists' is fundamentally over the *theory* of how the economy works, and the role of money in particular, or over the relevance to the real world of particular elements of an agreed body of theory. In other words is it a theoretical or empirical dispute?

To begin with, it should be emphasized that nobody on either side apparently believes that money is *in theory* irrelevant to the determination of income, employment and the price level. The Keynesians have for many years used a model with a monetary sector, such as the two-sector model in Chapter III, and it does them rather less than justice to suggest that their analysis of income determination is limited to the derivation of the simple multiplier. If it is agreed then that money *is* relevant the debate must be over *either* how it operates, that is the mechanism by which it affects the real variables and the price level, *or* how much it affects these variables in practice.

The Keynesians are agreed that the mechanism by which money can affect $Y$ and $P$ is as described by the two-sector model together perhaps with the Pigou effect as incorporated into the *IS–LM* analysis in section 5.2.1. An increase in the supply of money affects $Y$ and $P$ through its impact on 'the' rate of interest and on the real value of cash balances held by consumers. In the Keynesians' interpretation 'the' rate of interest is the rate on short term financial assets thought to be close substitutes for money. The monetarists view the influence of money on expenditure decisions as being more pervasive. They see money as a substitute for financial and real assets alike so that an increase in the supply of money is expected to alter the prices (yields) of a wide range of assets. This interpretation of the impact of monetary changes would not lead one to expect the demand for money to be elastic with respect to the yields of any particular group of assets such as the financial assets whicq are important to the Keynesians' theory.

When considering the monetarists' attitude towards the mechanism by which monetary changes are transmitted to the real variables and the price level, it is necessary to insist that the means by which additional money enters the system be specified. If, as Friedman has postulated,† the money were dropped from helicopters and if money is a close substitute for real rather than financial assets, individuals would balance their portfolios of real and financial assets by directly substituting goods for money through the purchase of more goods. However, Keynesians have protested that a more realistic method of injecting money must be assumed and have argued that if the money is injected by open market operations the interest rate on bonds will fall (their price rise) and will fall more the less substitutable is money for financial assets. Much seems to

† Friedman (1969), p. 4, *et seq.*

hinge, therefore, on whether money is a close substitute for other financial assets or for real assets.

The outcome of this discussion is that the effect of money is transmitted to expenditure via the marginal rates of return on some group of assets. The Keynesians regard the financial rate as important and the monetarists favour the (real) rates on a wide range of real and financial assets. But this does not seem to be a drastic disagreement in terms of the structure of our formal models. This may explain why the model presented by Friedman as representative of the monetarists' theory has a distinctly Keynesian flavour.† The view of one critic of the extreme monetarist position is that 'there is nothing in what he [Friedman] says to make anyone change his view that changes in the monetary stock can exert an influence only if they change people's wealth or interest rates'.‡

If the theoretical disagreement is of debatable significance what can be said of the empirical sources of disagreement? Friedman has said that 'the basic differences among economists are empirical, not theoretical',§ and the question to be considered here is whether we can identify the parameters whose magnitudes are disputed and which determine the influence of money.‖

An important initial point to make is that there are two quite separate questions concerning the influence of monetary changes on aggregate money income:

(1) Is there convincing evidence that in practice the deliberate control of the supply of money has exerted a significant influence on income in money terms?

(2) Is there convincing evidence that the influence of money (if significant) has been stronger than that of changes in fiscal instruments?

In answering question (1) it is necessary to distinguish between two types of evidence.¶ The first type establishes whether the parameter values have provided an environment in which the level of money income could *theoretically* be controlled by manipulating the supply of money. In general the evidence is that the demand for money function has been stable in the United States and less certainly so in Britain, with the interest sensitivity $L_r$ fairly low. These are conditions favourable to monetary policy.†† In addition there is accumulating evidence that consumption and investment decisions are sensitive to changes in interest rates. So the *possibility* of an influence of money of the kind predicted (in the absence of limiting cases) by the formal models discussed in earlier

† Friedman (1970).
‡ Hahn (1971).
§ Friedman (1970).
‖ Two lucid surveys of econometric work in this area are: Crockett and Goodhart (1970), and Laidler (1971).
¶ This important point is made by Laidler (1971), p. 80, *et seq.*
†† See section 8.2.2.

chapters is admitted. What is not clear is how this evidence discriminates between the monetarists' and Keynesians' views on *how* the impact of money is transmitted, since tests of the *relative* significance for expenditure decisions of the interest rate on financial assets and of the yields on real assets have not been made. However, the estimates of demand for money functions do suggest that the sensitivity of the demand to changes in the rate of interest on financial assets is non-zero but small. The limiting case of the liquidity trap ($L_r \rightarrow -\infty$) and the extreme monetarist view of interest-insensitivity ($L_r = 0$) are both refuted. Some adjustment resulting from a change in the supply of money is in holdings of financial assets but money and these assets are not nearly perfect substitutes. The best guess perhaps is that money could operate partly through the interest rate on financial assets and partly through the yields on real assets.

Turning to the second type of evidence, it should be clear that the existence of an appropriate environment of parameter ($L_r$, $C_r$ and $I_r$) values does not mean that changes in the money supply *have* exerted a significant influence in practice. If the environment has been favourable we must ask whether in fact the supply of money has been manipulated deliberately by the monetary authorities and whether there has been any observable impact on money income. After an intensive survey of the evidence Laidler concludes that in various 'test' periods for the United States the money supply did change independently of aggregate income, and that correlations between $M$ and $Y$ do support a direction of causation, at least in some instances, from changes in the money supply to changes in income. For Britain, however, the evidence that the money supply has been an exogenously determined influence on income is less convincing for two reasons. Firstly, it is probable that in an attempt to peg the interest rates on financial assets the Bank of England has allowed the money supply to vary in order to offset changes in the demand for money as income varied. In this context the money supply ceases to be exogenous and a correlation between $M$ and $Y$ represents a direction of causation from $Y$ to $M$. Secondly, the money supply has been altered by substantial changes in the flow funds from abroad (short-run monetary movements). For this reason it is plausible to argue that the money supply is not entirely exogenous even if the monetary authority does exert some control over it. To the extent that greater capital inflows are attracted during times of high income and demand for money, which raise the rate of interest, a correlation between $dM$ and $dY$ will be observed which is not indicative of monetary changes influencing the level of income. In the light of these two arguments some participants in the debate have denied that, at least in Britain, the money supply has in practice been an exogenous force affecting the level of economic activity.†

The answer to question (1) above can be given more briefly. The *relative* contributions of fiscal and monetary instruments have not been at issue in the

† See, for example, Kaldor (1970b).

theoretical part of the debate, but some implications for the relative contributions have been drawn from the empirical tests of the determinants of income changes. The argument has been that because the simple correlation between $C$, the only component of $Y$ presumed to be endogenous, and $\bar{M}$ has been higher than the correlation between $C$ and exogenous expenditure ($I_0 + \bar{G}$), monetary policy is more effective in controlling income than is fiscal policy which is assumed to operate on exogenous expenditure alone.† The point will not be pursued in detail but two counter-arguments should be apparent from the models of earlier chapters and from the previous section. First, fiscal and monetary instruments are not separate entities whose contribution to stability can easily be identified separately when the government operates under a budget constraint. Second, it is incorrect to assume that fiscal policy operates only by controlling exogenous expenditure. This is obvious from the fact that the direct tax rate enters the multiplier. A correlation between $C$ and ($I_0 + \bar{G}$) says nothing about the impact of fiscal policy since the policy would be expected to affect directly both the independent *and* the dependent variable.

In summary, three points may perhaps be agreed by a majority of economists:

(a) Changes in the supply of money have affected income in the United States, and, although the same cannot be said with certainty for Britain, nevertheless in this country there probably exists an environment favourable to the use of such policy in the future. One problem which we have not looked at, but which is important for short-run stabilization policy, is the length of lag with which monetary policy takes effect. The monetarists expect it to be long and variable and Friedman at least sees this as a serious obstacle to short-run monetary policy. But the evidence on lags in the expenditure and monetary sector equations is at present extremely uncertain.‡

(b) Fiscal instruments can be used to alter the level of money income. Numerous expenditure functions in econometric models have found fiscal variables to be significant determinants,§ but again our knowledge of the lags involved is weak.‖

(c) It is better not to view monetary and fiscal instruments as if they were competitive, even mutually exclusive. The futility of attempts to demonstrate the marginal superiority of one instrument over the other is apparent to those who are not committed to the exclusive use of one or the other.

† Friedman and Meiselman (1964). See also the subsequent controversy in *American Economic Review*, September, 1965.

‡ Laidler (1971), section IV, contains a critical evaluation of the present state of knowledge on monetary policy lags.

§ See, for example, Ando and Cary Brown (1968) and Ando and Goldfeld (1968), both papers being in the same volume edited by Ando, Cary Brown and Friedlaender.

‖ The Ando *et al.* volume referred to in the previous footnote provides some evidence on the lags for the United States. Some British evidence can be found in Dasgupta and Hagger (1971), Ch. 6, section 6.6.

One has only to look beyond the models with a single target variable, for example to the problems of internal and external balance (section 6.5.2), to see that the objective should be to *coordinate* the use of the instruments rather than to choose between them.

### 8.2.2   The monetarist limiting case

Let us pursue further the theoretical implications of the controversy by introducing into the two- and three-sector models a monetarist limiting case. This is the complete insensitivity of the demand for money to changes in the financial rate of interest, $L_r \to 0$. In section 3.4, we found that the slope of the *LM* curve is

$$\frac{\partial r}{\partial Y} = -\frac{L_Y}{L_r} > 0 \tag{3.7}$$

Setting $L_r \to 0$ we see from (3.7) that the monetarist *LM* curve has a slope approaching infinity, that is the curve approaches the vertical. Since the demand for money does not respond to changes in the rate of interest no compensating change in income is required to keep the demand for money equal to the given money supply.

Consider now the significance of the monetarist limiting case for the main comparative static results of the two-sector model. Setting $L_r \to 0$ in the solutions of the model for $dY$ and $dr$, equations (3.19) and (3.20), we have the following effects of expenditure and monetary changes:

$$\frac{\partial Y}{\partial C_0} = \frac{\partial Y}{\partial I_0} = \frac{\partial Y}{\partial G} \to 0 \tag{8.5}$$

$$\frac{\partial r}{\partial C_0} = \frac{\partial r}{\partial I_0} = \frac{\partial r}{\partial G} \to \frac{-1}{(C_r + I_r)} > 0 \tag{8.6}$$

$$\frac{\partial Y}{\partial \bar{M}} = -\frac{\partial Y}{\partial L_0} \to \frac{1}{L_Y} > 0 \tag{8.7}$$

$$\frac{\partial r}{\partial \bar{M}} = -\frac{\partial r}{\partial L_0} \to \frac{1 - C_Y(1 - T_Y) - I_Y}{(C_r + I_r)L_Y} < 0 \tag{8.8}$$

The most obvious significance of the monetarist limiting case is that it eliminates the impact on income of changes in expenditure plans, including changes in government spending, as (8.5) shows. This limiting case is therefore the theoretical converse of the Keynesian liquidity trap, neutralizing the fiscal instrument as a means of controlling income in the model just as the liquidity trap neutralizes monetary policy. The impact of expenditure changes is entirely on the rate of interest; an expansion of expenditure raises the interest rate as indicated by (8.6) and by Figure 8.1. With $L_r \to 0$ the demand for money is a function only of the level of income and, given that the supply of

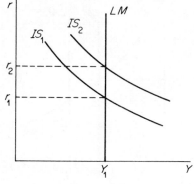

*Figure 8.1*

money is fixed, there will be only *one* income level, $Y_1$ in the figure, at which the demand for money equals the supply. Any increase in income resulting from the expansion of expenditure would raise the demand for money above the supply, and two-sector equilibrium requires that the rate of interest rise sufficiently, from $r_1$ to $r_2$, to restrict expenditure plans to the level $Y_1$ which is consistent with monetary equilibrium at income level $Y_1$.

*Qualitatively* the impact of monetary policy on income and the rate of interest is unaffected by the monetarist limiting case. An expansion of the money supply still raises income and reduces the rate of interest, as (8.7) and (8.8) show. However, the *size* of the impact of a change in the money supply on income (and also the impact on the rate of interest) is increased. The impact on income in the absence of the limiting case is given by equation (3.31), which can be rearranged as

$$\frac{\partial Y}{\partial \bar{M}} = \frac{1}{(1 - C_Y(1 - T_Y) - I_Y)\frac{L_r}{(C_r + I_r)} + L_Y} \qquad (8.9)$$

Comparing (8.9) with (8.7) it is apparent that the former is the smaller because the positive left-hand term in the denominator makes the denominator larger than that of (8.7). Figure 8.2 illustrates the situation with expansionary monetary policy shifting the $LM$ curve from $LM_1$ to $LM_2$. Given that the demand for money is interest-insensitive income must rise from $Y_1$ to $Y_2$ to raise the demand for money to the new level of the supply of money. This is achieved as the excess supply of money at income level $Y_1$ drives down the rate of interest until expenditure plans are stimulated to the level $Y_2$ at the new equilibrium rate of interest $r_2$.

The analysis of the monetarist limiting case can be extended a little by considering the three-sector model. If the two-sector equilibrium income level, $Y_1$ in Figure 8.1, is below full employment income there is no common point

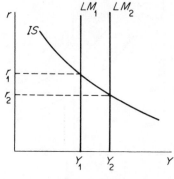

*Figure 8.2*

of intersection between *IS, LM* and $Y_f$, that is no *overall* equilibrium. Since changes in expenditure cannot, as we have seen, alter the two-sector equilibrium level of income, fiscal policy cannot be used to achieve full employment. Monetary policy, on the other hand, can be used to overcome the inconsistency of the system by shifting the *LM* to the right. If, for example, $Y_2$ in Figure 8.2 is the full employment income, then expansionary monetary policy sufficient to shift the *LM* curve from $LM_1$ to $LM_2$ is required for full employment.

## 8.3   DYNAMIC ANALYSIS OF STABILIZATION POLICY

The Samuelson multiplier–accelerator model discussed in section 7.2, assumed government expenditure to be exogenous and constant through time, and omitted any consideration of money. In order to extend this no-policy model to examine the effect of fiscal and monetary policies on the time path of income we shall have first to introduce a monetary sector and second to decide the way in which the two instruments are manipulated in an attempt to control income.†

The monetary sector incorporated is of the conventional kind analysed in Chapter III except that the variables now have time period subscripts, the demand for money being a function of the current rate of interest and income in the previous period. Using the linear form the demand for money function is

$$l_t = l_0 + l_Y Y_{t-1} + l_r r_t \qquad (8.10)$$

where $l_0 > 0$, $l_Y > 0$, $l_r < 0$. In the one-sector dynamic model planned spending was assumed to be realized within each period. We now assume also that within each period planned money holdings are achieved

$$l_0 + l_Y Y_{t-1} + l_r r_t = \bar{M} \qquad (8.11)$$

† Smyth (1963) was one of the first to extend the multiplier–accelerator model to include money.

The link between the monetary sector and expenditure decisions is provided by the interest sensitivity of investment, $i_r$ (consumption being assumed insensitive, that is $c_r = 0$). The investment function is:

$$I_t = a(C_t - C_{t-1}) + i_r r_t \tag{8.12}$$

where $i_r < 0$. Comparing equation (8.12) with equation (7.15) it is apparent that the new function is of the accelerator form but modified to allow an influence of changes in the rate of interest. With the consumption function unchanged as

$$C_t = c_0 + c_Y Y_{t-1} \tag{7.1}$$

this no-policy two-sector multiplier–accelerator model (with constant prices) can be solved for $Y_t$ in the usual way:

$$Y_t = (1 + a) c_Y Y_{t-1} - a c_Y Y_{t-2} + i_r r_t + (c_0 + \bar{G}) \tag{8.13}$$

In order to convert this into a second-order difference equation we must eliminate $r_t$, which can be achieved by solving the monetary sector equation (8.11) for $r_t$ and substituting for $r_t$ in equation (8.13). This yields the no-policy expression for $Y_t$:

$$Y_t = \left[ (1 + a) c_Y - \frac{i_r l_Y}{l_r} \right] Y_{t-1} - a c_Y Y_{t-2} + (c_0 + \bar{G}) - i_r \left( \frac{l_0 - \bar{M}}{l_r} \right) \tag{8.14}$$

Equation (8.14) can usefully be compared with the one-sector no-policy expression for $Y_t$, equation (7.17), to illuminate the effect on the system of introducing money. The coefficient for $Y_{t-2}$ is unchanged so that the boundary between damped and explosive cycles is not affected. Consequently boundary (2) in Figure 7.2 is repeated in Figure 8.3 which represents the system with a monetary sector. On the other hand the boundary between $a$, $c_Y$ combinations producing cycles and those which produce smooth growth or decline of income *is* affected. The coefficient for $Y_{t-1}$ is reduced (since $i_r l_Y/l_r$ in equation (8.14) is positive) and this pushes up boundary (1), as Figure 8.3 shows.[†] There is an increase in the number of $a$, $c_Y$ combinations which yield cyclical time paths of income.

We can now introduce first fiscal and then monetary policy into this model. Before outlining the characteristics of the fiscal policy to be studied it is necessary to define two extra variables. Let $Y_t^N$ be the level of income which would occur in period $t$ if the government did *not* undertake any stabilization policy in the current period. $Y_t^N$ is therefore the *no-policy income level* in the subsequent analysis. It will be assumed that the government has in mind a constant *target level of income* $Y^*$ and that fiscal policy consists of adjusting the level of government spending according to the gap between the income which would occur without policy and the target level of income, $Y^*$. That is, the government's level of spending in period $t$ is

$$G_t = G_0 + \mu(Y^* - Y_t^N) \tag{8.15}$$

---

† This argument assumes that the monetary effect is not strong enough to reverse the sign of the $Y_{t-1}$ coefficient; this assumption is retained throughout.

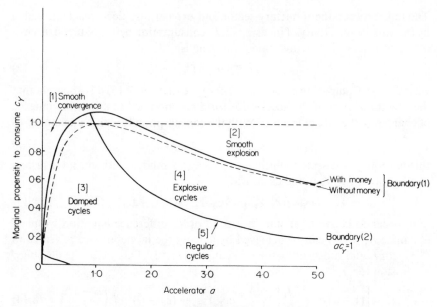

*Figure 8.3*

Equation (8.15) is the government's *reaction function*,† in which $G_0$ is the exogenous component of $G_t$ and $\mu$ is the fiscal reaction coefficient which determines the extent to which the government reacts to a given gap between $Y_t^N$ and $Y^*$. It will be assumed in the analysis to follow that $0 < \mu < 1$, which means that the fiscal authority reacts only partially to the gap. A similar partial adjustment will be assumed for monetary policy, and the objective of the analysis of the two instruments will be to compare the impact on the cycle of *partially* adjusted instruments which operate without time lags and which are based on excellent forecasting. $Y_t^N$ is assumed to be perfectly forecast when the instrument changes are made to take effect in period $t$.‡ The assumption of *partial* adjustment is plausible given the constraints on stabilization policies imposed by other policy objectives and given the likelihood of caution in the manipulation of instruments for stabilization purposes.

Substituting the expression (8.15) for the previously exogenous government expenditure in equation (8.14) we have

$$Y_t = \left[(1+a)\,c_Y - \frac{i_r\,l_Y}{l_r}\right] Y_{t-1} - ac_Y\,Y_{t-2} + (c_0 + G_0)$$
$$+ \mu(Y^* - Y_t^N) - i_r\left(\frac{l_0 - \bar{M}}{l_r}\right) \qquad (8.16)$$

† More complicated reaction functions can be devised; see Allen (1967), p. 350, *et seq.* on the work of Phillips in this area.

‡ It is assumed also, for simplicity, that the target income level coincides with the equilibrium level, i.e. $Y^* = Y^e$.

Remembering that $Y_t^N$ is the no-policy income level and is therefore equivalent to equation (8.14), we can substitute (8.14) for $Y_t^N$ in equation (8.16) and obtain the expression for $Y_t$ with fiscal policy operating:

$$Y_t = (1 - \mu)\left[(1 + a)c_Y - \frac{i_r l_Y}{l_r}\right]Y_{t-1} - (1 - \mu)ac_Y Y_{t-2} + (1 - \mu)(c_0 + G_0)$$

$$+ \mu Y^* - (1 - \mu)i_r\left(\frac{l_0 - \bar{M}}{l_r}\right) \tag{8.17}$$

If $\mu$ were equal to unity $Y_t$ would be reduced to a constant at the target income level by the perfect policy. But since $\mu$ has been restricted to less than unity the effect of fiscal policy on the basic difference equation is to reduce the absolute size of *both* the $Y_{t-1}$ and the $Y_{t-2}$ coefficient, as a comparison of equations (8.17) and (8.14) shows. This effect on the structure of the model has consequences for the income paths in the various areas of $a,c_Y$ combinations in Figure 8.3. It is most interesting, however, to investigate the consequences for *cyclical* time paths (areas [3], [4] and [5]). Three effects of policy can be identified:

(a) Within the area of cyclical $a,c_Y$ combinations the boundary (2) between damped cycles and explosive cycles is shifted upwards (see Figure 8.4). Now there are more combinations which lead to *damped* cycles than there were in the absence of policy.

(b) For any $a$, $c_Y$ combination which yielded a damped cycle in the absence of policy the cycle becomes *more damped* with fiscal policy operating. What is

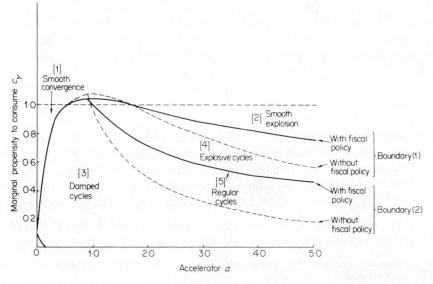

*Figure 8.4*

more, the combinations previously yielding regular cycles (i.e. those on boundary (2) in Figure 8.3) now produce *damped* cycles. This dampening effect can be regarded as stabilizing and can be illustrated with the combination $a = 2\cdot0$, $c_Y = 0\cdot5$ by finding the income time path numerically.† The result is that the no-policy income path in Figure 8.5 is eliminated and the more-damped income path is substituted.

(c) The increase in dampedness of the cycle, which is desirable because it reduces the deviations of income from the target, is accompanied by an increase in the *frequency* of the cycle.‡ The fiscal policy income path in Figure 8.5 is more damped than the no-policy path but the peaks and the

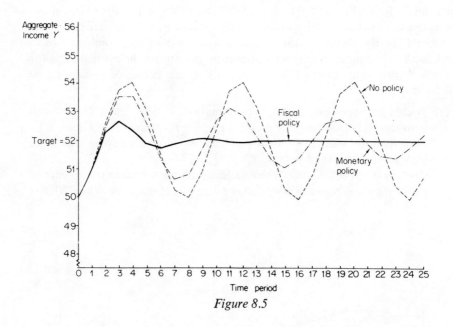

*Figure 8.5*

troughs occur more rapidly when policy is operating than when it is not. However, this frequency effect probably does not constitute a cost to society because the stabilized income path in Figure 8.5 always has a lower gradient than the original income path. The increase in frequency need not, therefore, impose any higher costs of adjustment on society.

Turning to monetary policy, we need to postulate some reaction function of the monetary authority which is analogous to equation (8.15) for fiscal policy.

† The assumed values of the other parameters $l_Y = 0\cdot25$, $l_r = -5\cdot0$, $i_r = -1\cdot5$ and $\mu = 1 - c_Y$. The assumed income target is $52\cdot0$.

‡ The frequency effect was first observed by Baumol (1961).

It will be assumed that the supply of money is manipulated proportionately to the gap expected between no-policy income and the target:

$$M_t = M_0 + m(Y^* - Y_t^N) \tag{8.18}$$

where $M_0$ is an exogenous component of the total money supply, $m$ is the monetary authority's reaction coefficient, and $0 < m < 1$ (for reasons previously stated). If there *is* a gap between the no-policy income level expected in period $t$ and the income target, then the supply of money is varied from the level $M_0$, which is associated with an equilibrium income at the target level. If there is no gap the supply of money is *left* at $M_0$ (in the case of that amount of money being in circulation in period $t - 1$) or is *returned* to $M_0$ (in the event of the money supply not being equal to $M_0$ in period $t - 1$). This implies a particular interpretation of monetary policy in cases where the target level of income is expected to be achieved without policy intervention. 'No monetary policy' requires the monetary authority to *actively* return $M_t$ to the level $M_0$, if $M_{t-1} \neq M_0$. In the case of fiscal policy if $G_0$ is the required level of spending in period $t$ the government just stops spending any amount in excess of $G_0$, but since the supply of money in excess of $M_0$ does not exhaust itself (being a stock rather than a flow as in the case of government spending) the government must actively reduce the supply of money to return us to $M_0$. If the government did not do this but rather operated on a reaction function similar to (8.18) but with $M_{t-1}$ replacing $M_0$, the effect of monetary policy in the previous period would 'hang over' into the current period, so that $M_{t-1}$ would enter the difference equation for $Y_t$ and quite different effects of monetary policy would be observed.†

Substituting $M_t$ from equation (8.18) into the expression for $Y_t$, equation (8.14), the equation for income with monetary policy operating is obtained in a similar way to the derivation of the fiscal policy income equation (8.17). The result is:

$$Y_t = \left(1 - \frac{i_r m}{l_r}\right)\left[(1 + a)c_Y - \frac{i_r l_Y}{l_r}\right] Y_{t-1} - \left(1 - \frac{i_r m}{l_r}\right) a c_Y Y_{t-2}$$
$$+ \left(1 - \frac{i_r m}{l_r}\right)\left(c_0 + \bar{G} - \frac{i_r(l_0 - M_0)}{l_r} + \frac{i_r m Y^*}{l_r}\right) \tag{8.19}$$

This rather forbidding second-order difference equation, which determines the time path of income when monetary policy is operating, can in fact be interpreted fairly simply to provide a comparison with the situation under fiscal policy as expressed in equation (8.17). Comparing equation (8.19) with the no-policy equation (8.14) it is apparent that the impact of policy depends on the term $[1 - (i_r m/l_r)]$. It should be said straight away that there is an important

---

† The equation for $Y_t$ in this case could not be solved algebraically and we would have to rely on simulations to produce numerical results for the income path.

difference between fiscal and monetary policy as regards their effect on the structure of the equation for $Y_t$. The condition that $0 < \mu < 1$ is *sufficient* to guarantee that the absolute sizes of the coefficients for $Y_{t-1}$ and $Y_{t-2}$ are reduced by fiscal policy. By contrast the condition $0 < m < 1$ is *not* sufficient to guarantee that the two coefficients are reduced by monetary policy. They will be reduced as long as $[1 - (i_r m/l_r)] > -1$. Let us pause for a moment to consider the significance of this expression. The impact of monetary policy is determined by the combination of the parameters $i_r$, $m$ and $l_r$. This can be seen if we ask what happens in the limiting cases which the comparative static theory showed to nullify monetary policy. If we set either $i_r = 0$ or $l_r \rightarrow -\infty$ (or of course $m = 0$ which implies no reaction by the monetary authority) then the expression $[1 - (i_r m/l_r)]$ reduces to 1 and policy has no effect on the income time path because the $Y_{t-1}$ and $Y_{t-2}$ coefficients are unaltered. Now, the greater is $i_r m$ relative to $l_r$ the greater is the risk that $[1 - (i_r m/l_r)] < -1$. If for example investment is very sensitive to changes in the rate of interest ($i_r$ large) and the demand for money is very insensitive to such changes ($l_r$ near to zero) then this possibility will occur. But what does it imply?

Let us divide the analysis of the impact of monetary policy into two cases:

(1) If $[1 - (i_r m/l_r)] > -1$ then the absolute sizes of the $Y_{t-1}$ and $Y_{t-2}$ coefficients are reduced and the impact of monetary policy is *qualitatively* similar to fiscal policy. Monetary policy also brings about the consequences (a)–(c) identified on page 175. Using the same example $a, c_Y$ combination as before ($a = 2 \cdot 0$, $c_Y = 0 \cdot 5$) the income time path of monetary policy is as shown in Figure 8.5. Comparing the fiscal and monetary policy income paths in the diagram it is apparent that with the parameter values assumed† fiscal policy dampens the cycle more rapidly than monetary policy. However, results more favourable to monetary policy can be obtained by assuming, as the monetarists would wish, a lower value for $l_r$ or a higher value for $i_r$. Setting, for example, $l_r = -1 \cdot 0$ instead of $l_r = -5 \cdot 0$, we find, in Figure 8.6, that the speed with which income is damped to the target is much the same for fiscal policy as for monetary policy. This illustrates the important point that the effectiveness of stabilization policy in dampening the cycle is determined by the underlying structure of the economy. The importance of econometric work on the estimation of demand for money functions, investment functions and so on is apparent. Without a sound knowledge of the size of the central parameters no estimate can be made of the *quantitative* impact of policy instruments on the target variables.

(2) If $[1 - (i_r m/l_r)] < -1$ then the absolute sizes of the $Y_{t-1}$ and $Y_{t-2}$ coefficients are *increased* with the result that monetary policy *reduces* the dampedness of a damped cycle, converts regular cycles into explosive cycles and increases the rate of explosion of explosive cycles. It is worth remembering that

† The same as in the first footnote on page 176, plus $m = 0 \cdot 33$.

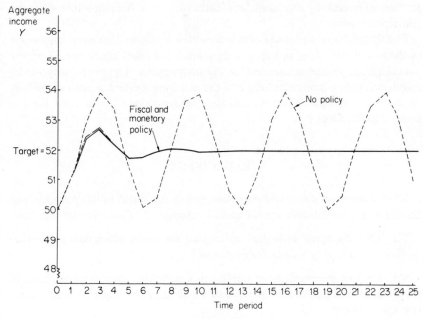

*Figure 8.6*

the risk of this destabilizing policy effect is greater the nearer is $l_r$ to zero. The danger of monetary policy which is effective in terms of the size of the policy multiplier is that in a dynamic context the instrument could be de-stabilizing. The reason why this risk is attached to monetary policy more than fiscal policy is that, by its nature, monetary policy is *indirect* in its impact on expenditure decisions and is determined by the parameters $i_r$ and $l_r$ as well as $m$. Establishing the limitation $\mu < 1$ on the fiscal reaction coefficient is sufficient to prevent de-stabilizing fiscal policy in the model without lags and forecasting errors. Establishing a similar constraint on $m$ is, as we have seen, *not* sufficient. For de-stabilizing policy to be avoided a more severe constraint on $m$ is necessary, which is, from the expression $[1 - (i_r m/l_r)] > -1$, that $l_r/i_r > (1/2)m$. The smaller is $l_r$ (or the greater is $i_r$), and therefore the more sensitive is expenditure to a change in the supply of money, the smaller must be the monetary reaction coefficient $m$ if de-stabilizing policy is to be avoided. Both of the numerical examples we have used, $l_r = -5 \cdot 0$ or $-1 \cdot 0$, $i_r = -1 \cdot 5$ and $m = 0 \cdot 33$ satisfy the condition for monetary policy to be stabilizing.

If $[1 - (i_r m/l_r)] = 0$ we have the special case which is equivalent to $\mu = 1$ for fiscal policy. The impact of monetary stabilization policy then is to reduce income to a constant at the target level, which is perfect stabilization policy. This requires the monetary authority to set $m = l_r/i_r$ which may or may not be compatible with the requirements of other policy objectives and with the caution exercised by the monetary authority, that is compatible with the restrictions on $m$.

Finally, perhaps we should conclude with a reminder that our comparison of fiscal and monetary policy in a dynamic model has concentrated on the partial nature of the adjustment of the instruments. The probability of destabilizing policy is increased either if the instrument operates with a time lag, or if the government bases its decisions on inaccurate forecasts of the no-policy income level $Y_t^N$.

## EXERCISES

**8.1** 'The use of fiscal and monetary policy for stabilization purposes too readily assumes that inflation is demand-determined.' Comment on this view.

**8.2** Do you agree with the verdict that the main differences separating monetarists and Keynesians are empirical?

**8.3** Outline the problems of stabilization policy which become apparent in the dynamic analysis of such policy but which are not evident from comparative static theory.

# CHAPTER IX

# An Introduction to Growth Theory

In previous chapters the main concern has been with short-run changes in macroeconomic variables. The models presented were used to explain the use of fiscal and monetary instruments to control the economy in the short run. The short-run analysis is obviously limited by the severe assumption that changes in production are achieved only through variations in the degree of utilization of a given labour force, with the stock of real capital, $K^R$, constant. It is now time to consider the effects of changes in both the size of the labour force and the size of the real capital stock, which brings us to the process of economic growth. The objective of this chapter is to explain the development of two models of growth, which will enable us to identify some of the theoretical problems of using policy instruments to control growth. No attempt is made to examine a range of growth models which is representative of the present state of the theory of growth.† But an effort will be made to express the models discussed in terms which make clear the features that they have in common with the static models. This may help to bridge the gap between the static macroeconomic theory and the advanced theory of growth.

## 9.1 THE HARROD–DOMAR GROWTH MODEL

### 9.1.1 Assumptions

The assumptions of the Harrod–Domar model in the basic form considered here are that

(1) there is no monetary sector and the price level is constant;

† Sen (1970), provides a lucid survey in his introduction. More comprehensive surveys of growth models can be found in Allen (1967), Ch. 10–16, and in Hahn and Matthews (1965).

(2) the existing labour force is offered for employment with perfect elasticity at a constant real wage rate;

(3) the proportion of income saved (that is the average propensity to save) does not alter as income changes. This implies of course a proportional relationship between $S$ and $Y$;

(4) the ratio of labour units to capital units required to produce one unit of output, that is, the capital–labour ratio, $K^R/N$, is fixed. The relative capital or labour intensity of the production process cannot be varied;

(5) there is no technical progress.

### 9.1.2  Output and capital

The first step is to drop the assumption of Chapter IV that labour is the only variable input in the production process. We can postulate a production function of the general form:

$$Y = Y(K^R, N) = \min(vK^R, zN) \tag{9.1}$$

where $K^R$ and $N$ are the quantities of capital and labour employed, and $v = Y/K^R$ and $z = Y/N$, the output–capital and output–labour ratios, are fixed. The expression 'min' on the right-hand side means that the maximum output achievable is determined by the size of the *smaller* of the two terms $vK^R$ and $zN$. If, for example, $vK^R < zN$ then the availability of capital limits output to a level less than could be achieved if all labour were employed with adequate capital.

Since the factor proportions are fixed for all levels of output we can state

$$\frac{Y}{K^R} = \frac{dY}{dK^R} = v \tag{9.2}$$

and

$$\frac{Y}{N} = \frac{dY}{dN} = z \tag{9.3}$$

Note that the derivatives $dY$, $dK^R$ etc. in this chapter are read as *derivatives with respect to time*, that is as $dY/dt$, $dK^R/dt$ etc. Equations (9.2) and (9.3) state that the average equals the marginal output–capital ratio; and the average equals the marginal output–labour ratio.

From equation (9.2) we have

$$Y = vK^R \tag{9.4}$$

which implies

$$dY = v\,dK^R \tag{9.5}$$

This says that the total output *supplied* is equal to output per unit of capital input $v$ times the capital input. Changes in the output supplied at any price level (assumed constant in this model), and therefore the extent of the shift to the right of the aggregate supply curve, are determined by the amount of output produced by a unit of capital and by the increase in the capital stock, the level of investment.

We have considered so far the changes in the *maximum* output which can be produced as the capital stock is increased. If capital is to be fully employed it is necessary (starting from a position of equilibrium between aggregate supply and demand) for the growth of output supplied to be matched by a growth in the level of aggregate demand.

The representation of the determinants of aggregate demand is typically extremely simple in growth models, many of the developments in the more complex models having been on the supply side. It is common to adopt an expenditure sector which makes consumption a function of income alone and investment exogenous, and omits the public sector altogether. This lack of interest in expenditure decisions is not surprising with the recent concentration on models in which planned investment is magically equated (automatically) to the level of saving planned out of full employment income.[†] With the same degree of simplification as that used by the more sophisticated models, we can define aggregate *demand* as

$$Y = C + I = C + dK^R \tag{9.6}$$

or

$$Y = \frac{1}{1 - C_Y} dK^R = \frac{1}{S_Y} dK^R \tag{9.7}$$

Taking the differential of equation (9.6) we have for a change in output demanded:

$$dY = \frac{1}{1 - C_Y} dI = \frac{1}{S_Y} dI \tag{9.8}$$

As we have said, the requirement for the maintenance of the full employment of capital is that changes in the potential output supplied be equal to changes in output demanded. Therefore, setting supply from equation (9.4) equal to demand from equation (9.7) yields:

$$Y = vK^R = \frac{1}{S_Y} dK^R \tag{9.9}$$

or

$$\frac{dK^R}{K^R} = vS_Y \tag{9.10}$$

This is the rate of growth of the capital stock which secures equilibrium in the product market and the full employment of capital This can be converted into

† See Hahn and Matthews (1965), section 1.4, p. 12. Models which make this classical type of assumption are called 'neo-classical'.

a required rate of growth of income. With $v$ constant rearranging equation (9.2) yields:

$$\frac{dY}{Y} = \frac{dK^R}{K^R} \qquad (9.11)$$

which implies that the required income growth rate is:

$$\frac{dY}{Y} = vS_Y = g_w \qquad (9.12)$$

Both capital and income must grow at the same rate $g_w$ which is known as the *warranted rate of growth*. With a constant savings ratio the rate of growth of saving is the same as the income growth rate. At the same time investment must grow at the same rate as the capital stock so that in equilibrium the rates of growth of planned saving and investment are equal.

### 9.1.3  Output and labour

We have referred so far only to the employment of capital. The next task is to establish the conditions for the full employment of the labour force ($N = N_f$) as income, aggregate demand and the capital stock grow. Using the output–labour restriction represented by equation (9.3) we find, by the rearrangement of that equation, the amount of labour demanded in order to produce a given output $Y$:

$$N^D = \left(\frac{1}{z}\right) Y \qquad (9.13)$$

which, with $z$ constant, implies also that

$$dN^D = \left(\frac{1}{z}\right) dY \qquad (9.14)$$

Turning to the supply of labour (at a given real wage rate) it will be assumed that the size of the labour force grows at a constant percentage rate $n$ which is exogenously determined:

$$\frac{dN^S}{N^S} = n \qquad (9.15)$$

For the labour market to be kept in equilibrium it is necessary for the rate of growth of the demand for labour to be equal to the rate of growth of the labour supply. The rate of growth of labour demand is found from equations (9.13) and (9.14):

$$\frac{dN^D}{N^D} = \frac{dY}{Y} \qquad (9.16)$$

Equating this rate to the rate of growth of supply of labour, equation (9.15), we have the condition for the maintenance of full employment of the labour force:

$$\frac{dN^S}{N^S} = \frac{dN^D}{N^D} = \frac{dY}{Y} = n \tag{9.17}$$

Income must grow at the same rate as the labour force, and this is called the *natural rate of growth* $g_n$.

### 9.1.4 The condition for steady growth

In the static analysis of earlier chapters much of the effort was directed at establishing the conditions to be satisfied for the system to be in equilibrium, and at a comparison of different equilibrium positions (comparative statics). One of the characteristics of static equilibrium is that the values of the variables in the system will remain constant unless the equilibrium is disturbed.

By analogy with the static theory, growth theory attempts to establish the conditions under which the *rate of growth* of the variables in the system will remain constant. This is the counterpart of static equilibrium and is known as *steady-state growth*. The extension of the analysis which is closest to comparative statics is a comparison of the rates of growth of the variables in different steady states, referred to as comparative dynamics. In the discussion which follows we will be concerned mostly with the conditions for a steady state to exist, although the characteristics of different equilibria will be compared briefly in section 9.3.

It should be clear from the analysis of section 9.1.2 that the rate of growth of income cannot permanently exceed or fall short of the rate of growth of the capital stock. Because, in this model, the output–capital ratio is fixed a rate of growth of income in excess of the rate of growth of capital cannot be maintained due to a shortage of capital, and one lower than the rate of growth capital leads to capital being unemployed. Similarly, if labour is to be fully employed the rate of growth of income cannot exceed or fall short of the rate of growth of the labour force. Consequently if an income growth rate is to be sustained, the requirement for a steady state, it must satisfy the condition:

$$\frac{dY}{Y} = g_w = g_n = vS_Y = n \tag{9.18}$$

The warranted and natural rates of growth must be equal. But unfortunately the three factors which enter this condition, the average propensity to save and output–capital ratio parameters, and the (exogenous) rate of growth of the labour force, are determined independently of each other. There is no guarantee that they will take on values which satisfy equation (9.18), and in the model which has been described there is no adjustment mechanism which operates to move the values towards a combination which would produce a steady state.

The Harrod–Domar model is a rigid construct and growth models have since been developed which do not use the same restrictive assumptions.† It is possible with rather minor modifications to introduce policy instruments into the model. For example, the rate of growth of aggregate demand may be made a function of government spending and tax rates simply by introducing a government into the expenditure sector, and the rate of growth of capital creation may be affected by government fixed investment.‡ However, it is doubtful whether minor changes in the Harrod–Domar model are productive as a means of analysing policy for growth, particularly since much of the recent interest in growth theory has centred on models which relax the crucial assumption of the fixed output–capital and output–labour ratios. It is to a model of this kind that we now turn.

## 9.2   THE NEO-CLASSICAL MODEL

### 9.2.1   Developing the basic model

A divergence of the warranted rate from the natural rate of growth means that the simultaneous full employment of both factor inputs is not achieved. Naturally we would like to know whether there exists any equilibrating mechanism to eliminate such a divergence or whether government intervention will be required to achieve this end. A glance at equation (9.18) suggests that adjustments might be made in the output–capital ratio $v$, the savings ratio $S_Y$, or the rate of growth of the labour force $n$. When account is taken of labour-saving technical progress the equilibrium condition (9.18) can be rewritten as

$$vS_Y = n + \phi \qquad (9.19)$$

where $\phi$ is the proportional rate of technical progress. In this case there is a fourth possible means of bringing the warranted and natural rates into equality. Much literature has been generated by the investigation of the possibility of automatic adjustments in $v$, $S_Y$, $n$ or $\phi$. Since these efforts are well surveyed elsewhere§ let us concentrate on adjustments in $v$ as envisaged by the neo-classical model.‖

In contrast to the Harrod–Domar model, the neo-classical model assumes that capital and labour can be substituted for each other. In fact the extreme assumption is made that there are an indefinitely large number of production processes available, so that the ratio of capital to labour used in producing a

---

† See Hahn and Matthews (1965), pp. 6–7.
‡ See Peacock and Shaw (1971), pp. 99–101.
§ Sen (1970), p. 16, *et seq.*; Hahn and Matthews (1965), p. 6, *et seq.*
‖ Originating in the work of Solow (1956) and Swan (1956).

given output can be varied continuously. The resulting production function is of the form

$$Y = Y(K^R, N) \qquad (9.20)$$

It is assumed that an increase in the input of one factor, while the other remains constant, is subject to diminishing returns. That is:

$$Y_K' = \frac{\partial Y}{\partial K^R} > 0, \qquad Y_K'' = \frac{\partial^2 Y}{\partial (K^R)^2} < 0$$

and

$$Y_N' = \frac{\partial Y}{\partial N} > 0, \qquad Y_N'' = \frac{\partial^2 Y}{\partial N^2} < 0$$

It is the assumption about the variability of the capital–labour ratio which constitutes the basic difference between the Harrod–Domar and neo-classical models. In other respects they are the same: the expenditure sector is similar, with its assumed constant savings ratio, and the rate of growth of the labour force is exogenous to both models. But while the condition to be satisfied for steady state growth proves to be the same in both models (as we shall see) the emphasis in the neo-classical case is more on *how* the system will move from a disequilibrium (unsteady state) situation to a steady state. The analysis then centres on establishing the direction in which the factor mix used, i.e. the capital–labour ratio $K^R/N$, will alter in disequilibrium, and by implication the (equilibrium) condition on which the capital–labour ratio will not change at all.

In the literature the analysis is sometimes couched in terms of the absolute values of $Y$ and $K^R$, and sometimes in *per capita* $Y$ and $K^R$ terms. This can be confusing and we will present *both* forms to show that the two analyses lead to the same result.

The demand side of the model can be taken straight from the Harrod–Domar model. Consequently, we have from equation (9.7):

$$dK^R = S_Y Y \qquad (9.21)$$

Setting the supply of output equal to the demand for output we can substitute for $Y$ in the demand equation (9.21) using $Y$ from the supply equation (9.20). The result is the change in the capital stock which is consistent with the full employment of capital:

$$dK^R = S_Y Y(K, N) \qquad (9.22)$$

At this point the emphasis of the analysis departs from that of the Harrod–Domar model. We wish to find the determinants of changes in the capital–labour ratio, $K^R/N$. To begin with, the rate of change of the capital–labour ratio can be defined as the difference between the rates of change of $K^R$ and $N$.

Using the quotient rule, differentiate $K^R/N$, divide through by $K^R/N$ and you have:

$$\frac{d(K^R/N)}{K^R/N} = \frac{\dfrac{N\,dK^R - K^R\,dN}{N^2}}{K^R/N} = \frac{dK^R}{K^R} - \frac{dN}{N} \tag{9.23}$$

But $dN/N = n$ and $dK^R = S_Y\,Y(K^R, N)$ from equation (9.22), so that:

$$\frac{d(K^R/N)}{K^R/N} = \frac{S_Y\,Y(K^R, N)}{K^R} - n \tag{9.24}$$

which says that the rate of change of the capital–labour ratio is equal to the difference between the first term which is the warranted rate of growth $g_w$, and the second term, the natural rate of growth $g_n$. If the two growth rates are equal the rate of change of $K^R/N$ will be zero. The requirement for a constant $K^R/N$ is therefore

$$\frac{S_Y\,Y(K^R, N)}{K^R} - n = 0$$

or

$$\frac{Y}{K^R} = \frac{n}{S_Y} \tag{9.25}$$

Since $Y/K^R = v$ equation (9.25) can be rewritten as the equation (9.18) previously derived:

$$vS_Y = n \tag{9.18}$$

The condition for a constant $K^R/N$ is therefore the same as the condition for a steady state in the Harrod–Domar model. In equilibrium the two models are the same, but the neo-classical model explains what happens if $g_w \neq g_n$. Two cases can be distinguished. If

$$\frac{S_Y\,Y(K^R, N)}{K^R} - n = g_w - g_n > 0$$

then a labour shortage results. If factor prices are flexible labour will become more expensive relative to capital, and capital will be substituted for labour at the margin. This reduces the output–capital ratio and reduces $(Y/K^R)S_Y$ towards $n$; that is the warranted falls towards the natural rate. If, on the other hand:

$$\frac{S_Y\,Y(K^R, N)}{K^R} - n = g_w - g_n < 0$$

then a capital shortage results. Capital becomes more expensive relative to labour and labour is substituted for capital so that $Y/K^R$ is increased. The warranted rate then rises towards the natural rate.

Only if the capital–labour ratio reaches the level $n/S_Y$ is equilibrium achieved and does the adjustment of $Y/K^R$ cease. The neo-classical model is therefore characterized by stable equilibrium, but it should be noted that all of the adjustment is towards the *natural* rate of growth. Since the natural rate is exogenously determined the model is unable to *explain* the determinants of the equilibrium rate of growth of income $n$.†

### 9.2.2   An alternative exposition in *per capita* terms

The main result of the neo-classicists can be restated in *per capita* terms and this does have certain advantages when we consider further the characteristics of the model in equilibrium in section 9.3.‡

It is necessary at this point to be more specific about the form of the production function. It will be assumed that there are constant returns to scale, that is the function is homogeneous of degree one. This means that increasing *both* of the inputs $K$ and $N$ together by the same multiple $\lambda$ increases output by the same multiple.§ Consequently

$$Y = Y(K^R, N) \tag{9.20}$$

becomes

$$\lambda Y = Y(\lambda K^R, \lambda N) = \lambda Y(K^R, N) \tag{9.26}$$

If we set $\lambda = 1/N$ the production function can be written in terms of output and capital input *per capita*:

$$\frac{Y}{N} = Y\left(\frac{K^R}{N}, 1\right) \tag{9.27}$$

The condition for a constant capital–labour ratio can now be rewritten. Equation (9.21) becomes

$$\frac{dK^R}{N} = S_Y \frac{Y}{N} \tag{9.28}$$

and substituting in (9.28) for $Y$ from equation (9.27) we have the *per capita* equivalent of equation (9.22)

$$\frac{dK^R}{N} = S_Y\, Y\left(\frac{K^R}{N}, 1\right) \tag{9.29}$$

Following equation (9.23), but substituting *per capita* capital $K^R/N$ for $K^R$ the percentage change in $K^R/N$ is:

$$\frac{d(K^R/N)}{K^R/N} = \frac{dK^R/N}{K^R/N} - \frac{dN}{N} \tag{9.30}$$

† This is true also where the model is extended to make the natural rate of growth dependent on $n$ and on the rate of growth of labour-saving technology $\phi$. Typically $\phi$ is assumed exogenous also. See Sen, p. 25.

‡ The formal exposition here may also assist in the understanding of *per capita* growth models expressed diagrammatically, such as Johnson (1967), Ch. IV.

§ See Allen (1967), p. 315, and section 1.4.2 above.

or

$$\frac{d(K^R/N)}{K^R/N} = \frac{S_Y\, Y\!\left(\dfrac{K^R}{N}, 1\right)}{K^R/N} - n \tag{9.31}$$

which is the equivalent of equation (9.24) in *per capita* terms. It will be convenient to express this in terms of the absolute change in $K^R/N$ rather than the proportionate rate of change, so we multiply equation (9.31) by $K^R/N$ and obtain

$$d\!\left(\frac{K^R}{N}\right) = S_Y\, Y(K^R/N, 1) - (K^R/N)n \tag{9.32}$$

The change in the capital–labour ratio, i.e. capital per head, is the difference between the amount of capital per worker created (equals saving *per capita* $S_Y\, Y(K^R/N, 1)$) and the amount by which the level of capital per worker is reduced by the increase in the labour force, $(K^R/N)n.$†

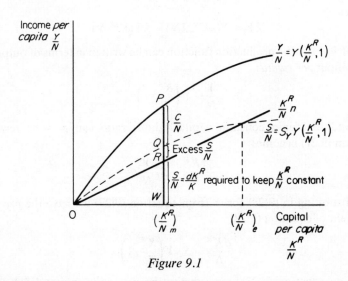

*Figure 9.1*

The neo-classical model in *per capita* terms is illustrated in Figure 9.1 where income (equals output) *per capita* is on the vertical axis and capital *per capita* on the horizontal axis. The purpose of the analysis of the neo-classical model

† 
$$d\!\left(\frac{K^R}{N}\right) = \frac{dK^R N - dN K^R}{N^2}$$

and therefore with $dK^R = 0$ the change in the capital–labour ratio attributable to a change in the size of the labour force is:

$$d\!\left(\frac{K^R}{N}\right) = \frac{-K^R}{N}\frac{dN}{N} = -\frac{K^R}{N}n$$

has been to show that $K^R/N$ will converge on an equilibrium value which sets the income growth rate equal to $n$. In the diagram the $Y/N$ curve represents the *per capita* production function. The $S/N$ curve is saving *per capita* and is derived from the $Y/N$ curve given the constant savings ratio $S/Y$ which in the figure is equal to $QW/PW$. The $S/N$ curve is of course the amount of capital created *per capita*, the first term on the right-hand side of equation (9.32). Finally, the $(K^R/N)n$ curve, with a slope equal to $n$, is the amount by which $K^R/N$ is reduced by the increase in the labour force, the second term in equation (9.32), and can alternatively be viewed as the amount of capital creation required to keep $K^R/N$ constant.

Consider the situation if the capital–labour ratio is $(K^R/N)_m$. At this point output *per capita* is $WP$ and saving and capital creation *per capita* are $WQ$. But $WQ$ is in excess, by the amount $RQ$, of the capital creation (*per capita*) required to keep $K^R/N$ constant which is $WR$. The excess $RQ$ can be used to *raise* the $K^R/N$ ratio, and a similar adjustment will occur at any capital–labour ratio below $(K^R/N)_e$. Analogously, at capital–labour ratios above $(K^R/N)_e$ the capital creation *per capita* is *less* than that required to keep the capital available to each worker constant, and the $K^R/N$ ratio must decline. These adjustments in the $K^R/N$ ratio will occur in response to changes in the relative factor prices as previously explained.

The system adjusts to $(K^R/N)_e$. At this point in the diagram we have

$$\frac{S}{N} = S_Y \frac{Y}{N} = \frac{K^R}{N} n \qquad (9.33)$$

Multiplying (9.33) through by $N$ we see that at $(K^R/N)_e$ the condition $n = S_Y Y/K^R$, for the equality of the warranted and natural rates, holds. The adjustment mechanism in the neo-classical model moves the system to a steady rate of growth of income equal to $n$.

## 9.3 THE ROLE OF MONETARY AND FISCAL POLICY

Both the Harrod–Domar and the neo-classical models make many abstractions from reality as the list of assumptions in section 9.1.1 indicates, but the neo-classical model does require in addition the assumption that factor prices are perfectly flexible. Even with capital and labour being *technically* substitutable, factor price rigidities, such as the downward inflexibility of the real wage rate or the real rate of interest, will prevent the automatic adjustment of $K^R/N$ towards $(K^R/N)_e$ through the substitution of one factor for the other at the margin. But even if the capital–labour ratio does adjust the warranted rate automatically, a case can still be made for government intervention in the form of monetary or fiscal policy, though of course the case would be strengthened by the existence of factor price rigidity.†

† Ignoring for simplicity other possible adjustment mechanisms such as variations in the savings ratio $S_Y$. See Allen (1967), p. 215, and Kaldor (1970a).

In the neo-classical model with its automatic adjustment there are two possible roles for fiscal or monetary policy:

(1) to speed up the movement towards the steady state growth;
(2) to change the income and consumption *per capita* characteristics of the steady state.

The discussion of policy will concentrate on these two roles but it should be borne in mind that, outside the framework of the basic neo-classical model with an exogenous natural rate of growth, further functions of policy can be imagined. For example, if the natural rate depended on the rate of technical progress embodied in new investment, fiscal investment incentives would have long-run growth effects. If, to take another example, investment were not automatically equated to planned saving as it is in the neo-classical model, fiscal and monetary policy would be needed to adjust the rate of growth of aggregate demand to equal the rate of growth of supply so that capital would be fully employed.†

Considering first the speed of adjustment, the neo-classical models predict that the warranted rate of growth will adjust to the natural rate, but they do not indicate whether the adjustment process would be rapid enough to be acceptable in practice. It has been argued that, given realistic values of the parameters of the model, the adjustment would be exceedingly slow—perhaps up to a hundred years.‡ While this estimate of the adjustment period has been challenged, the possibility remains that adjustments in the warranted rate of growth will take a considerable time to work themselves out.§ The role of fiscal policy in this context would be to speed up the adjustment. This could be done by attempting to alter the relative prices of capital and labour. If an increase in $K^R/N$ is needed, subsidies to the introduction of labour-saving capital equipment or employment taxes could help the factor prices, and thereby the $K^R/N$ ratio, to adjust. Monetary policy to alter the rate of return on capital relative to the real wage rate could have similar consequences. Alternatively, the government could leave the factor prices to be market determined, but alter the *amount* of adjustment in $K^R/N$ required by altering the savings ratio and, as a result, the equilibrium capital–labour ratio. While this type of policy would reduce the adjustment time, it would also affect the *per capita* income and consumption characteristics of equilibrium so it can be examined in connection with the role (2) mentioned previously.

In Figure 9.1 we plotted income and saving *per capita* curves and a capital creation requirement line $(K^R/N)n$, with consumption per head at any level of $K^R/N$ being the vertical distance between the $Y/N$ and $S/N$ curves. One advantage of the exposition of the model in *per capita* terms is that it shows the

† See Cornwall (1963).
‡ Sato (1963).
§ Sato (1966) and Conlisk (1966).

variability of $Y/N$ and $S/N$ even though the rate of growth $n$ does not change. With a given savings ratio $S_Y$ in Figure 9.2 income *per capita* rises as $K^R/N$ rises and consumption *per capita* increases up to $LM$, which is achieved at the $K^R/N$ ratio $(K^R/N)_1$. At $(K^R/N)_1$ the $Y/N$ and $(K^R/N)n$ curves are parallel, which satisfies the condition for maximum consumption *per capita*, that the marginal product of capital (*per capita*) in terms of income (*per capita*) be just equal to the growth rate $n$. This condition for maximum consumption per head is known as the 'golden rule' of capital accumulation.

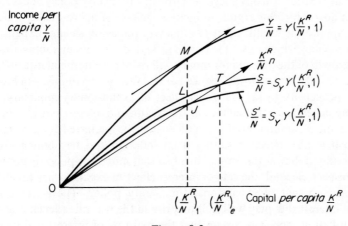

*Figure 9.2*

With the savings ratio $S_Y$ the steady state equilibrium at $(K^R/N)_e$ does not maximize consumption *per capita*. But a reduction in the capital–labour ratio to $(K^R/N)_1$ could be achieved if fiscal or monetary policy were used to pivot the $S/N$ function to $S'/N$, creating a new equilibrium at $J$. Compared with $T$ the position $J$ has a lower level of income and saving but higher consumption *per capita*.

In the basic neo-classical model which has been presented formally there is no government and no public sector. A full analysis of fiscal and monetary policy would therefore require an elaboration of the model, but it is sufficient for this brief discussion to outline the implications of such an exercise. The introduction of a government in the simple form implies a savings function of the kind used in Chapter II:

$$S = S_Y Y(1 - T_Y) \qquad (9.34)$$

so that adjustments in the direct tax rate $T_Y$ alter the proportion of pre-tax income saved (and invested) in the private sector. In addition the government may employ as an instrument variations in the proportion of government spending used for the creation of capital. Either way, the capital creation curve $S/N$ can theoretically be altered towards $S'/N$, while the curve is now interpreted as the sum of private and government saving channelled into private and government investment.

The use of monetary policy to alter the saving-consumption characteristics of the steady state is more difficult to interpret and can be analysed only within a model with variable prices. If the nominal money supply is expanded at a rate greater than $n$ then inflation will result, which reduces the demand for real cash balances as holders of cash expect to incur real capital losses. The decline in real wealth held is accompanied by a decline in the proportion of (*per capita*) income consumed, an increase in the saving (*per capita*) available for capital creation.† Conversely, deflationary monetary policy shifts the $S/N$ function down. But this argument ignores the rate of interest effect which will tend to oppose the wealth effect of monetary policy on saving. Expansionary monetary policy which raises the rate of growth of the money supply above the rate of growth of the demand for money will reduce the nominal rate of interest and (due to inflation) *a fortiori* reduce the real rate, which in turn will lower the average propensity to save. The *net* effect of expansionary monetary policy on saving depends on the balance of the wealth and interest rate effects. Since the outcome is ambiguous fiscal policy may be preferred for two reasons. First, real wealth effects resulting from inflation can be obtained by any expansionary policy at full employment so that monetary policy is not unique in this respect. Second, the rate of interest effect of expansionary fiscal policy is opposite to that of expansionary monetary policy. The increase in the nominal interest rate may well lead to a rise in the real rate (depending on the rate of inflation) and it is certain that the real rate of interest will be higher with expansionary fiscal policy than with equally expansionary monetary policy. In the case of fiscal policy, therefore, the effect of expansionary policy is unambiguously to increase $S/N$ as long as the real rate of interest is raised. Referring back to Figure 9.2, fiscal policy can move us towards equilibrium at $(K^R/N)_1$ and thereby increase consumption *per capita* while the rate of growth of income remains equal to $n$.

## EXERCISES

**9.1** 'The Harrod–Domar model is too pessimistic, and the simple neo-classical model too optimistic, about the likelihood of sustained, stable growth being achieved.' In this view fallacious?

**9.2** Demonstrate that the condition for a constant capital–labour ratio in the neo-classical model is the same as the condition for sustained growth in the Harrod–Domar model.

† Arguments about the impact of monetary policy on the average propensity to save through the effect on prices and real wealth have been made by Tobin (1965); and Johnson (1967), Ch. IV.

# Table of Symbols[†]

| Symbol | Mathematical definition | Economic definition |
|---|---|---|
| $a$ | | Linear accelerator |
| $A$ | | Arbitrary constant (in difference equations) |
| $b$ | | Parameter in difference equation solutions, determined by parameters of the model |
| $B$ | $X - F$ | Balance of trade |
| $B_\gamma$ | $\dfrac{\partial B}{\partial \gamma}$ | Marginal response of balance of trade to a change in the exchange rate |
| $B_Y$ | $\dfrac{\partial B}{\partial Y} = -F_Y$ | Marginal response of balance of trade to a change in income |
| $c_0$ $c_r$ $c_Y$ | | Respectively $C_0$, $C_r$, $C_Y$ in linear functions |
| $C$ | | Total consumption in real terms (equals money consumption in constant-price model) |
| $C_M$ | $\dfrac{\partial C}{\partial \left( \dfrac{M}{P} \right)}$ | Marginal response of consumption to changes in real cash balances |
| $C_0$ | | Exogenous component of consumption |
| $C_r$ | $\dfrac{\partial C}{\partial r}$ | Marginal response of consumption to a change in the rate of interest |
| $C_Y$ | $\dfrac{\partial C}{\partial Y}$ | Marginal propensity to consume |
| $D_J$ | | Utility of the $j$th worker |
| $F$ | | Value of imports |

† Greek letters are listed at end of table.

| Symbol | Mathematical definition | Economic definition |
|---|---|---|
| $F_\gamma$ | $\dfrac{\partial F}{\partial \gamma}$ | Marginal response of the import bill to a change in the exchange rate |
| $F_0$ | | Exogenous component of imports |
| $F_Y$ | $\dfrac{\partial F}{\partial Y}$ | Marginal propensity to import |
| $g_n$ | $=n$ | Natural rate of growth |
| $g_w$ | | Warranted rate of growth |
| $G$ | | Government expenditure on goods and services in real terms (equals money government expenditure in constant price models) |
| $H$ | $B + K$ | Balance of payments |
| $\left.\begin{array}{c} i_0 \\ i_r \\ i_Y \end{array}\right\}$ | | Respectively $I_0, I_r, I_Y$ in linear functions |
| $I$ | | Total investment in real terms (equals money investment in constant models) |
| $I_0$ | | Exogenous component of investment |
| $I_r$ | $\dfrac{\partial I}{\partial r}$ | Marginal response of investment to a change in the rate of interest |
| $I_Y$ | $\dfrac{\partial I}{\partial Y}$ | Marginal propensity to invest |
| $k$ | | Multiplier |
| $K$ | $K^F - K^X$ | Net inflow (or outflow) of financial capital to (or from) a country |
| $K_r$ | $\dfrac{\partial K}{\partial r}$ | Marginal response of net capital inflow (or outflow) to a change in the rate of interest |
| $K^F$ | | Capital imports |
| $K^R$ | | Total stock of real capital |
| $K^X$ | | Capital exports |
| $\left.\begin{array}{c} l_0 \\ l_r \\ l_Y \end{array}\right\}$ | | Respectively $L_0, L_r, L_Y$ in linear functions |
| $L$ | | Demand for money in real terms (equals demand in money terms in constant price models) |
| $L_0$ | | Exogenous component of demand for money |
| $L_r$ | $\dfrac{\partial L}{\partial r}$ | Marginal response of the demand for money to a change in the rate of interest |
| $L_Y$ | $\dfrac{\partial L}{\partial Y}$ | Marginal response of the demand for money to a change in income |
| $m$ | | Monetary authority's reaction coefficient |
| $M$ | | Total supply of money in nominal terms |
| $\dfrac{M}{P}$ | | Real supply of money |

| Symbol | Mathematical definition | Economic definition |
|---|---|---|
| $n$ | | Rate of growth of the labour force |
| $N$ | | Level of employment |
| $N_f$ | | Full employment level of employment |
| $N^D$ | | Demand for labour |
| $N^S$ | | Supply of labour |
| $N^S_M$ | | Maximum supply of labour |
| $P$ | | General price level |
| $P^C$ | | Supply price of capital goods |
| $P_D$ | | Price of domestic goods |
| $P_F$ | | Price of foreign goods |
| $\dfrac{dP^*_t}{P^*_{t-1}}$ | | Current *expected* rate of inflation |
| $Q_i$ | | Output of the $i$th firm |
| $r$ | | Rate of interest |
| $\sum R_j$ | $R_1 + R_2 + \cdots + R_n$ | Sum of expected earnings from an investment |
| $s_0$ $s_r$ $s_Y$ | | Respectively $S_0$, $S_r$, $S_Y$ in linear functions |
| $S$ | | Total saving in real terms (equals money saving in constant-price models) |
| $S_0$ | | Exogenous component of saving |
| $S_r$ | $\dfrac{\partial S}{\partial r}$ | Marginal response of saving to a change in the rate of interest |
| $S_Y$ | $\dfrac{\partial S}{\partial Y}$ | Marginal propensity to save |
| $t$ | | Time subscript to date variables |
| $t_0$ $t_Y$ | | Respectively $T_0$, $T_Y$ in linear functions |
| $T$ | | Total tax revenue in real terms (equals money tax revenue in constant-price models) |
| $T_0$ | | Exogenous component of tax revenue |
| $T_Y$ | $\dfrac{\partial T}{\partial Y}$ | Marginal response of tax revenue to a change in income, equals tax rate in case of proportional income tax |
| $v$ | $= \dfrac{Y}{K^R}$ | Output–capital ratio |
| $W$ | | Money wage rate |
| $\dfrac{W}{P}$ | | Real wage rate |
| $\left(\dfrac{W}{P}\right)_f$ | | Full employment real wage rate |
| $\left(\dfrac{W}{P}\right)_M$ | | Real wage rate at which maximum supply of labour is offered |
| $X$ | | Value of exports (except in section 7.4; see the footnote on page 156) |

| Symbol | Mathematical definition | Economic definition |
|--------|------------------------|---------------------|
| $X_\gamma$ | $\dfrac{\partial X}{\partial \gamma}$ | Marginal response of export earnings to a change in the exchange rate |
| $Y$ | | Total income in real terms (equals money income in constant-price models) |
| $Y_f$ | | Full employment income |
| $Y^c$ | | Complementary function |
| $Y^d$ | $Y - T$ | Disposable income in real terms |
| $Y^e$ | | Equilibrium income (particular integral in dynamic model) |
| $Y^H$ | | Permanent income |
| $Y^N$ | | No-policy income in dymamic model |
| $Y^z$ | | Transitory income |
| $Y'_N$ | $\dfrac{\partial Y}{\partial N}$ | Marginal product of labour |
| $Y''_N$ | $\dfrac{\partial^2 Y}{\partial N^2}$ | Change in the marginal product of labour as employment changes |
| $\hat{Y}$ | | Previous peak income |
| $Y^*$ | | Target level of income in dynamic model |
| $Y^{\max}$ | | Income (output) ceiling |
| $Y^{\min}$ | | Income (output) floor |
| $z$ | $= \dfrac{Y}{N}$ | Output–labour ratio |
| $\alpha$ (alpha) | | Non-linear accelerator |
| $\beta_1$ (beta) | | Response of absolute price level to a change in absolute excess demand |
| $\beta_2$ | | Elasticity of price level with respect to changes in excess demand |
| $\gamma$ (gamma) | | Rate of exchange |
| $\gamma_e$ | | Equilibrium rate of exchange |
| $\delta$ (delta) | | Elasticity of aggregate demand with respect to changes in exogenous expenditure |
| $\lambda$ (lambda) | | Arbitrary constant |
| $\rho$ (rho) | | Elasticity of price expectations with respect to changes in the actual previous price level |
| $\phi$ (phi) | | Rate of labour-saving technical progress |
| $\sigma$ (sigma) | | Elasticity of aggregate supply with respect to changes in wage cost |
| $\mu$ (mu) | | Fiscal reaction coefficient |
| $\Omega_0$ (omega) | | Exogenous element in $C/Y$ function (relative income hypothesis) |
| $\Omega_Y$ | | Parameter in $C/Y$ function (relative income hypothesis) |

# Answers to Exercises

**1.1** $x_1 = 1$, $x_2 = 2$, $x_3 = 0.5$

**1.2** $\dfrac{dY}{dt} = Y_K{}^R \dfrac{dK^R}{dt} + Y_N \dfrac{dN}{dt}$

**1.3** $\dfrac{\partial y}{\partial g} = \dfrac{\partial y}{\partial x_1}\dfrac{\partial x_1}{\partial g} + \dfrac{\partial y}{\partial x_2}\dfrac{\partial x_2}{\partial g}$; $\quad \dfrac{\partial y}{\partial h} = \dfrac{\partial y}{\partial x_1}\dfrac{\partial x_1}{\partial h} + \dfrac{\partial y}{\partial x_2}\dfrac{\partial x_2}{\partial h}$

**1.4** $\dfrac{\partial P}{\partial g} = \dfrac{-M}{Xg^2} < 0$; $\quad \dfrac{\partial P}{\partial X} = \dfrac{-M}{X^2 g} < 0$; $\quad \dfrac{\partial P}{\partial M} = \dfrac{1}{Xg} > 0$

**2.1** (a) $\begin{bmatrix} 1 & -1 & -1 \\ -0.60 & 1 & 0 \\ -0.20 & 0 & 1 \end{bmatrix} \begin{bmatrix} Y \\ C \\ I \end{bmatrix} = \begin{bmatrix} 10 \\ 10 \\ 20 \end{bmatrix}$

     (b) $Y = 200$, $C = 130$, $I = 60$

**2.2** (a) 100 (b) surplus of $23\frac{1}{3}$ (c) 1

**2.3** (a) $Y = 100 - 20r$

     (b) $Y = 116.67 - 20r$

     (c) $Y = 175 - 30r$

        Slopes $-1/20$ and $-1/30$

**3.1** (a) $Y = 300 + 10r$

     (b) Slopes $1/10$ and $1/1000$

**3.2** $Y = 1000$, $r = 0.10$

**3.3** As $1_r \to 0$

$\dfrac{\partial Y}{\partial \bar{G}} \to 0$

$\dfrac{\partial r}{\partial \bar{G}} \to -\dfrac{1}{(c_r + i_r)} > 0$

$\dfrac{\partial Y}{\partial \bar{M}} \to \dfrac{1}{l_Y} > 0$

$\dfrac{\partial r}{\partial \bar{M}} \to \dfrac{1 - c_Y(1 - t_Y) - i_Y}{(c_r + i_r)l_Y}$

**4.1** (a) See section 4.5, and Table 8.1

# Bibliography

Aitken, A. C. (1956). *Determinants and Matrices*, 9th ed., Oliver and Boyd.

Allen, R. G. D. (1962). *Mathematical Analysis for Economists*, Macmillan.

Allen, R. G. D. (1967). *Macroeconomic Theory: A Mathematical Treatment*, Macmillan.

Ando, A., and Cary Brown, E. (1968). 'Personal income taxes and consumption following the 1964 tax reduction', in *Studies in Economic Stabilization* (A. Ando, E. Cary Brown, and A. Friedlaender, Eds.), Brookings Inst.

Ando, A., and Goldfeld, S. (1968). 'An econometric model for evaluating stabilization policies', in *Studies in Economic Stabilization* (A. Ando, E. Cary Brown, and A. Friedlaender, Eds.), Brookings Inst.

Archibald, G. C., and Lipsey, R. G. (1967). *An Introduction to a Mathematical Treatment of Economics*, Weidenfeld and Nicholson.

Artoni, R. (1970). 'The coordination of fiscal and monetary policies', *Public Finance*, September.

Bailey, M. J. (1971). *National Income and Price Level*, 2nd ed., McGraw-Hill.

Baumol, W. J. (1961). 'Pitfalls in contracyclical policies: Some tools and results', *Review of Economics and Statistics*, February.

Burrows, P. (1974). 'The upward sloping *IS* curve and the control of income and the balance of payments', *Journal of Finance*, March.

Chiang, A. C. (1967). *Fundamental Methods of Mathematical Economics*, McGraw-Hill.

Christ, C. (1968). 'A simple macroeconomic model with a government budget restraint', *Journal of Political Economy*, January/February.

Conlisk, J. (1966). 'Unemployment in a neo-classical growth model: The effect of speed of adjustment', *Economic Journal*, September.

Cornwall, J. (1963). 'Three paths to full employment growth', *Quarterly Journal of Economics*, February.

Crockett, A. D., and Goodhart, C. A. E. (1970). 'The importance of money', *Bank of England Quarterly Bulletin*, June.

Dasgupta, A. K., and Hagger, A. J. (1971). *The Objectives of Macroeconomic Policy*, Macmillan.

Evans, M. K. (1969). *Macroeconomic Activity: Theory, Forecasting and Control*, Harper.

Floyd, J. E. (1969). 'Monetary and fiscal policy in a world of capital mobility', *Review of Economic Studies*, October.

Friedman, M. (1957). *A Theory of Consumption Function*, Princeton University.

Friedman, M. (1969). *The Optimum Quantity of Money*, Macmillan.

Friedman, M. (1970). 'A theoretical framework for monetary analysis', *Journal of Political Economy*, March/April.

Friedman, M., and Meiselman, D. (1964). 'The relative stability of monetary velocity and the investment multiplier in the United States, 1897–1958', in Commission on Money and Credit, *Stabilization Policies*, Prentice-Hall.

Gelting, J. (1941). 'Nogle Bemaerkninger om Financieringen af Offentlig Virksomhed', *Nationalökonomisk Tidsskrift*, Volume 79.

Goodwin, R. M. (1951). 'The non-linear accelerator and the persistence of business cycles', *Econometrica*, January.

Haavelmo, T. (1945). 'Multiplier effects of a balanced budget', *Econometrica*, October.

Hahn, F. H. (1971). 'Professor Friedman's views on money', *Economica*, February.

Hahn, F. H., and Matthews, R. C. O. (1965). 'The theory of economic growth: A survey', in *Surveys of Economic Theory*, Vol. II, American Economic Association and Royal Economic Society, Macmillan.

Hicks, J. R. (1939). *Value and Capital*, 1st ed., Clarendon Press.

Hicks, J. R. (1950). *A Contribution to the Theory of the Trade Cycle*, Clarendon Press.

Johnson, H. G. (1967), *Essays in Monetary Economics*, Unwin University Books.

Johnson, H. G. (1971). *Macroeconomics and Monetary Theory*, Lectures in Economics 1, Gray-Mills Publishing Ltd.

Kaldor, N. (1970a). 'A model of distribution', Reading 3, in *Growth Economics* (A. Sen, Ed.), Penguin.

Kaldor, N. (1970b). 'The new monetarism', *Lloyds Bank Review*, July.

Krueger, A. O. (1965). 'The impact of alternative government policies under varying exchange systems', *Quarterly Journal of Economics*, May.

Laidler, D. (1971). 'The influence of money on economic activity—survey and some current problems', in *Monetary Theory and Monetary Policy in the 1970s* (G. Clayton, J. C. Gilbert, and R. Sedgwick, Eds.), Oxford University Press.

Laidler, D. (1969). *The Demand for Money: Theories and Evidence*, International Textbook Company.

Laidler, D. (1968). 'The permanent-income concept in a macroeconomic model', *Oxford Economic Papers*, March.

Lindauer, J. (1968). *Macroeconomics*, J. Wiley and Sons Inc.

Liu, Ta-Chung (1963). 'An exploratory quarterly econometric model of effective demand in the postwar US economy', *Econometrica*, July.

Mueller, M. G. (1967). *Readings in Macroeconomics*, Holt, Rinehart and Winston.

Mundell, R. A. (1962). 'The appropriate use of monetary and fiscal policy for internal and external stability', *I.M.F. Staff Papers*, March.

Patinkin, D. (1956). *Money, Interest and Prices*, Row, Paterson and Co.

Peacock, A. T., and Shaw, G. K. (1971). *The Economic Theory of Fiscal Policy*, Allen and Unwin.

Pesek, B. P., and Saving, T. R. (1967). *Money, Wealth and Economic Theory*, Macmillan.

Pigou, A. C. (1943). 'The classical stationary state', *Economic Journal*, December.

Samuelson, P. A. (1939). 'Interactions between the multiplier analysis and the principle of acceleration', *Review of Economic Statistics*, May.

Samuelson, P. A. (1967). *Foundations of Economic Analysis*, Atheneum.

Sato, K. (1966). 'On the adjustment time in neo-classical growth models', *Review of Economic Studies*, July.

Sato, R. (1963). 'Fiscal policy in a neo-classical growth model: An analysis of time required for equilibrating adjustment', *Review of Economic Studies*, February.

Sen, A. (1970). *Growth Economics*, Penguin.

Shapiro, E. (1970). *Macroeconomic Analysis*, Harcourt, Brace and World.

Silber, W. L. (1971). 'Monetary policy effectiveness; The case of a positively sloped *IS* curve', *Journal of Finance*, December.

Simkin, C. G. F. (1968). *Economics at Large*, Weidenfeld and Nicholson.

Suits, D. (1962). 'Forecasting and analysis with an econometric model', *American Economic Review*, March.

Smyth, D. J. (1963). 'Monetary factors and the multiplier–accelerator interaction', *Economica*, November.

Solow, R. M. (1956). 'A contribution to the theory of economic growth', *Quarterly Journal of Economics*, February.

Swan, T. (1956). 'Economic growth and capital accumulation', *Economic Record*, November.

Takayama, A. (1969). 'The effects of fiscal and monetary policies under flexible and fixed exchange rates', *Canadian Journal of Economics*, May.

Tinbergen, J. (1952). *On the Theory of Economic Policy*, North-Holland.

Tobin, J. (1958). 'Liquidity preference as behaviour towards risk', *Review of Economic Studies*, February.

Tobin, J. (1965). 'Money and economic growth', *Econometrica*, October.

Vanek, J. (1962). *International Trade: Theory and Economic Policy*, Irwin.

Whitman, M. Von Neumann (1970). *Policies for Internal and External Balance*, Special Papers in International Economics, Princeton University.

Willett, T. D., and Forte, F. (1969). 'Interest rate policy and external balance', *Quarterly Journal of Economics*, May.

Williamson, J. H. (1971). 'On the normative theory of balance-of-payments adjustment', in *Monetary Theory and Monetary Policy in the 1970s* (G. Clayton, J. C. Gilbert, and R. Sedgwick, Eds.), Oxford University Press.

# Author Index

203

# Subject Index